Contents

Alexander Pope

Alexander Pope by Michael Dahl, *c.* 1727. From the collection of the Earl of Pembroke, Wilton House

Alexander Pope

The evolution of a poet

Netta Murray Goldsmith

Ashgate

1004660983.

Published by
Ashgate Publishing Limited
Gower House
Croft Road
Aldershot
Hants GU11 3HR
England

Ashgate Publishing Company
131 Main Street
Burlington, VT 05401–5600 USA

Ashgate website: http://www.ashgate.com

British Library Cataloguing in Publication Data

Goldsmith, Netta Murray
    Alexander Pope: The evolution of a poet – (Studies in early modern English literature)
    1. Pope, Alexander, 1688–1744   2. Poets, English – 18th century – Biography
    I. Title.
    821.5

US Library of Congress Cataloging-in-Publication Data

Goldsmith, Netta Murray.
    Alexander Pope: The evolution of a poet / Netta Murray Goldsmith.
        p.   cm. – (Studies in early modern English literature)
    ISBN 0-7546-0310-5 (alk. paper)
    1. Pope, Alexander, 1688–1744. 2. Authors and readers – England – History 18th century. 3. Poets, English – 18th century – Biography. 4. Creation (Literary, artistic, etc.) 5. Creative ability. I. Title. II. Series

    PR3633 .G58 2002
    821'.5–dc21
    [B]   2001046423

ISBN 0 7546 0310 5
Series cover design after *Dr Thomas Morell* by William Hogarth
This book is printed on acid-free paper
Typeset in *Times New Roman* by N^{2}productions
Printed in Great Britain by MPG Books Ltd., Bodmin, Cornwall.

In memory of Ernest

List of Figures

In the case of the portraits of John Gay, Lord Bolingbroke and Colley Cibber, the author will be pleased to clear the copyright with the present owners if they make themselves known.

Abbreviations

BL	British Library.
Corr.	*The Correspondence of Alexander Pope*, ed George Sherburn, 5 vols (Oxford: Clarendon, 1956).
PRO	Public Records Office.
Spence	Joseph Spence, *Observations, Anecdotes, and Characters of Books and Men*, ed J. M. Osborn, 2 vols (Oxford: Clarendon, 1966).
TW	*Poems of Alexander Pope*, The Twickenham Edition (London: Methuen and New Haven: Yale University Press, 1938–69). I *Pastoral Poetry and An Essay on Criticism*, ed E. Audra and Aubrey Williams (1961); II *The Rape of the Lock*, ed Geoffrey Tillotson, 3rd edn (1962); III-i *An Essay on Man*, ed Maynard Mack (1950); III-ii *Epistles to Several Persons*, ed F. W. Bateson, 2nd edn (1961), IV *Imitations of Horace*, ed John Butt, 3rd edn (1961); V *The Dunciad*, ed James Sutherland, 3rd edn (1963); VI *The Minor Poems*, ed Norman Ault, completed John Butt, 3rd edn (1964); VII–VIII *The Translations: The Iliad*, ed Maynard Mack et al. (1967); IX–X *The Translations: The Odyssey*, ed Maynard Mack et al. (1967); XI *Index Volume*, ed Maynard Mack (1969). This edition has been used for all quotations from the poems, except where otherwise stated in the notes.

General Editor's Preface

Studies in Early Modern English Literature

The series focuses on literary writing of the seventeenth and eighteenth centuries. Its objectives are to examine the individuals, trends, and channels of influence of the period between the Renaissance and the rise of Romanticism. During this period the English novel was invented, poetry began to tackle its unsteady relationship with non-literary discourse, and post-Shakespearean drama reinvented itself.

Alongside studies of established figures, the series will include books on important but lesser-known writers and those who are acknowledged as significant but given slight attention: typically, William Cartwright, James Shirley, John Denham, Edmund Waller, Isaac Watts, Matthew Prior, William D'Avenant, Mark Akenside and John Dyer. Also of particular interest are studies of the development of literary criticism in this period, monographs which deal with the conditions and practicalities of writing – including the practices of the publishing trade and financial and social circumstances of writing as a profession – and books which give special attention to the relationship between literature and other arts and discourses.

Monographs on a variety of writers and topics will be accepted; authors are invited to combine the best traditions of detailed research with astute critical analysis. The use of contemporary theoretical approaches will be acceptable, but every book will be founded upon historical, biographical and textual scholarship.

Professor Richard Bradford,
University of Ulster

Preface

Three biographies of Alexander Pope were written in the last century. The first two, George Sherburn's in 1934 and Peter Quennell's in 1968 did not say what happened to their subject after 1728. Only Maynard Mack's *Alexander Pope: A Life* was fully comprehensive, going from the poet's birth in 1688 until his death in 1744. In telling Pope's story again, I have also covered the whole period and, like Mack and Sherburn I have discussed the poet's work as well as his actions as a man. In other respects however my book is somewhat different from its predecessors.

In it I have attempted a relatively new approach to literary biography. You could call this study a psychobiography, except that it does not put the poet on a psychoanalyst's couch. Instead it makes use of recent research into creativity. Human creativity is an intriguing subject which currently interests a varied group of men and women, including geneticists, biologists, sociologists and computer scientists, as well as psychologists. One reason they are interested is that we are all of us creative, whilst occasionally there appears amongst us that mysterious phenomenon, a creative genius, such as Pope. When I say Pope was a genius, I am recalling Dr Johnson's *Dictionary* definition of one as 'a man endowed with superior faculties'. Modern psychologists have identified a number of features we can expect to find in the personalities of these rare individuals.

There are two primary aims in this biography. The first has been to bring Pope the man clearly before our eyes. Bearing in mind the observations of researchers into creativity enables us to see Pope in relation to his intellectual peers and so understand his complex and often perplexing character.

The second aim has been to show how it was that Pope succeeded so triumphantly as a poet in his own lifetime, becoming celebrated throughout the Western world. Admittedly he was endowed with a high degree of linguistic ability, but most of us have come across gifted people who have never achieved anything of value. Pope could have used his verbal facility to hold forth brilliantly in taverns and coffee houses, without ever writing a line. Mere genius is not enough. Furthermore, given that he had the necessary character traits, as well as the talent, to be a poet, he might yet have suffered the fate of the many creative geniuses who are unrecognized until after they are dead – had it not been for the way he related with his society.

The relationship between a creative genius and society has interested several modern researchers. One of these is the psychologist Mihalyi Csikszentmihalyi who argues that genius is in the eye of the beholder. To be more precise, he has formulated a theory, known as the Systems Perspective, to explain how a creative work comes to be recognized. Recognition is all because without it the public does not realize the work exists.

Csikszentmihalyi's starting point in *Creativity: Flow and the Discovery and Invention* (1996) is to ask not 'What is creativity, but where is it'? He locates it in a system that has three parts. The first part is the Domain, the body of knowledge and rules an individual must learn before he or she can contribute to it. The second part is the Field, which includes the institutions and judges who decide whether the individual's work is of value. Csikszentmihalyhi calls these experts the Gatekeepers. In the case of a writer they are usually the editors and critics. Finally, the third component in the Systems Perspective is the individual. Creativity occurs when the individual has a new idea or sees a new pattern and this is accepted by the Gatekeepers in the Field for inclusion in the Domain. Csikszentmihalyi, who often writes about scientists, stresses originality as a distinguishing feature of true creativity.

R. Ochse, however, in *Before the Gates of Excellence: the determinants of creative genius* (1990), points out that in the Arts the new idea or pattern is not necessarily so dramatic as it is in the Sciences. Originality can occur within an existing tradition without causing a major shift and he gives Bach and Mozart as examples. With Ochse's proviso, Pope's career is a copybook illustration of how the Systems Perspective works.

Csikszentmihalyi's theory has been endorsed and developed by other psychologists, including Howard Gardner and Howard Gruber, writing about great scientists and artists of all kinds. Both these men have also helped me in tracing the pattern of Pope's career.

In *Creating Minds: An Anatomy of Creativity* (1993), Howard Gardner points out that creative people normally look for allies and support groups among people who will encourage them and with whom they can share their ideas. Thinking about Pope, it seemed to me that for him support groups were particularly important. He had two kinds. From the first kind, such as the Scriblerus Club where he met Swift and Gay, he looked for literary encouragement. From the second kind, consisting of his VIP friends, he looked for the political protection he needed as a vulnerable Papist and suspected Jacobite subversive.

Pope also devised umpteen, varied methods for dealing with his enemies – he is famous for it. But he was not alone in this. Howard Gruber in *Darwin on Man: A Psychological Study of Scientific Creativity* (1974), has described his subject taking immense pains to forestall and circumvent his opponents.

However, Pope had a much clearer idea than many creative people have of how important the Field is and he tried to influence it. Indeed he became a Gatekeeper himself, decreeing the literary standards for his era.

Looking at Pope in the light of what modern psychologists have to say about creativity enables us to place him, with all his good and bad points, along with Darwin, Freud, Einstein, Stravinsky and T.S. Eliot, in which, different as the members of that family are, you can still see that they are kin.

As well as being indebted to the psychologists, I owe a great deal to Pope scholars, as the notes to this book will show. There are so many of these that it is impossible to mention them all here but I would like to pay my personal tribute to Maynard Mack who died in 2001 after a long and distinguished career. Presiding over a golden age in American scholarship which he helped to create, he, more than anyone else, has added to my understanding of Pope.

Because Maynard Mack included every known fact about the poet in his 1985 biography of him, I have felt free to be selective in my shorter book, concentrating on those aspects of his life that show his evolution as a creative artist, rather than include every detail about him. Nor have I made any new discoveries. Not even Maynard Mack was able to do that, apart from revealing a few letters from the unidentified female admirer of the poet who called herself Amica. The ground has now been gone over so thoroughly that one suspects that only serendipity – the chance discovery in an attic or provincial record office – will produce fresh information.

I do however offer various hypotheses about aspects of Pope's life that still remain obscure and hope these will be considered worthy of consideration, while my interpretation of those poems I discuss is, for better or worse, my own.

The staff of the British Library, the Cambridge University Library and the London Library have, as ever, dealt courteously and patiently with my many enquiries. At the CUL I am especially grateful to Neil Hudson of the Periodicals Department, who went to Addenbrooke's Hospital and found a newly published paper on Pope's medical condition for me.

It seemed at first that collecting illustrations for this book might prove complicated. However any difficulties that arose were resolved smoothly by James Kilvington of the National Portrait Gallery, as well as by Sibylle Beck, Melanie Blake and Barbara Thompson of the Witt Library at the Courtauld Institute, London. May I thank them for their special efforts on my behalf and also all the private individuals who kindly gave their permission to reproduce pictures they owned.

Finally I would like to say how much I appreciate the generosity of the Authors Society who gave me a grant for research expenses.

Postscript. I hope I may be forgiven for referring to Martha Blount as Patty throughout this book. My excuse for doing so is that Pope's friend was hardly ever known by the name she was given at birth. Nor is Patty a familiar form of Martha but an entirely separate appellation and, presumably, the one she chose to go by.

disposed towards him, were moved to amend his self portrait.[31] As for his enemies, they continued to give their own partisan picture.

Those who were the targets of Pope's satire refused to believe that he was motivated by a 'strong antipathy of Good to Bad.'[32] Instead, they insisted he was venomous and vengeful, a man who never forgot a slight, so that the attacks he launched in his verse were merely a matter of paying off old scores. They denied he did not care about money, accusing him of being mercenary with an unpleasant way of heaping contempt on writers less well off than himself, as if, one of his victims said, 'want of a dinner made a man a fool, or riches and good sense only kept company.'[33]

Far from being honest and forthright, those Pope had injured maintained he was a 'Stabber in the Dark', who professed candour and friendship in a face to face encounter with a man, before going away to try and destroy him with his pen.[34] While even friends agreed he was secretive and devious, someone who could 'hardly take tea without a stratagem.'[35]

Last, but not least, hardly anyone believed him when he said, 'Sworn to no Master, of no Sect am I', or his claim that he was prepared to give praise where praise was due to a man, whatever his religion or politics.[36] As the years went on his Whig and Protestant opponents insisted the house at Twickenham, where he entertained those old friends he spoke of, was actually the Tory opposition headquarters, while Pope himself, being a Roman Catholic, was the Jacobite subversive he had always been.[37]

Amidst the flickering images of Pope, conjured up by himself and others, is it possible to see him plain? The answer to this question is 'Yes, perhaps', if we keep in mind the one thing that was constant in him, which is that he was a poet, first, foremost and always. This obvious fact is the thread which can guide us through the labyrinth of contradictions that made up his personality.

A biographer of Pope can be baffled and exasperated, just as his contemporaries were, because he was serious and high minded one day, frivolous and bawdy the next, both compliant and aggressive, self-deprecating and arrogant, tender-hearted and cruel and so on. Furthermore he was a man of 'so little moderation' when he displayed such contrasting qualities.[38] However the inconsistencies become less puzzling if we accept a suggestion, made recently, that complexity is the trait that, more than any other, distinguishes creative men and women. This means 'that they show tendencies of thought and action that in most people are segregated. They contain contradictory extremes – instead of being an "individual," each of them is a "multitude." Like the color white that includes all the hues in the spectrum, they tend to bring together the entire range of human possibilities within themselves.'[39]

It is an advantage for the poet as a creative individual to be like this. One has only to think of Shakespeare, who could enter into the feelings of a Falstaff, Hamlet or Lady Macbeth. Keats once said 'if a Sparrow comes before my window I take part in its existence and pick about the Gravel.'[40] The same was true of Pope who entered into the sensations of a spider with its touch 'exquisitely fine!' as it 'Feels at each thread and lives along the line.'[41] For the poet as man, however, this receptivity and power of comprehensive empathy has its disadvantages because it makes him unsure of his own character, or whether he even has a character.

Keats's description of this state of affairs is the best known. He declared 'A Poet is the most unpoetical of any thing in existence; because he has no Identity – he is continually [informing] and filling some other Body. The Sun, the Moon, the Sea and Men and Women who are creatures of impulse are poetical and have about them an unchangeable attribute – the poet has none,' and he went on to warn the friend he was writing to, 'It is a wretched thing to confess; but is a very fact that not one word I ever utter can be taken for granted as an opinion growing out of my identical nature – how can it, when I have no nature?'[42]

Keats's apologia was written in 1819. A hundred years before that Pope was debating with Swift, Dr Arbuthnot and the other members of the Scriblerus Club the question of whether or not any human being had an abiding self. This topic had come up because John Locke in his *Essay concerning Human Understanding* (1690) had discussed identity in such a way as made it possible to doubt whether anyone could say he had an essential personality which he was born with and retained to the end of his life.[43] Pope, aware of the contradictions in his own nature, was the most sympathetic of the Scriblerians to Locke's ideas.[44]

Twenty years later he dealt at length with the subject of identity in the *Epistle to Cobham* (1733). In the first 170 lines or so of that poem he depicts human beings as inexplicable because they behave so inconsistently. This brings him to the conclusion that 'Our spring of action to ourselves is lost' (l. 42), and man 'A bird of passage! gone as soon as found' (l. 156). In all probability Pope was moved to make these observations partly for subjective reasons. As he says himself 'All Manners take a tincture from our own' (l. 25).

However Pope refuses to let the matter rest there. In the remainder of the poem he suggests it is possible to understand another human being once we discover his ruling passion, be it lust of praise or lechery, because this determines his every action.[45] A problem with this argument is that it is hard to believe that the majority of people are so single minded that they are motivated in everything they do by any one thing such as vanity or acquisitiveness, or love of food, even if they do have a reputation for being vain, materialistic or gourmands. Nevertheless, Pope's hypothesis is of interest if we relate it to creative individuals. Those people, be they scientists, inventors or artists, who make their mark in the world by their outstanding achievements, are often noted for their utter dedication to their chosen calling and for the fact that it comes before everything else in their lives.

Pope had his ruling passion. It was his calling as a poet. This was so, not just because he was gifted, but for several other reasons, including the pressure exerted by external circumstances. So, for instance, it is relevant that he was born to be an outsider in the society he determined to conquer by his art. Many creative individuals have been marginalized by class or religion or geography, while some twenty per cent have suffered from physical handicaps.[46] Pope was marginalized three times over, by physical deformity, as well as by his middle class origins and because he was a Papist in a Protestant country. All these things were the source of affliction to him as a man but they were of no disadvantage to him as a poet. If anything they gave him an incentive to work hard at what he proved to be good at so as to make those inclined to view him with contempt and distrust, admire or fear him.

Pope found his vocation early and soon dreamed of being a great poet. Thereafter, from the age of twelve he began educating himself for this purpose. Like many poets, before and since, he did this by reading voraciously all the verse and criticism he could lay his hands on. It was necessary to acquaint himself with the cultural domain in this way, because he had to know what had been done before, whether he wanted to follow faithfully in the footsteps of his predecessors, or whether he decided to expand or break with tradition.[47] At the same time that he was reading, Pope taught himself the craft of composing verse by writing in various genres and imitating his favourite poets. Finally, he concentrated, as most of his contemporaries did, on imitating the classics of ancient Greece and Rome and on practising the heroic couplet which, for much of the eighteenth century, was used by the majority of poets.

As a poet Pope was fortunate to live in the right place at the right time, in a period when the literary tradition was temporarily stable and in a country where the rules that determined that tradition were fairly flexible. Before the end of the century popular culture and romanticism raised the neoclassical fortress in England to the ground but while he lived it still stood, even if the besiegers were at the gates. This meant that when Pope focused on writing heroic couplets to the best of his ability, he could do so undistracted. By the age of sixteen he had made himself a master of that particular verse form. Eventually he would become a technical virtuoso who could make the couplet do anything he wanted, whether it was reproducing what his enemies called the language of Billingsgate, or conveying Apocalyptic grandeur in the finale to *The Dunciad*.

Becoming a master however was not enough. It is the mark of creative individuals that they do not go on doing exactly what others have done before them; they try something new. Pope did not wish to break with the neoclassical tradition but, from early on in his career, he wanted to expand and develop it in untried ways. As Dr Johnson said, he 'had a mind active, ambitious and adventurous, always investigating, always aspiring; in its widest reaches still longing to go forward, in its highest flights still wishing to be higher, always imagining something greater than it knows, always endeavouring more than it can do.'[48]

If we wonder sometimes why Pope behaved as he did we need only ask ourselves how his actions fitted into or protected his role as a poet and we can usually find the answer. He used everything and everyone to feed his talent. He made many friends and ensured they all helped him in one way or another. Some of them he put into his verses, others he went to for literary advice or ideas for more poems. Often the men and women he knew gave him practical assistance, copying and storing his manuscripts, or acting as a cover when he feared the publication of a work might lead to him being sued for libel.[49] When he launched his devastating and occasionally unfair attacks on his literary enemies he was safeguarding a tradition and his reputation as the leading exponent of it. Eventually he found a way to make these enemies serve his purpose directly when he orchestrated their clamour to publicise *The Dunciad*.

Right from the beginning of his career Pope realized that it was one thing to write poems which he thought were good and quite another to see that they were recognized as such by other people. It may happen that a work of genius bursts upon the firmament in a shower of stars like a rocket, but someone has to have set a match to the touch paper first. Sooner or later a creative work has to be approved by those deemed competent to judge, if it is to become part of our cultural heritage. Furthermore, no poet wishes to blush unseen. Even Emily Dickinson, who kept her poems hidden in drawers and cupboards, tried to get some of them published when she was a girl. She was unsuccessful in this attempt because she was ahead of her time and because she lacked influential contacts who were both perceptive and energetic enough to promote her work.

Pope was fortunate, as we have already said, in being born at the right time when the public was familiar with neoclassical verse. Nevertheless, when he decided to embark on his career as a poet, he realized he was likely to meet with indifference or prejudice because he was an unknown country boy and a Papist to boot. He went about overcoming these problems with noteworthy efficiency. Before he made his debut with *The Pastorals*, he sought the approval of the accepted field of literary judges by sending the manuscript of his poems to be read by a dozen influential Protestant gentlemen.[50] This exercise in generating advance publicity might not have worked if the poems had been egregiously bad, but they were not and, as a result of their author's preparatory efforts, they were being talked about favourably even before the general public was able to see them on the printed page. As time went on he set himself up as the leader in the field of literary judges, so as to establish all the more clearly the criteria by which his own poetry should be evaluated. He succeeded in this endeavour, so that his enemies, not without justification, said he was a literary dictator, in the words of one of them the 'Lord Paramount-wou'd-be of Mount Parnassus.'[51]

Living in an age when the concept of a professional writer who made an adequate living by his pen was still in its infancy, Pope proved an adept at career management. It is doubtful whether any writers nowadays are better than he was at this, even with all the modern machinery of public relations at their disposal.

As well as being his own best publicity agent, Pope knew instinctively that he needed freedom if he was to develop his full potential as a poet. The prerequisite for this was to establish a measure of independence. He set about doing so in a number of ways.

In the first place he made money, reaping about £5,000 when he translated the *Iliad* while he was in his twenties, and as much again when he went on to publish a translation of the *Odyssey*.[52] This meant that he did not have to rely on the vagaries of patronage. It did not mean that he ignored the market. Throughout his career he was willing to consider ideas for poems that would interest one or other section of the public. When he embarked on the Homer he knew there was a need for an English version of the epics which a polite audience could read easily, if only because many gentlemen had forgotten whatever Greek they had learned at school and the ladies had never been taught it anyway. The only reason a translation to meet the modern taste had not been made already was that it was thought to be a 'prodigous' undertaking, 'which not all the Poets of our Island durst jointly attempt.'[53] But Pope never lacked confidence in his own abilities. Nor was this confidence misplaced. Because of the sizeable sum of money which the successful completion of his task brought, he was able to choose whether or not he wrote verses on topics and personages suggested to him by others. It also meant that, as well as not having to rely on a patron, he was not tempted to become one of Robert Walpole's hacks, as so many of his contemporaries were, even those inimical to the Government, including Henry Fielding.[54]

Pope actively maintained his marginality, realizing instinctively that the outsider has more space and freedom than a regular and accepted member of any community. So he resisted suggestions that he abandon his religion, even though going on for half the English Catholics in the eighteenth century defected to the Church of England.[55] His conversion need only have been nominal, as it was with some of his other co-religionists, and Anglicanism would have brought him certain practical advantages such as no longer having to pay the double taxes imposed on Papists. However, it would also have brought him closer to the established order and he was always wary of any attempt to identify him too closely with a particular group, even one he sympathised with. He soon became incensed with Catholics when they reprimanded him for his lines about monkish superstition in *An Essay on Criticism*.[56] Later on, he lent his services to the Tory Opposition but was never subsumed by it, refusing insistent pleas by some members of it to write this, that or the other, if these did not fit in with his own plans.[57]

Pope was not unusual in seeking to maintain a certain distance between himself and society. Creative individuals who are not marginalized to begin with sometimes strive to make themselves so, for instance T.S. Eliot. He removed himself from his establishment background in America, choosing exile in London, where he distanced himself still further by adopting the religious and political stance of a minority.[58] In so doing, Eliot instinctively protected his vocation.

At the same time Pope guarded his chosen destiny as a leading poet by keeping out of serious political danger. He might be suspected of being a Jacobite but no one has ever been able to prove conclusively that he was one. This is as well because proven Jacobites could end up in gaol, if not on the gallows. Eventually too, when his satires in support of the Tory Opposition led to his windows being broken and the possibility of an investigation by the Whig Government, he wrote no more of them.[59]

That did not mean however that he stopped writing. With some relief he seized on a good excuse to pen no more overt Tory propaganda and turned to other projects. Pope might say sometimes that he wrote when he had nothing better to do, but we should not be deceived. Whenever he visited friends he insisted on having a writing desk placed by his bedside, in case ideas occurred to him during his hours of insomnia.[60] Even his chronic ill health did not deter him for long at a time. There was probably never a day in his adult life when he was free from pain.[61] Nevertheless he worked whenever he could, often early in the morning when he was at his best and at other times, according to Swift 'he had always some poetical scheme in his head.'[62] He composed verse quickly and then went over every work he wrote, making corrections and revisions, until he was satisfied it was ready for the printer, which might not be for two years. Thereafter he nursed the poem through the press, ensuring that each minute instruction he had issued for its presentation on the page was followed exactly. Towards the end of his career when he asked the question 'This subtle Thief of Life, this paltry Time, / What will it leave me, if it snatch my Rhyme?' he knew the answer.[63]

Pope was in love with poetry. At times he resented his bondage to an exacting mistress but she gave him more lasting satisfaction than anyone or anything else in life could have done. When he was in the throes of creation he could forget the cares and preoccupations of everyday existence, including the fact he was 'that little Alexander the women laugh at.'[64] While he translated Homer during the 1715 rebellion the fretful Jacobite struggles faded far away because he was spending all his waking hours in Troy or laying siege to its walls. On one occasion he described to a young friend how it was for him when he was in the process of creating a poem. During the bitter winter of 1712, when he was writing *Windsor Forest*, he said he could not always tell the difference between what was going on in his mind and what was going on around him, so that he spoke to his family of things as truths and real events, he had only dreamed of. He sat close to the fire in his parents' house, conjuring up 'a painted scene,' which he alone controlled, of 'trees springing, fields flowering, Nature laughing,' and compared himself in his entranced state to 'a witch whose Carcase lies motionless on the floor, while she keeps her airy Sabbaths, & enjoys a thousand Imaginary Entertainments abroad, in this world, & in others.'[65]

Creative work has its pains as all those engaged in it will admit. But artists keep going because of the sense of power, the feeling of being fully alive it can bring.[66] Of the many men and women who have testified to this, one of the most recent is Harold Pinter who, describing both the good and bad patches in his career as a dramatist, has said, 'When you can't write you feel banished from yourself', adding on another occasion, 'But my writing life ... has been one of relish, challenge, excitement.[67] Pope, who breathed by writing, would surely have understood these sentiments.

Pope had genius in that he had an extraordinary aptitude to excel in a particular domain and make a unique and valuable contribution to our cultural heritage. Without that he would not be on the roll of great poets more than 300 years after his birth. Civilization, however, often produces gifted individuals who do not fulfil their potential. Pope's genius might not have flowered if it had not been for the circumstances in which he found himself and, also, if he had not had certain traits in his character, including mental energy, a capacity for hard work, perseverance, resilience, unwavering confidence in his own abilities along with the habit of rigorous self criticism and a reasonably good, co-ordinating intelligence. It is also doubtful whether he would have achieved noteworthy material success and extraordinary fame in his own lifetime without other qualities as well, such as business acumen, an instinct for self-promotion, a combative spirit and guile.

This book tells the story of Pope's evolution as a poet, how he found people to help him and how he coped with an equal number of others who wanted to hinder him. It describes what he did when he suffered reversals, as well as how he prepared for and engineered his triumphs. By concentrating in this way on his essential being, it is hoped to look beyond the images of him which he and others conjured up and glimpse the man seen so often in distorting mirrors.

Notes

1. James Northcote, *Life of Joshua Reynolds*, 2 vols, 2nd edn (London, 1818), 1: 19–20.
2. 'Thomson', *Lives of the Poets*, 3 vols, ed G.B. Hill (Oxford: Clarendon, 1905), 3: 291.
3. William Walsh and Lord Lansdowne. *Corr.* 1: 7 and TW. 1: 59n.
4. Letter from Mather Byles, 7 October 1727, *Corr.* 2: 450–1.
5. Letter to Thieriot, 26 October 1726, quoted Spence, no. 527n.
6. *A Letter to Mr. C-b--r, On his Letter to Mr. Pope* , printed for J. Roberts, 19 August 1742, p. 25.
7. *The Works of Alexander Pope Esq.*, in nine volumes with Commentaries and Notes by William Warburton, 1751, 2nd edn (Dublin, 1752), 1: vii–viii.
8. John Dennis, *A True Character of Mr. Pope, And His Writings* (London, 1716).
9. Maynard Mack, *Alexander Pope: A Life* (Yale University Press, 1985) and D.

Greene, 'An Anatomy of Pope-bashing', *The Enduring Legacy: Alexander Pope Tercentenary Essays* (Cambridge University Press, 1988), pp. 241–81.

10. J.V. Guerinot, *Pamphlet Attacks on Alexander Pope 1711–1744: a descriptive bibliography* (London: Methuen, 1969), p. xxix.

11. John Dennis, *op. cit.*

12. *Corr.* 4: 521n.

13. *Verses Address'd to the Imitator Of The First Satire of the Second Book of Horace* (London, 1733), p. 4.

14. *Gulliveriana* (London, 1728).

15. John Dennis, *op. cit.*

16. W.K. Wimsatt, *The Portraits of Alexander Pope* (New Haven and London: Yale University Press, 1965). Wimsatt believes Pope 'was probably the most frequently portrayed English person of his generation, perhaps of the whole eighteenth century', p. xv.

17. James Prior, *Life of Edmund Malone* (London, 1860), pp. 428–9.

18. Charles Gildon, *Memoirs Of the Life of William Wycherley Esq.* (London, 1718).

19. Letter to Thomas Cromwell, 19 October 1709, *Corr.* 1: 73.

20. Spence, no. 59 and note.

21. *Letters*, ed B. Dobrée (1932), no. 36.

22. *Complete Letters of Lady Mary Wortley Montagu*, ed Robert Halsband, 3 vols (Oxford University Press, 1967), 3: 57.

23. Edward Roome, *Dean Jonathan's Parody On The 4th Chapter of Genesis* (London, 1729) and *The Poet Finish'd in Prose. Being A Dialogue Concerning Mr. Pope And His Writings* (London, 1735).

24. *A Letter to Mr. Cibber* (London, 1742).

25. *A Letter From Mr. Cibber, To Mr. Pope* (London, 1742).

26. *An Epistle to Dr. Arbuthnot*, l. 120.

27. *Sixth Epistle of the First Book of Horace*, ll. 32–3.

28. *First Epistle of the First Book of Horace*, l. 162.

29. *Second Satire of the Second Book of Horace*, l. 138.

30. Ibid., ll. 139–40.

31. William Kent was one of several of Pope's contemporaries who denied he was abstemious, see *Corr.* 4: 150. Modern critics who dwell on Pope's affluence, which permitted him to have an aristocratic life style at Twickenham, include Brean S. Hammond, *Pope* (Brighton: Harvester Press, 1986) and Leopold Damrosch Jr, *The Imaginative World of Alexander Pope* (University of California Press, 1987).

32. *Epilogue to the Satires, Dialogue II*, l. 198.

33. James Ralph, *Sawney. An Heroic Poem* (London, 1728), p. vii.

34. John Dennis, *op. cit.*

35. Johnson, 'Pope', *Lives of the Poets*, 3: 200.

36. *First Epistle of the First Book of Horace*, ll. 24ff.

37. *A Hue and Cry After Part of a Pack of Hounds, which broke out of their Kennel in Westminster* (London, 1739).

38. Johnson, *Lives of the Poets*, 3: 215.

39. Mihaly Csikszentmihalyi, *Creativity: Flow and the Psychology of Discovery and Invention* (New York: HarperCollins, 1996), p. 57.

40. *The Letters of John Keats*, ed M.B. Forman, 3rd edn (Oxford University Press, 1947), p. 169.

41. *Essay on Man*, 1: 217–18.

42. *Letters, op. cit.*, p. 228.

43. Book 2, ch. 27.

44. Christopher Fox, 'Locke and the Scriblerians: the Discussion of Identity in early Eighteenth-Century England', *Eighteenth-Century Studies*, 16 (1982), 1–25.
45. Pope's theory was not original. See Introduction to *An Essay on Man*, TW. 3.2: xxxvi ff.
46. V. Goertzel and M.G. Goertzel, *Cradles of Eminence* (Boston: Little, Brown, 1962), quoted by R. Ochse, *Before the Gates of Excellence: the determinants of creative genius* (Cambridge University Press, 1990), ch. 4.
47. Csikszentmihalyi, *op. cit.*, pp. 27ff.
48. *Lives of the Poets*, 3: 217.
49. TW. 5: xxviii.
50. Spence, pp. 616–17.
51. Sir Butterfly Maggot [pseud], *The Gentleman's Miscellany. In Verse and Prose* (London, 1730), Dedication.
52. Maynard Mack, *Alexander Pope: A Life* (New Haven and London, Yale University Press, 1985), p. 416.
53. Thomas Burnet and George Duckett, *Homerides: Or A Letter To Mr. Pope, Occasion'd by his intended Translation of Homer* (London, 1715), p. l.
54. Donald Thomas, *Henry Fielding* (London: Weidenfeld and Nicolson, 1990), p. 141 and *Champion*, 13 December 1739.
55. 'The 115,000 Catholics of 1720, had shrunk to 69,000 by 1780' as stated by Roy Porter, *English Society in the Eighteenth Century* (Harmondsworth: Penguin Books, 1982), p. 194.
56. Letter to John Caryll, 25 June 1711, *Corr.* 1: 122.
57. *Corr.* 4: 138–9.
58. Howard Gardner, *Creating Minds* (New York: Basic Books, 1993), ch. 7.
59. *Epilogue to the Satires, Dialogue II*, ll. 248–9 and note, TW. 4: 327.
60. Johnson, *Lives of the Poets*, 3: 209.
61. E.M. Papper, 'The Influence of Chronic Illness upon the Writings of Alexander Pope', *Journal of the Royal Society of Medicine*, 82 (June, 1989), 359–61.
62. Johnson, *Lives of the Poets*, 3: 208–9.
63. *Second Epistle of the Second Book of Horace*, ll. 76–7.
64. Letter to John Caryll, 25 January 1710, *Corr.* 1: 114.
65. *Corr.* 1: 163 and 168.
66. Csikszentmihalyi, *op. cit.*, p. 75.
67. *Various Voices* (Faber, 1998).

PART I

How Alexander Pope Became a Poet

CHAPTER ONE

On Being a Papist

Alexander Pope was born on Monday 21 May 1688 at 6.45 pm when England was on the brink of a revolution. Much of his character and life were to be determined by that revolution and by the decision his father had taken to become a Roman Catholic. From birth he was destined to be an outsider.

Mr Pope, whose first name was also Alexander, probably converted to Catholicism when he was a young man, during the early, easy years of the Restoration. Later, during the agitated reign of James II, he bought and read all that was being written on both the Protestant and Papist sides but, when he had finished reading, he found no way he could change his mind.[1] After the revolution Mr Pope's decision to remain a Catholic made him a religious and political outcast, ever careful to avoid attracting the attention of the authorities, or of hostile neighbours. He had virtually no civil rights. In modern terminology he was a non-person. His son would live all his life as a potential enemy alien in the land of his birth.

Mr Pope was an unlikely martyr. He was not reckless, impractical, or an obvious rebel, but he thought for himself and his education in a puritan setting failed to indoctrinate him against the Church of Rome. He was born posthumously in 1646, the year in which Charles I lost at Edgehill and surrendered to Parliament. His father had been the energetic and zealous Rector of Thruxton in Hampshire, who once rejoiced in bringing the daughter of a local Catholic landowner 'unto our Church of England.'[2] After the Rector's death his widow returned with her newborn child, and his brothers and sisters, to Micheldever where her father, the Rev. William Pyne, had his parish. The theological views of Mr Pope's grandfather can be guessed at from the fact he kept his living throughout the Cromwellian era.

Mr Pope rejected his family's Protestant faith, but not the Protestant work ethic. He grew up to be industrious, thrifty and ambitious. At the beginning of 1688 he was a successful linen merchant. Twenty years earlier he and his brother William had used the few hundred pounds they had inherited from their father to start a business, dealing in 'Hollands wholesale.'[3] After a while William had disappeared and Mr Pope carried on alone, selling cloth in England, then expanding his operations so as to export goods to the American colonies, steadily increasing his initial capital of £500 until he was worth several thousand.[4] In this respect he was a typical member of the rising, mercantile, middle class.[5] He was also a typical and worthy descendant of men who were hard working and knew how to make and look after money, in whatever field they laboured – and, as we shall see, his son would carry on this family tradition.

Since the sixteenth century the Popes had moved a few steps up the social ladder with each generation. The first one we know anything about was a blacksmith in Andover. He did well enough to enable his son Richard to buy The Angel Inn, the leading hostelry in the town. Richard prospered, played an active part in Andover's public affairs and sent his son Alexander to Oxford. This was the Alexander who became the Rector of Thruxton who, dedicated to his calling as he was, still looked after his worldly interests.[6] Before his sudden death he was on the brink of securing an income of more than £400 a year, which was six to eight times as much as the average parson received.[7] It was in order to obtain the standard of living the Rector would have enjoyed, had he lived, that Mr Pope had gone into trade. When he did so he did not expect to find that his religious convictions would get in the way of his commercial success.

He married twice, choosing Catholic women on both occasions. His first wife died in 1679, leaving a daughter Magdalen who survived, and a son (another Alexander) who died three years later. While Mr Pope looked for a second wife he had sent his children to be cared for by his sister, not minding that her husband was the Anglican Rector of Pangbourne. When he remarried Mr Pope chose Edith Turner, a plain, affable woman, three years older than himself. She came from a highly respected, middle class family in Yorkshire, but was unlikely to inherit much money because she was one of seventeen children who lived to maturity. There were fourteen girls, half of them Protestants. Like her husband, Edith never let religious differences prevent her getting on with her relatives.[8] One of her Catholic ancestors was Margaret Clitherow who was canonized, after embracing an excruciating martyrdom in 1586.[9] Mrs Pope, however, was simply a devout woman who later won the respect of Jonathan Swift because she was that rare being, 'a good Christian.'[10]

Mr Pope took Edith and Magdalen to live in the house he had rented in Plough Court, off Lombard Street in the City. His landlord John Osgood was another linen merchant.[11] He was also a Quaker but this did not stand in the way of his having a cordial relationship with his tenant. The Popes and the Turners were perhaps unusual in numbering both Catholics and Protestants in their families, but they were not unusual in being able to get on with people from other denominations. During the reign of Charles II Protestants often lived and worked alongside Catholics without friction, turning a blind eye when they knew their neighbours celebrated Mass, even though this was against the law. Catholics were in the minority, amounting to less than two per cent of the population. As individuals practising their faith, they were not feared. Trouble arose, when it did, because Roman Catholicism was not just a matter of private belief. It was also a political system which English Protestants were determined should never be re-imposed on them.

houses to avoid the attention of any reveller who, like the man in Ward's verses, might conclude if he saw a darkened home, 'This House I'm sure without a Light / Belongs to some damn'd Jacobite.'[20]

William III made it clear at the beginning of his reign that he did not want Catholics to be harmed but he could not give them financial security or peace of mind because of repeated plots to restore James (and subsequently his son and grandson) to the throne, in which it was assumed Catholics took part. During the next fifty years or so there were a dozen Jacobite conspiracies, most of which involved invasion plans with the help of foreign troops.[21]

The consequences for Mr Pope's son of being born a Catholic in eighteenth-century England were pervasive and complex. His religious status affected his mental and emotional development, as well as his material circumstances. He never left the Church of Rome for which his father had made sacrifices, although he did not share his parents' unwavering religious conviction. When, as a boy, he read through the polemical literature Mr Pope had collected, he found himself 'a Papist and a Protestant by turns' as he finished each book.[22] From the beginning he detested religious zeal.

He was however every bit as meticulous as Mr Pope in obeying the Penal Laws, far more so than some of his Catholic friends, worrying, for example, when one of them gave him a horse worth more than five pounds.[23] In all probability, because of his father's experiences, he was haunted by the fear he might be summoned to take the Oaths. He was aware that even a trivial transgression might result in such a summons, such as being found in possession of a rosary. One year before he died, he surprised Joseph Spence, who had brought him a small present of 'some beads and medals', by laying them gently aside, and saying 'Those would be good presents for a Papist.'[24]

Pope had Jacobite sympathies. It would have been surprising if he had not, because life was obviously more comfortable for a Catholic if his king was a Stuart. However, all Jacobites, whether active or fellow travellers, kept their feelings hidden unless they were sure they were with their own kind. Pope was no exception. As we shall see, references to the Stuarts and a second Restoration in his works are always expressed obliquely in covert messages, that are meant to be understood only by those familiar with Jacobite symbolism. This habit of mind spilled over into all his working and personal relationships. He was always wary and became super subtle. The deviousness, that friends as well as enemies complained of, was due in part to the fact that he had to survive in a world where he knew it was often dangerous for him to be frank and direct. Although he was not a cold man, he learned to be calculating. Living his life as if it were a game of chess, he always looked several moves ahead and tried to work out what the other player was likely to do.

Not all the consequences of Pope living as a Catholic in the years after the Revolution were negative. The Penal Laws meant that he was denied a standard education. But if he had gone to one of the major schools which were available only to Anglicans, and then to the university, from which he was barred as a Papist, he could hardly have begun at the age of twelve educating himself intensively for his chosen vocation as a poet. Furthermore, it was easier for him to choose that vocation than it would have been if he had been a Protestant, when he would have had so many more promising opportunities for making his way in the world than by literature. As it was most other careers were closed to him. Being a Roman Catholic, therefore, in eighteenth-century England was one of the factors that determined Alexander Pope's future as a poet.

Notes

1.   *Corr.* I. 453. According to family tradition Mr Pope had become a Catholic while serving an apprenticeship on the Continent. See Joseph Warton, *Essay on the Genius and Writings of Alexander Pope* (1806), 2: 255–6.
2.   Chancery Proceedings, Charles I, W88/61.
3.   Spence, 11.
4.   Chancery Proceedings, Reynardson 86/84. In 1684 Mr Pope was in court, trying to get a Virginian factor to pay for a valuable cargo sent him.
5.   Peter Earle, *The Making of the English Middle Class* (Methuen, 1989), pp. 14–16.
6.   F.J. Pope, *Notes and Queries*, 11 Series (12 April 1913), pp. 281–3, 441.
7.   Gregory King, *Natural and political observations and conclusions upon the state and condition of England* (1696). Fifty years after the Rector's death King gives the usual income for clergy as £45 to £60 a year.
8.   Valerie Rumbold, 'Alexander Pope and the Religious Tradition of the Turners', *Recusant History* (May, 1984), pp. 17–37.
9.   Katharine M. Longley, 'Saint Margaret and Alexander Pope: An unexpected Link', *Recusant History* (October, 1986), pp. 143–8. The saint was the poet's second cousin, three times removed. She was sentenced to be crushed to death with stones.
10.   *Corr.* 2. 394.
11.   Information about John Osgood comes from an anonymous article, 'The Birthplace of Pope' in the *Illustrated London News* (7 December 1872).
12.   The following historical details for the time of the Revolution have been compiled from *Bishop Burnet's History of his Own Times* (1723), the 1688 entries in John Evelyn's *Diary*, Lord Macaulay's *History of England from the Accession of James II* (1848) and J.C.D. Clark, *English Society 1688–1832* (Cambridge University Press, 1985).
13.   Spence, 12.
14.   George Sherburn, 'New Anecdotes of Alexander Pope', *Notes and Queries*, n.s. 5 (1958), 348–9.
15.   Maud D. Petre, *The Ninth Lord Petre* (London, 1928), pp. 86–92.
16.   Spence, 12.
17.   Petre, *op. cit.*
18.   Spence, 192 and 13.
19.   Petre, *op. cit.*
20.   *Hudibras Redivivus* (1708), Part 8, vol. 2, canto 7.

21. Paul Kléber Monod, *Jacobitism and the English People 1688–1788* (Cambridge University Press, 1989).
22. *Corr.* 1. 453–4.
23. John Caryll gave Pope a horse in December, 1713. For a history of what happened to it, before and after the 1715 rebellion, see *Corr.* 1. 128, 203, 241 and 340.
24. Spence, 353.

CHAPTER TWO

The 'Itch of Poetry'

Alexander Pope had no idea where his poetic gift came from. 'What sin to me unknown / Dipt me in ink' he asked, 'My Parents, or my own?'[1] His parents, who showed no signs of having any literary talent, would have denied responsibility. Nevertheless his special aptitude almost certainly had a genetic origin which, because he had certain other mental attributes, meant he could, in the right circumstances, develop into a genius. However, the huge number of genes contributed by each parent, and the innumerable ways they can be combined, makes the probability of producing a child who turns out to be a genius less likely than buying a lottery ticket with the six winning numbers on it.[2] Furthermore, notwithstanding all the investigations by geneticists, psychologists and many others, creativity itself remains 'a puzzle, a paradox, some say a mystery.'[3] Still, if Pope the poet is fundamentally an enigma to us, as he was to himself, it is possible to say something about the specific nature of his gift.

It is now thought that as well as the logical-mathematical intelligence revealed in the old IQ tests, there are several other kinds of intelligence, one of which is linguistic.[4] In the normal course of events all human beings possess linguistic intelligence. Hence children learn to talk. In addition, a few individuals, at an early age, show a fascination with the sound of words and delight in playing games with them, and some of these children may become poets, in whom a love of language is prerequisite and pre-eminent. John Keats was just such an infant. A neighbour of the Keats family remembered how, when John was still under five, 'instead of answering questions put to him, he would always make a rhyme to the last word people said, and then laugh.'[5] There are signs that Pope too showed a marked interest in verbal patterns when he was very young. He said himself he 'lisp'd in Numbers, for the Numbers came.'[6] And there is evidence this was so, for the earliest known verse by him appears to have been composed when he was little more than an infant.

He wrote four lines when he was six, though they were not printed until ten years later, by which time they may well have been polished. The subject of this quatrain was political and referred to Queen Mary and Marshal Luxembourg, who had recently died within a week of one another. It ran as follows:

Behold Dutch Prince here lye th'unconquer'd Pair
Who knew your Strength in Love, your Strength in War!
Unequal Match, to both no Conquest gains,
No Trophy of your Love or War remains.

This is very much an occasional poem, topical in 1695 when the point of the lines would have been immediately clear. The Marshal, who was William's rival among the French generals had, by dying, cheated the Dutch Prince of the glory of conquest, just as Mary's death from smallpox had deprived him of the chance of an heir.[7]

As well as the surprising sophistication this short poem shows, the fact that it is political satire, mocking William, tells us something about the attitude to the new king in the boy's home. In the lines the monarch has been demoted to Prince. Clearly Mr Pope was bringing up his son to be critical of the current situation and sympathetic to the Stuart cause. Indeed it is likely that, after the departure of James II, Alexander's home in Plough Court was a political hothouse, much as James Joyce's Dublin home was to become after the fall of Charles Stewart Parnell. Then, it will be remembered, the nine-year-old James wrote a poem 'Et Tu, Healey,' arraigning one of the bishops he blamed for driving Parnell to his death. John Joyce was so pleased that he had his son's verses printed and distributed to his friends.[8] No doubt Mr Pope was equally pleased with Alexander's achievement, even if he did not risk having the poem published.

Mr Pope watched over his son intently at every stage of his development during these early years. It is easy to understand why. The normal love a father might feel for his child was heightened for a number of reasons. To begin with, there was the memory of that other Alexander, the son who died after he was placed in the care of relatives. To a man of Mr Pope's religious temperament it must have seemed that the boy born in 1688 was a gift from God. He had been given a second chance and was unlikely to be given another, because Edith was already forty-five when she gave birth. Given how important the arrival of this son was, Mr Pope was somewhat unusual in that he does not seem to have had any preconceived idea of how he wanted his heir to develop. That the child had a poetic turn must have come as rather a surprise, but the father nurtured his son's talent from the start, devoting all the more time to the task because his own career had been brought to an abrupt end. Although Mr Pope was no poet himself, he emerges as one of Alexander's earliest mentors – and a good one, in that he was not over indulgent. Edith described how her husband set their son 'to make verses very young', adding, 'he was pretty difficult in being pleased and used often to send him back to new turn them. "These are not good rhymes", he would say.'[9]

Alexander was fortunate in his early childhood. Not only did he have a discerning father with time to devote to him, he was surrounded by affectionate adults, several of whom encouraged him. If he gave signs of being precocious, no one minded in an age when childhood was regarded as a stage to be got through as quickly as possible. Mr Pope had given a home to one of Edith's sisters, Elizabeth, who taught Alexander to read. After which he taught himself to write by copying the words in his hornbook. He did this painstakingly so that eventually he was able to reproduce a near facsimile of any printed page.[10] Aunt Christiana, another of Edith's sisters, who lived nearby, was pleased to find that Alexander not only enjoyed writing verses, but was good at drawing. She was the widow of the distinguished miniature portrait painter Samuel Cooper, and she left her nephew, who was also her godson, her husband's painting materials, as well as her books and pictures, when she died in 1694.[11]

Apparently Edith herself did not play any part in Alexander's education and so, compared with her husband, she remains a shadowy figure. We know however that she was easy to live with. She may well have provided a point of rest in the household, for she was a placid, amiable woman who was able to get on with everyone, including her moody stepdaughter. Even her son's enemies rarely said anything unpleasant about her. Lady Mary Wortley Montagu, comparing her with the poet on one occasion, declared tartly, 'She allways appeared to me to have much better sense than himselfe.'[12]

As was customary among middle class women at that time, Edith did not feed her baby herself. The Popes had hired a wet nurse. This was Mary Beach who found being with her adopted family so congenial that she never left, going on to live with her charge for the rest of her long life. Mary Beach was already a middle aged woman when she came to Plough Court and Aunt Christiana had been sixty-five when the poet was born. Indeed none of the people mentioned so far, who watched over Alexander's development, was under forty. He had no sibling rivals. His half sister Magdalen was at least nine years older than he was and she was approaching adolescence while he was still an infant.

In 1692 a Jesuit priest arrived at the house in Plough Court. He was Edward Taverner, who sometimes called himself Bannister and sometimes Davis. As a member of a proscribed class he was in need of a refuge. Mr Pope provided this, passing him off as one of the servants.[13] Eventually he became Alexander's first tutor, giving him lessons in Greek and Latin, so laying the foundation for that knowledge of the classics which was mandatory for all educated men in the eighteenth century. Father Taverner gave his pupil lessons in both ancient languages at the same time. This method worked and Pope said later that this first tutor was the only one from whom he learned anything.[14]

Father Taverner had no sooner arrived at Plough Court than the family was forced to leave, because in 1692 a law was passed forbidding Papists to live within ten miles of the seat of Government. We next hear of Mr Pope in Hammersmith, then a village which had long provided a haven for Catholics. It even had a convent school for girls, which had survived a visit from Titus Oates.[15] Mr Pope spent the next eight years in Hammersmith, and we have no idea how he passed his time there. It is hard to imagine him idle though, and as the area was famous for its market gardens, he could have been producing and selling some of the fruit and vegetables that supplied half London.[16] We know that by the time he left the area he had become something of a horticultural expert, interested, among other things, in growing white strawberries.[17]

Meanwhile someone gave Alexander a lavishly illustrated Homer in John Ogilby's translation. It was an inspired gift. Nearly fifty years later when Pope recalled the pleasure reading Ogilby had given him as a child, it was 'with a sort of rapture only on reflecting on it.'[18] It is impossible to exaggerate the importance the discovery of the *Iliad* and *Odyssey* had for the eight-year-old boy who, up till then had been living in a house in which, as he said, there were no books apart from the religious tracts bought by his father.[19] In the first place, while he read, he was transported from the loving, but claustrophobic confines of his London home onto the windy plains of Troy and wished himself in Homer's battles.[20]

Howard Gardner has suggested that the stories we come upon when very young affect us ever after. These stories often involve a struggle between individuals or opposing forces and later on, no matter how educated or sophisticated we become, we tend to see certain basic situations in the light of values we absorbed as children from these tales.[21] For a modern child this seminal influence might be *Star Wars* or *Harry Potter*. For Pope it was the *Iliad* and *Odyssey*. In the epics he found heroes to live by. When he was an adult, shades of the valiant Hector or (more often) the resourceful Odysseus hovered in the background as role models when he sallied forth onto the literary battlefield.

Ogilby's translation of the Greek epics also had another crucial effect on Pope. Homer himself became his hero, from whom he caught 'the itch of poetry.'[22] Educational psychologists can often identify a particular occasion when talented individuals fall in love with a particular subject. Alfred North Whitehead called this moment the 'initial romance'. More recently David Feldman has defined it as a 'crystallizing experience.'[23] Both these terms aptly describe Alexander's reaction on first reading the *Iliad* and *Odyssey*. He already knew he had a facility for writing verse. This knowledge had enabled him to cross the barrier that many children meet when they are about seven years old. Up to that age most children are exuberantly creative. They paint, talk, write and sing without inhibition. After that there is a drop in creativity as they learn to be self-critical.[24] Alexander's creative urge did not dwindle because he had already reached an unusual level of competence and was 'a child at promise.'[25] The fact he could write his poem on the Dutch Prince, by the time he was six, shows he had no reason to become discouraged. Reading Homer in an accessible translation gave direction to his talent. Before he went to school he had found his vocation.

The Ogilby book may well have been a farewell present from Father Taverner who left Hammersmith in 1696, after which Alexander was sent to school. If the family had been Protestant, Mr Pope, like other middle class parents ambitious for their sons, would probably have sent the boy to Westminster. Then, as now, a major public school had more to offer than education, a fact Pope later brought out clearly, in recreating a conversation he had with his publisher. Lintot, on being asked about his son, replied:

> I spare nothing for his education at Westminster. Pray don't you think *Westminster* to be the best school in *England*? Most of the late *Ministry* came out of it, so did many of this *Ministry*; I hope the boy will make his fortune.[26]

The 'best school in England' was for Anglicans only and, strictly speaking, schools for Catholics were illegal, though there were a few – mostly second rate. Twyford, near Winchester, had the one with the highest reputation, so Mr Pope sent his son there.[27]

The venture was not a success. Clever and imaginative, enthusiastic about literature and used to individual attention, Alexander became discontented with his pedestrian ushers who, subscribing to the educational theory of their day, concentrated on grammatical analysis when they taught the classics. He amused himself by writing a comic poem about the shortcomings of his teacher. One anonymous account, which he may have written himself, says this was at least a hundred lines long and was discovered in his pocket after another boy told on him. He was severely punished, whipped and locked in his room for a week.[28] Eighteenth-century parents regarded corporal punishment as a normal part of education but Mr Pope did not share this view. He went promptly to Twyford and brought his son home.

After rescuing Alexander from Winchester (where he had been for less than a year) Mr Pope looked for a place where his son could be educated in London, with the result that most of the remaining two years or so of the boy's conventional education was spent in the 'little schools' kept by Thomas Deane, first in Marylebone and then at Hyde Park Corner.[29]

Thomas Deane, like Mr Pope, was displaced when King William came in. He had been a Fellow of University College, Oxford, where he converted to Catholicism in 1685. He was then supposed to have written articles defending the Roman Church, which he printed privately in the Master's Lodge and, with the departure of James II, left Oxford with an anti-Papist mob at his heels. Thereafter, he became an object lesson to Catholics, showing them what could happen if they were not wary. He took up the Stuart cause with enthusiasm and in 1691 was made to stand in the pillory after he was found in possession of seditious literature.[30] He was also gaoled more than once, for he remained a rash optimist throughout his life. Even in his seventies he was writing and publishing Romanist and Jacobite papers, though by that time, having been without a regular income for years, he was in a debtors' prison.[31]

Alexander did not learn very much under Deane's tuition, but he was allowed to go his own way. Sometimes, while the other boys were playing games, 'he used to amuse himself with Drawing.'[32] At other times he sat writing a play. This was a dramatization of the *Iliad* with speeches from the epic 'tacked together' with verses of his own.[33] When it was finished, Thomas Deane let him put it on at school. The boys played most of the parts, but the master's gardener was specially chosen to be the massive Ajax. Obviously the play was no casual entertainment. Every care was taken with a production in which the cast wore costumes copied from the illustrations in Ogilby.[34]

With Deane's permission Alexander was also 'suffered to frequent the playhouse in company with the greater boys.'[35] The theatre with the biggest drawing power at the time was the playhouse in Lincoln's Inn Fields which opened in 1695 and had William Congreve as its resident dramatist. Congreve's *Mourning Bride* was the major success of the year there in 1697, and his *Way of the World* a striking failure in 1700. The theatre was managed by Thomas Betterton. Betterton was in his sixties but still some years off retirement, in command of a wide range of parts from Valentine in *Love for Love*, to Falstaff and Hamlet. Pope said later he was the best actor he ever saw.[36]

While Alexander was a pupil at Thomas Deane's school, Mr Pope commissioned a portrait of his son. This shows him to have been a good-looking child with a round, plump face and a fresh complexion. His mother said the picture was exactly like him.[37] In it he looks healthy and he was at the age of ten, when the portrait was done. The tuberculosis which would wreck his constitution did not manifest itself for another two years.[38] He was attractively dressed for the sittings as a young chevalier, so that he resembled James II's son as he appears in the portrait painted by Nicholas de Largillière at about the same time. The unknown artist, who shows us Alexander as a small boy, also succeeded in conveying something of his personality at that time, so that we see a self-confident child, who looks alert and cheerful as well. William Mannock, who used to see him on visits to the family, was delighted by him and said he had 'a particularly sweet temper' at this time.[39]

Mannock was probably a cousin. He was also the family priest of Alexander's sister. Soon after the Popes moved to Hammersmith, Magdalen had married a well-to-do fellow Catholic and possible Jacobite, Charles Rackett.[40] So by the time Alexander was six she had left home and by 1695 had given birth to her first child. Unlike Father Mannock she was not particularly charmed by her little brother. He received far more attention than she had ever had and she probably thought he was spoilt. When he was very young she said he was 'nice and whimsical as to eating.'[41] Later, when he was an adolescent, she noted that he had 'a maddish way with him', which suggests she found him excitable and too unconventional for her taste.[42] Pope, in his turn, never really felt at ease with his sister. Whereas to many people who knew him as a boy, he appeared 'excessively gay and lively', with Magdalen he was constrained, so that she once said she 'never saw him laugh very heartily' in all her life.[43]

Pope stayed in London until 1700, by which time his father was ready to move out of the capital with his family and live modestly as a country gentleman. In 1698 he bought Whitehill House in Binfield, near Windsor from his son-in-law for £445.[44] Catholics were forbidden to own property and, as we have seen, Mr Pope was always meticulous about not flouting the law. There were ways round the regulations however, so he laid plans which were

2.1   Alexander Pope, aged about ten years. Artist unknown

completed by 1700. In April of that year he transferred the house to Edith's Protestant nephews, Samuel and Charles Mawhood 'in trust for his only son, Alexander Pope.'[45]

The previous year, in 1699, an Act had been passed increasing the penalties for all those functioning as Catholic priests or teachers, so that now they were liable to life imprisonment. Thomas Deane's school closed and Mr Pope did not attempt to find another one for his son. Thereafter Alexander devised his own syllabus, designed to give him the education of an eighteenth-century gentleman and, above all, a vocational training in the craft of poetry.

He had already begun his apprenticeship as a poet before he went to Binfield, with desultory reading and by writing verses in imitation of poems by his favourite ancient and modern writers. The modern poet who pleased him the most was the greatest poet of the age, John Dryden, who was still living. Before Pope left London he was determined to see Dryden. So he asked a friend to take him to Will's coffee house.[46] Here the writer, now aging, ill and hard up, sat each day, in winter in his special chair by the fire and in summer by the window overlooking the street. One version of this story tells how the boy took one of his own poems with him – a version of the Pyramus and Thisbe story from Ovid – and Dryden gave him a shilling by way of encouragement.[47] Pope must have been tempted to take something he had written, but in a letter to William Wycherley later he did not mention it. He said he barely saw Dryden, though he also told Joseph Spence that nevertheless he 'observed him very particularly.' He regarded him with the 'greatest veneration' but this in no way dulled his powers of perception. He noted Dryden had a 'down look' and was not 'very conversible.' Later he decided his hero's lack of social polish was due to his having spent too much time with literary men.[48]

It is hardly likely that Dryden, surrounded by friends and respectful courtiers, looked so attentively at the boy who had come to pay him homage. On 1 May 1700 the old poet died, a few months short of his seventieth birthday. Soon afterwards Pope went with his parents to Binfield, there to begin in earnest his bid to succeed to the literary throne Dryden had left vacant.

At the age of twelve Pope was already better placed than most poets in the history of English literature to realize such an ambition. He not only had a talent for versifying, he wanted to perfect this gift, having found his vocation four years earlier. In addition, he had a supportive family, his father being particularly encouraging. It might have been otherwise if the family's religious and social status had not been what it was. If Mr Pope had been a Protestant he would not have given up his business when he did and might have wished his son to follow him, or he might have preferred him to take up one of the established professions, rather than try to make a living in an uncertain literary world. Then again, if the Popes had been higher up on the social scale (whether Catholic or Protestant) the wish by an only son and heir to be a professional writer would have been considered both eccentric and demeaning. In that case,

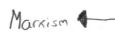

Alexander might well have written poems in his spare time, but would not have risen above the level of a score of aristocratic amateurs who were his contemporaries.

Alexander Pope, even as a child, revealed he had the psychological makeup of creative individuals who go on to fulfil their potential. Like a number of artists he had an independent spirit and rejected external regulation, as his disastrous term at the Twyford boarding school showed. His sister's comment about his whimsical eating habits also suggest he liked to get his own way and assert himself. On the other hand, he was saved from being merely wayward because with those he respected, such as his first tutor and his father, he was capable of self discipline and was able to learn. It is interesting that his father set him to write verses, presumably choosing the topic, as this suggests that Alexander enjoyed himself early on, employing his verbal skill, no matter what the subject was. A love of words came before an interest in content. This marks him out as a true poet in embryo. So does his capacity for taking infinite pains, as he did with the play, based on the *Iliad*, when he took care of every detail necessary for the successful production of it. Lastly in these childhood years he gives the impression that he was lively and eager. He had the mental energy as well as the determination he would need if he was going to succeed in life.

[handwritten margin note: So was ot a conscious thing? Or Just Pope's way?]

Notes

1.   *Epistle from Mr. Pope to Dr. Arbuthnot*, ll. 125–6.
2.   David T. Lykken, 'The genetics of genius' in *Genius and the Mind*, ed Andrew Steptoe (Oxford University Press, 1998), pp. 15–37.
3.   Margaret A. Boden, *The Creative Mind: Myths and Mechanisms* (Weidenfeld and Nicolson, 1990), the 'Preface'.
4.   Howard Gardner, *Frames of Mind: The Theory of Multiple Intelligences* (Heinemann, 1984).
5.   Andrew Motion, *Keats* (Faber, 1997), p. 20.
6.   *Epistle from Mr. Pope to Dr. Arbuthnot*, l. 128.
7.   David Nokes, 'Lisping in political numbers', *Notes and Queries*, n.s. 24 (June, 1977), 228–9. I have summarized Dr Nokes's argument about the occasional nature of the quatrain.
8.   Richard Ellmann, *James Joyce* (Oxford University Press, 1959), p. 33.
9.   Spence, 11.
10.   Spence, 14n.
11.   Traditional information, though not all these bequests are verifiable any longer. See Maynard Mack, *Alexander Pope* (Yale, 1985), p. 19.
12.   *Complete Letters of Lady Mary Wortley Montagu*, ed Robert Halsband, 3 vols (Oxford: Clarendon Press, 1956–67), 2: 101–2.
13.   London Public Records Office: Langbourne Ward, Box 36, MS. 12, p. 9.
14.   Spence, 14 and note.
15.   *Victoria History of the Counties: A History of Middlesex* (London, 1970), 1: 254.
16.   Ibid., vol. 2.
17.   *Corr.* 1: 443.

18. Spence, 30.
19. *Corr.* 1: 453–4.
20. Letter, 29 November, 1715. Reprinted in Maynard Mack, *Collected in Himself* (Newark, 1992), p. 467.
21. Howard Gardner, *Leading Minds* (HarperCollins, 1995), ch. 3.
22. *Corr.* 1: 297.
23. B. Bloom with L. Sosniak, *Developing Talent in Young Children* (New York: Ballantine Books, 1985). Also J. Walters and H. Gardner, 'The Crystallizing Experience', in R.J. Sternberg and J. Davidson, eds, *Conceptions of Giftedness* (New York: Cambridge University Press, 1986), pp. 306–31.
24. C. Scott Findlay and Charles J. Lumsden, 'The Creative Mind: Towards an Evolutionary Theory of Discovery and Innovation', *Journal of Social and Biological Structures*, 11 (1988), p. 43.
25. Howard Gardner, *Frames of Mind*, p. 35.
26. *Corr.* 1: 372.
27. Spence, 14.
28. Letter published by Edmund Curll in 1735 from a correspondent named 'E.P.' See Spence, 18 and Appendix.
29. Spence, 15.
30. Obituary in the *Whitehall Evening Post*, 18 November, 1735.
31. *Corr.* 2: 428–9.
32. Weaver Bickerton, *Life of Alexander Pope, Esq.* (1744), p. 14.
33. Spence, 33.
34. Owen Ruffhead, *The Life of Alexander Pope, Esq. Compiled from Original Manuscripts* ... (1769), p. 13.
35. Ibid.
36. Spence, 53.
37. Spence, 9.
38. Ibid.
39. Spence, 8.
40. Spence, 8n.
41. Spence, 16.
42. Spence, 28.
43. Spence, 10.
44. Lucius FitzGerald, 'Alexander Pope the Elder and the House at Binfield', *Notes and Queries*, 11th series, 25 July 1914, 65–6.
45. Ibid.
46. Spence, 57 and Appendix, p. 611.
47. Thomas Warton, *An Essay on the Genius and Writings of Pope*, 2 vols 3rd edn (London, 1772), 1: 82.
48. Spence, 59.

CHAPTER THREE

The Apprentice

'When about twelve' said Pope, 'I went with my father into the Forest.'[1] The forest was Windsor, not Arden, but it too had its brothers in exile. Mr Pope had taken his family from Hammersmith to another haven for Papists. The Catholic gentry, living in and around Binfield, came from old families that had helped shape the country's history and some, like the Blounts for instance, appear in the cast lists of Shakespeare's plays. Now, at the start of the eighteenth century, being excluded from public life, they filled their days hunting, fishing, reading and looking after their lands, if they had any. They put the world to rights over their dinner tables and toasted the king over the water. Outside their own homes most of them took care to be discreet, for all of them hoped to escape the notice of a Government presided over by a man many regarded as a usurper. When the retired linen merchant came to live among them, this beleaguered minority quickly accepted him as a fellow sufferer from the Penal Laws.

Nor was it very long before Protestants, in addition to Catholics in the locality, realized Mr Pope's son was an unusually gifted boy who deserved encouragement. A sign of the way the neighbours felt came within a few months when one of them, Gabriel Young, gave Alexander a handsome folio edition of Chaucer's *Works*, printed in 1598.[2] Up to 1700 the would-be poet's support group had been inside the family home. Now, in Binfield, he was to find a more extensive one, some of whose members had literary and scholarly interests, as well as access to influential people in London. As he approached adolescence, Pope made the maximum use of all this group had to offer in realizing his literary ambitions.

Whitehill House, which Mr Pope had bought for his family, stood on a slope with good views of the surrounding woods and fields and was itself clearly visible. Soon after moving in, he planted Scotch firs near the entrance – trees not often seen at that time in southern England – which would have told any passing Jacobite that here there was a safe house.[3] It had been built in the previous century of red brick in the same style as a number of farmsteads in the area. With only two storeys it was not as large as No. 2 Plough Court, where the family had lived in residential-cum-business premises with attics and a basement. Nevertheless, Alexander was allocated one of the small rooms in the new home as his own study and library.

In between cultivating the nineteen acres that went with the house and growing finer artichokes than any of his neighbours, Mr Pope continued to watch over his son, though he now had sufficient confidence in him to let him map out his own course of study. In any case, like many gifted children who have discovered their peculiar interest or talent, Alexander was 'intrinsically motivated', with a rage to learn.[4] Henceforth he forged ahead with his programme of self instruction at such a rapid pace that Mr Pope would have had difficulty keeping up with him. He occasionally offered advice, though it was not always followed by the boy as he grew older and more independent. This did not mean, however, that the two of them grew apart. The son knew his father was his never-failing ally and, as time went on, came to regard him as a friend as well as a parent.

To celebrate the arrival in his new home Pope wrote an *Ode to Solitude* in which he listed, in the Horatian tradition, all the advantages of an independent rural existence: sound sleep, simple food, 'health of body, peace of mind' and so on. This artfully artless poem, although written in the first person, says more about Mr Pope who has turned his back on the world than it does about the twelve-year-old boy, who had yet to make his way in it. So it celebrates the contentment of a man who is 'free from Care, the Business and the Noise of Towns,' and goes on to speak of living unseen and unknown. The poem is the son's compliment to his father, both congratulating him on what has been gained and consoling him for what has been lost by retirement. One doubts if Mr Pope sent the boy back to 'new turn' these verses. No writer need have felt ashamed of them, let alone at the age of twelve.

Meanwhile Alexander, who had dreams of being a great poet, devised a programme of self-tuition that was both rigorous and comprehensive. Between the ages of twelve and twenty he taught himself Latin and Greek and later (this time with help of a tutor), French and Italian. A part of his reading consisted of going 'through all the best critics, almost all the English, French and Latin poets of any name, the minor poets, Homer and some other of the greater Greek poets in the original, and Tasso and Ariosto in translations.'[5]

But this was not all. He was interested in religion and philosophy. He knew the Bible thoroughly of course, both the Douai and King James versions, and read the mainstream works of devotion by Thomas á Kempis, Aquinas and others. Having also devoured the religious tracts in his father's library, he tried to work out his own approach to faith, concluding that he was content to be a Catholic of the liberal kind, as represented by Erasmus. He read modern philosophers, such as Hobbes and Locke, and picked up a fair knowledge of ancient philosophy. He absorbed Neoplatonism through his reading of the English poets, many of whom, including Spenser, Chapman and Milton, were steeped in it.

Pope had two aims with his programme: to give himself the kind of education a gentleman usually received so that he could hold his own in genteel society, and to teach himself poetic craftsmanship. The process of teaching himself to be a poet went on at the same time he was reading for knowledge and enjoyment. As fast as he read, he wrote, translating, imitating, mastering literary techniques by practice.

He liked educating himself. He did not think that he had learned anything at the little schools he had attended, nor did he feel he could learn anything unless he enjoyed it. Later, remembering his early years in Binfield, he said, 'I followed everywhere as my fancy led me, and was like a boy gathering flowers in the woods and fields just as they fall in his way.'[6] The sheer excitement of discovery kept him going. He needed no external discipline, but he did realize when he was twenty that he had not been thorough. Earlier he showed how impetuous he was. Then he showed he could be patient, going over all the parts of his education again, from the beginning in a systematic way. It is hard to think of anyone else in the history of English literature who did more than Pope did to prepare himself for his chosen career.

He never thought he was at a disadvantage because he was self-taught. When he had a chance of comparing himself with his contemporaries, he considered the whole matter of education carefully and would have liked to write a treatise on it.[7] If he had done so, it would have been a somewhat radical document for its time. His method of studying languages, for instance, was unconventional. He leafed through dictionaries and grammars, but for the most part learned by embarking straightaway on a translation of passages by writers that impressed him in the best Greek and Latin. He believed it was the duty of a teacher to keep alive his students' capacity to enjoy their subject, and deplored arid over-emphasis on grammatical niceties in the study of the classics, at the expense of what those classics were actually saying. He never wrote the treatise but put some of his ideas into the *Dunciad*, where he has pedagogues boast of how they teach their charges:

> As Fancy opens the quick springs of Sense,
> We ply the Memory, we Load the brain,
> Blind rebel Wit, and double chain on chain,
> Confine the thought, to exercise the breath,
> And keep them in the pale of Words till death (4: 156–60)

Analysis and even drudgery had their place in education, as he realized when he organized his own re-training programme. But to begin too early, focusing exclusively on this approach to literature, was likely to produce a pedant, if it did not produce a George II, who never willingly opened a book again, once he had escaped his tutors.[8]

Pope was not unusual in being educated outside the system. During his lifetime one in three of the gentry, mentioned in the *Dictionary of National Biography*, went neither to school nor to university.[9] Some of that third of educated Englishmen had tutors and a knowledgeable, imaginative tutor might have saved Pope having to repeat his programme of instruction twice. Otherwise it is hard to see that he emerged any the worse a scholar because he worked

uncritical of the Administration, which he left in 1698 because the Lord Justices in Council had treated him 'more like a footman than a Secretary.'[37] Regarded as a somewhat timid politician by Pepys and others, he was nevertheless courted by at least one up-and-coming member of the younger generation, Henry St John Bolingbroke. The younger man came to him for advice and, while touring the Continent for nearly three years before 1700, had written him detailed letters about the political, cultural and moral scene in Europe.[38]

Sir William was the Fellow of All Souls to whom Pope lent Milton's early poems and on other occasions he enlisted his help in tracking down the source of obscure quotations. In general he enjoyed the boy's company and was impressed by him. As for Pope, his almost daily conversations with the scholar and statesman went some way to replacing the university education he could not have. Sir William was also another of the men in the Binfield area who offered Pope ideas for poems. As a verderer, responsible for maintaining the forestry laws, he knew the Windsor area well, including the history of its castle. One of the first things he did was suggest his young friend write *Windsor Forest* to celebrate the natural beauty and national significance of the place in which they took their rides.[39] Then, after reading the Sarpedon episode, Pope's first translation of a passage from Homer, he urged him to go on and put the whole of the *Iliad* into modern English.[40]

Sir William was in his mid-sixties when Pope got to know him. In Binfield, as in London, many of the boy's companions were elderly. Talking later about the amount of time he spent with old men in his youth, Pope decided it had 'brought some habits' upon him that were 'troublesome.'[41] He did not say what these habits were but it is not hard to hazard a guess about one or two of them. He became used to being indulged by these older friends who were far more solicitous than his own contemporaries would have been. If Sir William Trumbull's attitude is anything to go by, he was regarded almost as a pet. 'The little Creature is my darling more and more', Sir William wrote to his nephew.[42] And in another letter to the same correspondent he announced, 'Poor little Pope has been ill ... a Puff of wind had almost blown him away.'[43] All the adults around the boy worried about him overtaxing his strength. As a result Pope grew used to being ministered to and throughout his life remained very demanding of all his friends.

Furthermore, living in a predominantly adult world influenced Pope's behaviour. With his older mentors he was outwardly deferential, learning how to dissemble when necessary, just as adults themselves do in civilized society. Yet there was another less inhibited side to his nature, glimpsed by youths who occasionally visited Binfield. One of these was Edmund 'Rag' Smith, an unkempt student of Christ Church where he was usually in trouble, once when he was convicted of riotous behaviour and again when he published a lampoon on one of the dons. Pope, remembering his Twyford experience, found a kindred spirit in 'Rag' Smith who, in turn, said of the fourteen-year-old boy, 'Igad that young fellow will either be a madman, or make a very great poet.'[44]

Charles Wogan, a young Irish Jacobite, also came to Whitehill House. He knew something of the literary scene in London and the two of them concocted a plot whereby Wogan took Pope, then about sixteen, to London 'to dress à la mode, and introduce him to Will's coffee house.'[45] The fashionable clothes were borrowed, because while the family income was adequate for everyday expenses, there was little to spare for luxuries. So although Pope was becoming increasingly restless in Binfield, as he advanced into his teens, shortage of money, together with anxiety about his health, made his father reluctant to let his son go to London for any lengthy period. There were arguments for instance about the boy's 'wildish sort of resolution' to return to the capital to take lessons with a language tutor, so as to perfect the French and Italian he had been teaching himself. However 'he stuck to it' and 'went thither.'[46] Pope was nothing if not persistent and when he was about seventeen he obtained his father's permission to make an indefinite stay in London, in order to launch himself upon the literary world with a work carefully chosen for his debut, the *Pastorals*. He did not ask for new clothes and Mr Pope would not have to pay for lodgings for him because he would be staying with William Wycherley.[47]

In choosing to begin his public career with the *Pastorals* Pope was doing two things. On the one hand he hoped to win approval for his modesty by selecting for his first publication relatively simple poems celebrating an idealized version of country life. On the other hand, by beginning as Virgil had done with this particular genre, he was deliberately inviting comparison with his Roman precursor. It was a carefully thought out manoeuvre, designed both to disarm, and proclaim himself as the new heir to the throne of classicism.

He was deliberately limiting himself when he made his debut with the *Pastorals*. He could have begun his bid for recognition in any number of ways because, during the years of his apprenticeship to poetry, he practised most kinds of writing. He wrote odes, epigrams and love lyrics, in the style of his favourite English and Continental writers. He produced hymns and prayers. He translated sizeable chunks of Greek and Latin narrative verse, and laboured two years on an epic. He began a tragedy and completed another play about Genevieve, the heroic patron saint of Paris. He also maintained the habit (begun at the age of six) of writing political verse. 'To the Author of a Poem, intitled *Successio*', satirizing Elkanah Settle, was written when he was fourteen. It lamented the 1701 Act of Settlement, which dashed the hopes of those who thought the monarchy would revert in due course to the heirs of James II.

The hero of his epic was Prince Alcander, driven like James, from his throne and was the only juvenile work he destroyed. He was persuaded to do so by a friend, probably because of its Jacobite implications.[48] Otherwise he kept everything he wrote as a boy. Later on he published some of these early verses and they show that, by means of daily practice during his self-imposed apprenticeship, he had mastered much of the technique required to write in a number of genres, reaching the stage when he was well equipped to undertake almost any poetic enterprise. Furthermore, he not only taught himself the craft of versification, he found the subjects which would continue to preoccupy him, so that the themes of Pope's mature verse can be found in poems he wrote before he was sixteen.

In 'The River' Pope touched on the idea of a golden age and the transitory nature of all earthly things,[49] while in the lines 'To the Author of a Poem, intitled *Successio*' he enrolled Elkanah Settle as a founder member of the *Dunciad* when he told him 'Wit, past thro' thee, no longer is the same' / As Meat digested takes a diff'rent Name.' The stercoraceous image, along with several others from the same poem, would reappear too in later satires.[50] Nothing was wasted.

His juvenilia also reveals Pope veering between the ideal and the squalid, as he was to do throughout his career. So the Horatian 'Ode to Solitude', extolling a rural idyll, is balanced by Spenserian stanzas called 'The Alley' describing a slum in a small town on the edge of the Thames, where 'on the broken Pavement here and there, / Doth many a stinking Sprat and Herring lie' and hungry children are clamouring for bread near 'a Brandy and Tobacco Shop.' He also went from one extreme to the other when he wrote about girls, some days penning verses, in the style of Waller, to a perfect Serenissa, before whom 'The vanquish'd roses lose their pride', whose 'Soft looks of mercy grace the flatt'ring shade',[51] on another day, with Chaucer as his model, recounting a bawdy joke about a couple of country wenches who are rakes at heart.[52]

The contrasting, sometimes inconsistent qualities displayed in Pope's boyhood verses confirm a suggestion made earlier, when discussing his capacity to make favourites of diverse books. His choice of subjects to write about, like his varied reading tastes, reveal a nature that contained contradictory extremes. We should not therefore expect him to develop into an adult with fixed, unchanging attitudes and opinions. Like a number of creative people he was, as Mihaly Csikszentmihalyi has said, not so much an 'individual' as a 'multitude.'[53] Secondly, the fact Pope was willing to write about almost anything and take up different attitudes, suggests that he was primarily interested in problems of treatment and style, rather than in the content of his poems. He was a boy who enjoyed playing with language, seeing what he could make it do.

The time he spent in Binfield laid the foundation for Pope's outstanding achievements in the future. As well as storing his mind and learning the craft of poetry, he was helped by the widespread encouragement he received from an extensive circle of people, some of whom had useful contacts in the larger world. His father, meanwhile, continued to be supportive without being overbearing. There was no danger that Mr Pope would drive his son too hard and, in the process, destroy his gift by causing him to burn out before he became an adult. For one thing, he was a sensible parent. Furthermore he had no literary bent himself and would not have known where to begin, had he been tempted to direct his son's programme of vocational education.

In any case there was no need to drive Pope. He drove himself and he needed very little instruction. Like many gifted children he discovered his own way of doing things, which worked for him, as his unorthodox method of teaching himself Latin and Greek suggests. In boyhood he already showed he had those personal characteristics that enable creative individuals to fulfil their potential. To begin with, he was an independent spirit. No matter how compliant and deferential he might appear to the adults with whom he spent so much time, he was determined to go his own way. In addition, although he enjoyed company, it was not an essential. He was happy, possibly happier, in solitude, where he could be more fully himself, than he was in the society of others. Lastly he had unshakeable confidence in his ability as a poet.

Nothing happened in those early years in Binfield to dim his self confidence or optimism. They were, as he said, happy years. Yet they were not without stress and strain. Almost as soon as he moved to the country he fell ill, and not understanding the nature of his tuberculosis, thought he would soon die but, such was his determination, he fought back and then, facing his possible fate, did what he could to safeguard his reputation for posterity. That immediate crisis over his health passed. However, there were other causes of tension.

Pope knew that his father was a nervous victim of the Penal Laws who had been forced to retire from business precipitously and had already been driven out of one home. Through no fault of his own, Mr Pope had failed in what he set out to achieve in life, but this strengthened his son's resolve to succeed.

It was no bad thing for Pope as a poet that his boyhood was not entirely carefree. Stress in early life appears to be the grit in the oyster that produces the pearl for many artists. It has been estimated that three-quarters of the creative individuals who go on to achieve great things experience some kinds of extreme stress in their early family life, ranging from the death of one or both parents to having a father who fails professionally or goes bankrupt.[54] Undoubtedly, Pope would find that, when he left the forest and returned to the town, he would need every ounce of his resilience and fighting spirit.

Notes

1.   Spence, 14.
2.   Maynard Mack, *Collected in Himself* (University of Delaware Press, 1982), p. 401: 36.
3.   Paul Kléber Monod, *Jacobitism and the English People 1688–1788* (Cambridge University Press, 1989), p. 289.
4.   Ellen Winner, *Gifted Children* (Basic Books, 1996), p. 3.
5.   Spence, 44.

PART II

How Pope Courted the Judges

CHAPTER FOUR

Launching a Career

When Pope returned to London at the age of seventeen he wanted to conquer the literary world. He also hoped for sexual conquests – but more of that later.

As far as making his name as a poet was concerned, he had no intention of standing modestly back and waiting for the reading public to acclaim him. He was aware of the need to win the good opinion of the leaders of literary taste. He was also aware that the men who would judge him were subject to cultural and political bias. In this realization of the facts of literary life, he was unusual. Even now, three centuries later, many of us 'believe that a person who is creative will prevail regardless of environment. The Romantic idealization of the solitary genius is so solidly lodged in our minds that to state the opposite – that even the greatest genius will not accomplish anything without the support of society and culture – borders on blasphemy.'[1] Pope was fortunate in that he worked in a culture that was, on the whole, favourable to him and, as we shall see, he would soon make every effort to keep it so. Meanwhile, at the start of his career, he sought the support of society.

Pope arrived in London bringing with him a leather-bound manuscript into which he had copied his three pastorals, 'Spring', 'Summer' and 'Winter', leaving six pages blank for 'Autumn' which he had yet to finish. He also brought a plan of campaign with him. This did not involve following the normal course of sending his work to a printer in the hope it would be published. Although he intended to make sure the literary world knew he existed, he had no wish to rush into print. In fact he was nervous about putting himself to the test in this way. So when London's leading publisher made him an offer in 1706, he turned it down.[2] It would be 1709 before all four *Pastorals* appeared in Tonson's *Poetical Miscellanies, The Sixth Part*.

Tonson had heard about the poems as soon as he did because he was the secretary of the Whig Kit-Cat Club, where several members were shown the manuscript. Pope spent those early years in London preparing the ground for his literary debut and arranging his own advance publicity, by sending his manuscript to be read, and commented on, by a carefully chosen group of gentlemen. There were at least twelve of these readers.[3] They included peers and commoners, Tories and Whigs, but only one Catholic (the not very devout Wycherley) because Pope, having left behind the Papist enclave in Binfield, was looking for a wider public. Several of the readers were writers themselves, published ones including William Congreve and Dr Samuel Garth as well as Wycherley, also gentleman amateurs such as the Duke of Buckingham and

George Granville, while the Earl of Halifax, the Lord Chancellor, liked to think of himself as a patron of writers. They represented a cross section of the polite world and were the arbiters of taste, the gatekeepers.[4] In approaching these judges of literary merit Pope supposed that their approval would go some way to launching him on his career. Later on he said all these early readers gave him 'the greatest encouragement.'[5] So he gained a new support group to promote him. Up to a point therefore his advance publicity campaign was a success. However the fact he waged a campaign at all inevitably aroused resentment in some quarters. As he was to say himself, 'The life of a wit is warfare upon earth.'[6]

Pope continued revising the pastoral poems after he took them to London, in an effort to make them fault free, and he hoped that some of the men to whom he showed his manuscript would be his mentors as he proceeded with this task. The men who had helped and encouraged him in Binfield were not authors and it was authors who Pope believed could best advise him from now on.

He turned first to William Wycherley and asked him to tell him his faults 'as an unexperienced writer.'[7] However, Wycherley was incapable of this. His own achievements as one of the best of the Restoration dramatists were all in the past. Added to which, the creator of *The Country Wife* and *The Plain-Dealer* had lost his memory as a result of an illness in 1678.[8] By the time Pope sought him out he was liable to write down as his own the ideas of whatever author he happened to have been reading the previous night.[9] He had been handsome and successful with women. Now at sixty-three he was given to gazing at the portrait Lely had painted of him at the age of twenty-eight, and repeating with 'melancholy emphasis' the Virgilian motto he had ordered for it, 'Quantum mutatus ab illo' [How greatly changed from that].[10] Pope did not give up though. If Wycherley could not give him literary advice he could still provide him with useful contacts. Furthermore as the older dramatist had perfect courtly manners, he could be a social role model. Watching and listening to him, the boy in his rustic dress and own cropped hair received his first lessons on how to conduct himself in sophisticated London society.

For a while, the two of them were always together and the sight of them, in Will's, soon attracted attention. Few of the writers and critics who frequented that coffee house had any idea at first who Wycherley's companion was, and some of them disliked him on the spot. They noticed that, young and diminutive as Pope was, he appeared to dominate the older man who, even if his powers were failing, was still the most distinguished member of their circle. John Dennis conjured up an eerie picture of them with Pope as Wycherley's 'evil Genius,' and said 'while that Spectre hath haunted that ancient Wit, he has never been able to write or talk like himself.'[11] Others, when they realized the boy was 'setting up for a Wit and Poet' confounded his impudence.[12]

Nor was it long before the clientele at Will's realized that Pope's courtship of Wycherley was part of a scheme to get to know and win over influential men.

The genteel Charles Gildon, himself a struggling writer, was scathing about this endeavour by an unknown youth who, in his eyes, was a country bumpkin. Astonished, he noted how Pope, 'furnish'd with a very good Assurance, and a Plausible, or at least Cringing Way of Insinuation, first got acquainted with that Ingenious Gentleman and excellent Critick Mr. Walsh.'[13]

Pope 'got acquainted' with William Walsh quite easily because one of Wycherley's good deeds was to send the *Pastorals* to the man whom Dryden had considered 'the best critic of our nation.'[14] Walsh read the poems over several times with great satisfaction, and finding 'the Verses very tender and easy,' decided 'Virgil had written nothing so good' at the author's age. He told Wycherley he would be pleased to meet Pope, offering, if he called at his house, to go over his poems to give him his opinion on particular details.[15] So Pope found the mentor he was looking for, one who was neither abrasive or fulsome, 'To Failings mild, but zealous for Desert,' whom he eventually gave a place of honour in *An Essay on Criticism* as the 'Muse's Judge and Friend,' that is the ideal critic (l. 729).

Walsh was himself the author of pastorals as well as elegies and songs. He was also a Whig Member of Parliament and a courtier. Like his verses, his manners and dress were easy and elegant. Characteristically he confessed that in his youth he had been so susceptible to the charms of women, he had committed every amorous indiscretion, short of marriage.[16] He was totally lacking in originality and a little lacking in vitality. Possibly his health was not very good. He died at the age of forty-five, some months before the *Pastorals* were published.

Walsh was valuable to Pope at the start of his career as a perfect barometer of refined public taste. Indeed he was so much a man of his age that his reputation has not survived it. Few of us living now would have heard of him were it not for the advice he gave his young friend to whom he said, 'Though we had had several great poets, we never had any one great poet that was correct,' urging Pope to make that 'his study and aim.'[17] As a critic he had an excellent ear for the music of the line, as his detailed comments on the manuscript of the *Pastorals* show.[18] Guided by Walsh, Pope proceeded with the lengthy business of revising the *Pastorals*, concentrating on the versification, changing words and phrases to make the lines smoother, easier and more flowing, as well as precisely appropriate in connotation.

The *Pastorals* are interesting, however, not just because Pope turned them into a technical *tour de force* but because, within the tightly imposed limits of a particular verse medium, he expressed perennial feelings about the human lot. The four poems represent four times of the day, from dawn to midnight; four seasons of the year; four stages in the life of man, from innocence to maturity; and four stages in the history of the world, golden, silver, brazen and iron.[19] This scheme enables Pope to show that there is pain and sorrow even in Arcadia. No snake hides in its harmless groves but the serpent of unrequited love abides in the breast of the poet's *alter ego* Alexis, while Aegon, tormented by sexual passion, flings himself over the cliff – *et in Arcadia ego*. In 'Winter' the shepherds gather in the cold and darkness around a tomb to mourn the death of the fair Daphne. This was Pope's favourite out of the four pastorals. He makes the dead shepherdess represent the principle of order and harmony, now departed from the world. However, the mourners see that Daphne still reigns in a realm beyond the stars and Lycidas dedicates himself to her service, just as Pope was to do. In the rest of his career he kept on returning to the subject of an ideal order and harmony, trying to convince others – and himself – that it was divinely appointed. In *An Essay on Man* he reflected on the evidence for its existence. In the *Dunciad* he wrote an inverted pastoral about London where instead of the crystal streams of Arcadia, 'the fresh vomit runs forever green' (A. 2:148) and where a descent into chaos is a distinct possibility.

The view of life and aspirations expressed in the *Pastorals* were already in place before they were shown to Walsh. Pope praised his mentor for helping to make the verse 'sing.'[20] and to the end of his life considered these poems 'the most correct in versification and musical in numbers of all his works.'[21] As a further endorsement of the lyrical quality of the *Pastorals* one might add that, even if they do not have many general readers these days, there are few of us who have not heard the lines from 'Summer' that begin, 'Where-e'er you walk, cool Gales shall fan the Glade,' as these were borrowed by Handel and are sung regularly.

Underlying Walsh's advice to Pope to aim at correctness was the belief, shared by many of his contemporaries, that it was impossible to say anything new, the Greeks and Romans having said it all. Pope was already wondering though how he could add something of his own to the poems he wrote. It was his question about how far imitation should be carried which prompted Walsh to answer that aiming for technical perfection was the only task left for the modern English poet.[22] Pope did not argue but, without wishing to break with the neoclassical tradition, he was willing to expand it and take it in new directions and Walsh could not help him in this. However, not every writer at that time despaired of doing anything new. One of the more enterprising ones was Samuel Garth.

Dr Garth read the *Pastorals* without making any recorded comment, but provided their author with ideas for future poems and kept alive his social conscience. He did this indirectly when he gave the poet a copy of his mock epic *The Dispensary*, the work he had written making fun of the opposition of London's apothecaries to a scheme he supported to open a free clinic for the poor. Garth's updating of the burlesque mode, by giving it a topical theme and London setting, suggested a way of teaching and delighting readers which was naturally appealing to Pope who already had a keen sense of the ludicrous. *The Dispensary* provided one of the models for *The Rape of the Lock* and later for the *Dunciad*. Garth, who was inventive himself, encouraged his friend's inventive talent. Unlike Addison, for instance, he approved from the start of Pope's idea of adding the sylphs and gnomes to the poem about Belinda.[23]

To the young Lady Mary Wortley Montagu, Garth was a sardonic figure with a superior frown, striding round London in his red cloak.[24] To his friends he was the best of companions, amusing as well as humane and courageous. He was a free thinker and Pope, who almost certainly had not met one before, was a bit worried about this at first, until he decided that, all the same, Garth was the best of Christians, even if he did not know it.[25]

George Granville, was one of the most enthusiastic of Pope's early readers. As soon as he read the *Pastorals* he invited a friend 'Harry' to his lodging to drink a 'Bottle of good old claret' and meet Wycherley, who was bringing with him 'a young Poet, newly inspired, who promises miracles', comparing the boy, as Walsh had done, with Virgil.[26] If, as seems likely 'Harry' was Sir Henry Sheers, he presumably accepted the invitation and was soon reading the *Pastorals* for himself.

Granville was a gentleman amateur in the world of letters – one of several who promoted Pope early in his career. Like Walsh he combined writing with politics, though the two men were in opposing parties. During Anne's reign, when the Tories were in power, Granville was prominent in public life. He was included in the group of twelve peers created to safeguard the Administration in 1712, becoming Lord Lansdowne. The rest of the time he was either in eclipse or in disgrace. During the 1715 rebellion he was suspected of Jacobitism and was imprisoned in the Tower for two years where, with characteristic urbanity, he invited Pope to dine with him and see the lions free of charge.[27] Later, at the time of the Atterbury plot, he left England for the Continent where he stayed ten years, associating openly with Lord Mar and other supporters of the Pretender.

In his political sympathies Granville was representative of many of Pope's friends, two thirds of whom helped the Jacobite cause during at least part of their lives.[28] Granville's power and influence, when Pope first met him, encouraged him to think an eventual Stuart restoration was a practical possibility. At this stage several members of the Tory party hoped that the Act of Settlement might be rescinded, and that a Stuart prince, one who promised not to endanger the Church of England, would become heir to the throne. Meanwhile Granville was typical of those who served Anne loyally because she was herself a Stuart and fully supported English interests, unlike William.

The warm welcome Granville gave Pope was not entirely disinterested. Like other politicians of his day he saw how a promising writer could be useful. It comes as no surprise, therefore, to find him redirecting Pope's thoughts towards political verse. As well as the *Pastorals*, he had seen *Windsor Forest*, begun earlier at Trumbull's instigation. Sometime after 1710 Granville suggested how it might be converted from a mainly topographical poem, lauding the national heritage in general terms, into a work specifically celebrating the Tory Peace of Utrecht and an England blessed by the reign of Queen Anne.[29]

There was yet another man to whom Pope turned for advice during his early years in London. This was 'honest, hatless Cromwell with red breeches.'[30] Henry Cromwell had been one of the Dryden circle that gathered at Will's. Now he could be found most days at the Blue Ball near Drury Lane, or occupying a 'Speculative Angle' in Widow Hambleton's, another coffee house in the same area.[31] He divided his time between literature and women. His taste in the former was conservative, mainly the Latin classics, including Ovid, whom he translated. His taste in the latter was more eclectic, ranging from the Drury Lane 'nymphs' to more genteel ladies, including Elizabeth Thomas, a poet herself, whom he called Sappho. He was deaf, but this was not always a disadvantage. When he went to the theatre he could give all his attention to the females in the audience, without being distracted by the play.[32] He was a fondly regarded figure in coffee house society, caricatured several times in *The Tatler* as Squire Easy, the amorous Bard, and as Sir Timothy the Critick.[33]

As a critic Cromwell was a pedant, very concerned with grammatical niceties, and Pope teased his new friend about this. Nevertheless he consulted him about several of his boyhood translations and imitations, and he liked to discuss general literary principles with Cromwell, thereby testing reactions to views he would express in *An Essay on Criticism*.

Cromwell was also helpful in talking Wycherley round when the latter cooled off Pope for a while. Pope suspected that Gildon had been making ill-natured remarks about him and he probably had but, even without this intervention, the friendship with the old writer was destined to have its ups and downs. Ironically, instead of offering the young poet advice about his work, Wycherley asked him to revise some of his own poetic bits and pieces, so that they could be published and make a little money, as he was perennially hard up. When Mr Pope heard about the request he begged his son to refuse, saying very sensibly he would do 'nothing but get enemies by it', but Pope could not bring himself to say 'No.'[34] So for over two years from 1706 he struggled to give Wycherley's disordered and verbose lines unity and elegance. He succeeded in part, but not before he had antagonized their author who became all too humanly resentful, because there were far more corrections than he had envisaged.[35] Pope was upset as well but the estrangement was temporary. 'Soft, beneficent, Curteous Mr. Cromwell' effected a reconciliation with such success that Wycherley 'was for writing every Post' to the poet, and had to be reminded that two letters he had written already could hardly have reached him yet.[36]

Cromwell came down to stay with Pope in Binfield, where he impressed him by gaining the heart of Mrs Nelson, one of the family's Catholic neighbours, even though he appeared before her in an unfashionable 'long, black unpowder'd Perriwig, nay without so much as the Extremities of clean Linnen in Neckcloth and Cuffs!'[37] Pope was fascinated by Cromwell's amorous successes and would dearly have loved the same for himself. He flirted madly whenever he had the chance and told his friend about any encounter in which he

4.1   Teresa and Martha Blount. Charles Jervas, *c.* 1716

felt he had made some headway. In one letter he described an adventure he had had when he was travelling home from town one day. Sitting alone in the coach he realized a woman was about to join him. From the conversation in the roadway he gathered she was sick and was at first dismayed. However, as soon as she sat down and removed her hood, he saw she was remarkably good looking. To his surprise she addressed him by name and, although he did not remember her, he found out she was a young bride returning to the husband she had recently married in the Binfield area. Relishing by now the idea of an unexpected *tête à tête*, he set out to entertain her in a conversation where everything was said and nothing admitted. As he wrote to Cromwell:

> I ventur'd to prescribe her some Fruit (which I happen'd to have in the Coach), which being forbidden by Her damn'd Doctors, she had the more Inclination to. In short, I tempted, and she Eat; nor was I more like the Devil, than she like Eve. Having the good Success of the aforesaid Gentleman before my eyes, I put on the Gallantry of the old Serpent, & in spite of my Evil Forme, accosted her with all the Gayety I was master of.

Pope went on to report that the young lady recovered from her indisposition. 'In less than an hour she grew pleasant, her Colour return'd, & she was pleased to say, my Prescription had wrought an Immediate Cure. In a word I had the pleasantest Journey imaginable.'[38]

On this showing, if the seduction of women depended on the ability to use words alone, Pope might well have had a future as a libertine. However he had other encounters which brought home the brutal reality of sexual life. A year after the incident in the coach, Pope was at an assembly when a lady 'rally'd [his] Person so much, as to cause a total Subversion of [his] Countenance.' His confusion and silence at this public ridicule lasted until he was sitting alone with a pen in his hand. The next time he met the lady with the robust sense of humour in company, he presented her with the following 'Rondeau to Phillis':

> You know where you did despise
> (Tother day) my little eyes,
> Little Legs, and little Thighs
> And, some things, of little Size,
>   You know where.
> You, tis true, have fine back Eyes,
> Taper Legs, and tempting Thighs,
> Yet what more than all we prize
> Is a Thing of little Size,
>   You know where.

'Phillis' passed the verses round, and soon the poet's friends were asking for copies.[39] Pope could always win the war with words, though some of his victories were Pyrrhic ones.

On the whole Pope enjoyed life in London but he could not afford to stay there indefinitely. Lack of money drove him home periodically. Once there, he wrote letters to Cromwell telling him what he thought his urbane friend expected to hear, namely that Binfield was dull, where time was measured out by the seasons for peas and artichokes, peopled by hard-riding gentry, whose main contact with poetry came when they roared out the songs of the drinking man's bard Tom D'Urfey.[40] Yet at home he slipped back into the kind of behaviour expected of him by his pious parents. During Holy Week, when prayers were said in the house four times daily, he became 'an Occasional Conformist.' He was fully aware he was a social chameleon, explaining to Cromwell, 'Just as I am drunk or Scandalous in town, according to my Company, I am for the same reason Grave and Godly here.'[41] He was somewhat disconcerted by his own capacity for role playing and wondered if all men were as inconsistent as he was, concluding that life was 'a true Modern play, neither Tragedy, Comedy, nor Farce, nor one, nor all of these,' in which 'every Actor is much better known by his having the same Face, than by his keeping the same Character.'[42]

The one constant in Pope's nature was his function as a poet. It gave him his identity. For that reason he laboured during five years to make his poetic debut as perfect as possible and, having done all he could, was still apprehensive as the time approached for the *Pastorals* to appear in print. When publication was delayed in November 1708, he spoke of being 'mercifully reprieved by the Sovereign Power of Jacob Tonson, from being brought forth to Publick Punishment.'[43] Tonson's *Miscellanies* were finally published on 2 May 1709, with Pope making sure he was out of town for the occasion. Two weeks later Wycherley wrote to report that the *Pastorals* had 'safely run the Gauntlet, through all the Coffee-houses', adding in another letter that his young friend's verse gave 'a relish to the whole insipid Hotch-Potch' it was mingled with.[44]

Despite Wycherley's encouraging remarks, the truth was that Pope's publication fell flat. Those writers at Will's who had watched derisively as he courted Wycherley, Walsh and others, ignored his work. Apart from a possible wish to put the young man in his place, there were two reasons for this. To begin with, the *Pastorals* came out at the same time as the first number of Richard Steele's *Tatler*, and this 'whimsical new Newspaper' eclipsed Pope's debut as the main talking point in London's coffee houses.[45] Also, what Wycherley referred to as the 'hotch-potch' in the rest of the *Miscellanies*, included six pastorals by Ambrose Philips, peopled by English rustics, speaking an early version of 'mummerset.' These soon proved to be more popular than Pope's exquisite and strictly neoclassical poems, as well as receiving more critical attention after Addison praised them for breathing 'new life' into the genre.[46]

Pope was undaunted. Even when praise continued to be heaped on Philips's pastorals, he never doubted his own were superior. He had gained in confidence as a poet while he was in London because he had won the approval of several good judges of literary merit, even if he had not pleased others. The early signs of hostility he encountered, from other writers such as Gildon and ladies such as

'Phillis', came as a painful surprise after the unfailing good will he had met with in Binfield, but he did not wilt when he met with opposition. As his reaction to 'Phillis' showed, he fought back, with the only weapon available to him – words.

Notes

1. Mihaly Csikszentmihalyi, *Creativity* (HarperCollins, 1996), p. 330.
2. *Corr.* 1: 17.
3. Spence, pp. 616–17.
4. Csikszentmihalyi, p. 262.
5. TW. 1: 37n.
6. Preface to the *Works* 1717, l. 91.
7. *Corr.* 1: 5.
8. Spence, 90.
9. Spence, 87.
10. Spence, 77.
11. *Reflections Critical and Satyrical, Upon a Late Rhapsody, Call'd An Essay Upon Criticism* (1711).
12. Charles Gildon, *Memoirs of the Life of William Wycherley* (1718).
13. Ibid.
14. 'Postscript' to the *Aeneis* (1697).
15. *Corr.* 1: 7.
16. 'Letters & Poems, Amorous and Gallant' (1692) in the British Library's Manuscripts Department.
17. Spence, 73.
18. Maynard Mack, *The Last and Greatest Art* (University of Delaware Press, 1984), contains photographs of pages with Walsh's corrections.
19. Martin C. Battestin, 'The Transforming Power: Nature and Art in Pope's *Pastorals*', *Eighteenth-Century Studies*, 2 (1969), 183–204. This paper discusses the structure and theme of order in the *Pastorals*.
20. *Essay on Criticism*, 735–6.
21. Quoted TW. 1: 59.
22. *Corr.* 1: 20.
23. Spence, 105.
24. *Town Eclogue*, 'Saturday,' 78.
25. 'Farewell to London,' 15–16.
26. Lansdowne's *Works* (1732), 1: 437. Other suggestions to identify 'Harry' include Henry St John Bolingbroke and Henry Cromwell. See Carolyn D. Williams, 'Pope and Granville: Fictions of Friendship', *Notes and Queries*, vol. 236 (1991), 184–6.
27. *Corr.* 1: 287.
28. Howard Erskine-Hill, 'Alexander Pope: The Political Poet in his Time,' *Eighteenth-Century Studies*, 15:2 (1981–82), 123–4.
29. Spence, 102.
30. John Gay, 'Mr. Pope's Welcome from Greece' (1720), stanza 17.
31. *Corr.* 1: 70.
32. *Corr.* 1: 51.
33. *The Tatler*, nos 47, 49 and 165.
34. Spence, 82.

35. Spence, 83.
36. *Corr.* 1: 116 and 134.
37. *Corr.* 1: 47.
38. *Corr.* 1: 67.
39. *Corr.* 1: 129.
40. *Corr.* 1: 81.
41. Ibid.
42. *Corr.* 1: 71.
43. *Corr.* 1: 51.
44. *Corr.* 1: 59 and 62.
45. *Corr.* 1: 59.
46. *Spectator*, 523, 30 October 1712.

CHAPTER FIVE

A Poet's Manifesto

By the time Tonson's *Miscellanies* were in print and the *Pastorals* lay on the coffee house tables, buried under copies of the *Tatler*, another beautifully presented display manuscript was going the rounds of Pope's acquaintances. This was the 1709 version of *An Essay on Criticism*. Having read 'all the best Critics'[1] as a boy, he was now, at the age of twenty-one, prepared to issue his own literary manifesto. In it he would define poetry, decree the true relationship between a writer and his reader, and proclaim his faith in the power of literature to protect all that was best in civilization.

In the *Essay* Pope became a critic, motivated by an urge to command the field of competent judges of literature. He had this aim throughout his career, beginning at the age of sixteen when he wrote a *Discourse on Pastoral Poetry*, giving the criteria by which he thought his own pastoral poems should be judged. Tonson did not print the *Discourse* in the *Miscellanies*, but Pope made sure it was included among the prose pieces published in his *Works* in 1717. Right up to the end of his life, he was still seeking to shape public taste. Hence the *Art of Sinking* and the *Dunciad*.

When Pope set out to direct critical opinion in the *Essay*, he went to the heart of the matter by describing the creative process. His account of this was a comprehensive one, very far from being confined to the exclusively rational procedures sometimes associated with neoclassical theory. In particular he wanted to show that reason and judgement alone could not create good poetry. Imagination and feeling were every bit as important.

The role of imagination in the creative process was slighted by modern thinkers in Pope's day – as were intuition and inspiration. Instead the discursive faculty was extolled. Thomas Hobbes called the imagination 'decaying sense' and separated it firmly from judgement, writing that 'judgment begets the strength and structure, and Fancy begets the ornaments of a Poem.'[2] In this way the function of the imagination was limited to that of providing pleasing images to decorate ideas in poetry, ideas that could be expressed more honestly in plain language. Such a separation ruled out the possibility of imagination being a faculty that envisages and shapes.

Furthermore the association of poetic inspiration with religious enthusiasm made neoclassical critics shy away from the thought that there was anything mysterious about the way poetic imagination worked. Sir William Davenant, who admired Hobbes, thought the wise poet, like the wise general, was one who employed the most judgement, and he decried inspiration as a 'dangerous word.' He added it was an outmoded notion, 'deriv'd from the ancient Ethnick Poets', who pretended to be inspired to make their utterances appear to be religious revelations.³ A moderate spokesman for the Augustan attitude was Addison. He made a few timid steps in the direction of romanticism in his essays on 'The Pleasures of the Imagination', without ever suggesting that that faculty, which he described as an image making one, could transmute the ideas of sensation or see beyond their veil.⁴

In contrast the *Essay* described the creative power of the poet as 'th'informing Soul' that 'With Spirit feeds, with Vigour fills the whole, / Each Motion guides, and ev'ry Nerve sustains; *It self unseen*' (ll. 76–9). These lines suggest Pope did not think of the creative imagination and judgement as separate faculties. However, it is sometimes difficult to work out what the *Essay* is saying on this subject for two reasons. First of all there is the problem of terminology. Even now a reader can fail to notice that Pope discusses imagination at all because, in the whole poem, he uses the actual term 'imagination' once only – in line fifty-eight. Instead he speaks of 'wit', making the most of that word's protean nature. Second, when writing about aesthetics, Pope is deliberately gnomic, in the hope of warding off an attack from those who thought judgement was the pre-eminent poetic virtue. Hence those lines which have been a crux from the time they first appeared in print:

> Some to whom Heav'n in Wit has been profuse,
> Want as much more, to turn it into use (ll. 80–81)

The couplet makes sense if you suppose that wit in the first line means imagination, while in the second it means judgement. In these lines Pope was trying to find room for a concept of wit which he knew was no longer fashionable, as described, for instance, by Joseph Glanvill. Around the turn of the century Glanvill had said, 'For true Wit is a perfection of our faculties, chiefly in the understanding and imagination; Wit in the understanding is a sagacity to find out the nature, relations and consequences of things.'⁵ Another time he called it a 'faculty to dive into the depth of things, to find out their Causes and Relatives, Consonancies and Disagreements, and to make fit, useful and unobvious applications to their respective Relations and Dependencies.'⁶

A definition of wit which includes the idea of insight, on the lines suggested by Glanvill, clarifies another much debated couplet in the *Essay*:

> True Wit is Nature to advantage drest,
> What oft was Thought, but ne'er so well exprest (ll. 296–7).

This is sometimes taken to mean that it does not matter how banal poetry is, as long as it is elegantly worded. Some of Pope's contemporaries gave the impression they believed this, mainly because they despaired of ever having a new idea. So Addison wrote, 'We have little else left us but to represent the common Sense of Mankind in more strong, more beautiful, or more uncommon

Lights.'[7] However if wit includes the idea of insight and nature is truth, then poetry expresses something more than mere common sense. Pope believed it did. In the display manuscript he had written, 'ne'er before exprest.'[8] That 1709 definition would have been hard to sustain however. So, ever conscious of his audience, he made a cautious revision.

If Pope had been the matter-of-fact rationalist he is sometimes made out to be we might expect judgement to come into its own in those parts of the *Essay* where he discusses design in poetry. However, instead of going along with Hobbes who said 'Judgment begets strength and structure',[9] Pope said a poem grows organically. In the 1709 version of the *Essay* he used the image of childbirth to describe a work of true wit, which after '*A full Conception*' is '*brought forth with Ease*.'[10] The products of false wit, on the other hand, are not part of any natural process. When Pope condemns poets who to '*Conceit* alone their taste confine' (l. 289), it is because their work is purely cerebral, artificial and inorganic. False wit is what Hobbes had in mind when he spoke dismissively of 'Fancy' which 'begets the ornaments of a poem.'[11] In the *Essay* Pope speaks of poets who decorate their poems with fine metaphors and glittering thoughts – 'with Gold and Jewels cover ev'ry Part' when they are 'unskill'd to trace / The naked Nature and the living Grace' (ll. 293ff.).

The belief that the creation of a work of art is an organic process has a long history. It was held by Longinus and before him by Plato. Pope quotes over sixty people in the *Essay*, but he gave Longinus the place of honour at the end of his list of praiseworthy ancient critics. There was a bond between the two men because both thought of the creative faculty as an indivisible trinity comprised of judgement, imagination and feeling. So Pope made Longinus the tutelary spirit of his *Essay*.

In *Peri Hupsous*, the sole work that has survived by Longinus, the section on structure says, 'Composition is of the greatest importance in giving weight to noble passages, in the same way as the synthesis of the parts gives beauty to the body, for any member cut from the others and taken by itself is of no great account, but when they are all together they make a perfect harmony.'[12] In the *Essay* this simile, comparing a work of art to the human body, is repeated:

> In Wit, as Nature, what affects our Hearts
> Is not th'exactness of peculiar Parts;
> 'Tis not a *Lip*, or *Eye*, we Beauty call
> But the joint Force and full Result of all (ll. 243–6)

Later on, in the *Preface* to the *Iliad*, Pope used plant metaphors to describe the structure of Homer's epic.[13] The implications of seeing a poem in terms of a growing plant are many. The final form of the poem is inevitably contained in the initial idea for it, just as the root, stem and leaves to come are contained in the seed; the parts are inseparable from the whole. The process is complex in that the conscious and unconscious, the willed and spontaneous are present at the same time. The creative imagination, called 'Wit' in the *Essay* and 'Invention' in the *Preface* makes a work of art an organic unity. Speaking of this co-ordinating power at work in the *Iliad*, Pope described it as the 'strong and ruling Faculty' which 'like a powerful Star ... in the Violence of its Course, drew all things within its Vortex.'[14]

As that last image suggests, the poet works best when his imagination has been fired. Longinus provided Pope with an explanation of how emotion functions in the poetic process. As well as giving life to a poem, emotion helps to organize it into a unified whole, for when a poet feels deeply his imagination is directed to the essentials of his subject, enabling him to arrange his material in the most effective way. To illustrate this point Longinus quotes Sappho's 'That man seems to me,' in which she describes her feelings as she watches the woman she loves being courted by a male admirer. Sexual passion has so concentrated Sappho's mind that her many varied sensations are brought into unity, and her poem is all the more powerful as a result.[15] It is apparent from other passages analysed in *Peri Hupsous* that Longinus is not saying that all art arises out of personal experience as Sappho's seems to have done. It is important, however, that the poet enters fully into the life of his subject. Later, when Pope came to write about Shakespeare, he would say that passionate empathy was a feature of his plays, just as it was of Homer's epics.[16]

Peri Hupsous is usually translated as *On the Sublime* but, as Wordsworth realized long ago, its subject is actually 'animated, empassioned, energetic' writing.[17] Longinus believed that great literature moves the reader. For this to happen, the poet's passion must be genuine and profound. If a writer fakes an emotion outside his range, he will produce bombastic nonsense. While if his feelings are shallow, his work will shrivel and wither when it is reread.

During Pope's lifetime Cartesian rationalism, with its emphasis on whatever could be mathematically demonstrated, encouraged men to distinguish between how they responded emotionally and how they thought as rational creatures. Passion, as much as imagination, could only hinder logical thinking. However, just as Pope refused to separate wit and judgement, so he refused to separate wit and feeling. Like Longinus he argued that poetry must gain the reader's heart. Poets may sometimes break the literary rules but they must never transgress against this end. When, in the *Essay*, he urges critics not to focus their attention on petty faults, he tells them to respond to the feeling in the work they are reading, 'Where Nature moves, and Rapture warms the Mind' (1. 236). It is no use a poem being correct if it lacks energy and passion:

> ... such Lays as neither *ebb* or *flow*
> That shunning Faults, one quiet Tenour keep;
> We cannot *blame* indeed – but we may *sleep* (ll. 239–42).

Later, in the *Epistle to Dr. Arbuthnot*, he would dismiss anyone who wrote in this way as a mere 'Man of Rhymes,' extolling instead 'the Poet':

> ... who gives my breast a thousand pains,
> Can make me feel each Passion that he feigns,
> In rage, compose with more than magic Art;
> With Pity, and with Terror, tear my heart (ll. 340–43).

Those lines make it clear 'the Poet' is always disciplined and in control. Even 'in rage' he composes 'with more than magic Art.' In the *Essay* Pope makes a similar point, taking over Longinus's simile in which the poet is compared to the rider of a spirited horse. The rider has to use the bit more than the spur. Like Longinus Pope insists that when a poet controls passion, he does not suppress it. The emotional impact of his work is increased because:

> The wing'd Courser, like the gen'rous Horse
> Shows most true Mettle when you check his course.' (ll. 83–6)

No one who read, still less knew, Pope when he was alive, thought he lacked passion, though since his death far too much has been made of his own occasional claims to be a temperate man, ruled by the dictates of common sense. There are lines in the *Essay* where he gives the impression he is like this – lines in which he tells men, '*Avoid Extreams*,' 'At ev'ry Trifle scorn to take offence' and 'let not each gay *Turn* thy Rapture move' (ll. 384ff.). On the basis of such solemn injunctions we can decide 'a commitment to moderation was fundamental to Pope's temperament.'[18] This was true part of the time but we have also to bear in mind that the apostle of moderation wrote the Alps passage in the *Essay* and went on to write the apocalyptic finale to the *Dunciad*.

Pope is also the man who, in everyday life, all too often took offence at trifling matters and was easily moved to rapture. Lines in the *Essay* which advocate a temperate view of life are written by a man who struggled against the grain to be a dispassionate onlooker and, when they are applied to art, are designed to reassure readers who distrusted enthusiasm and had read the rationalist philosophers. Even so, the writer of them knew that passion is the life's breath of poetry.

If the majority of readers still think the *Essay on Criticism* makes artistic creativity sound a more banal activity than it is, this is largely Pope's own fault. He felt he could be explicit about the rational elements in poetry as these were unquestioned, while he expressed his more equivocal ideas about the nature of creative imagination in images and aphorisms. In the event he was too guarded. The *Essay*, which is supposed to be clear and straightforward, is actually ambiguous. John Dennis would say it was obscure and would fail to see that Pope admired Longinus as much as he did,[19] while it would strike Romantic and Victorian critics as being no more than a conventional neoclassical exercise. Pope had his own misgivings when he told John Caryll that his poem would not go into a second edition because it was a treatise 'which not one gentleman, even of a liberal education, can understand.'[20] He was wrong about the number of editions the poem would have, otherwise he was right. An *Essay on Criticism* was to become the most misunderstood poem in the language.

Notes

1. Spence, 44.
2. 'Answer to Davenant's *Preface to Gondibert*' (1650) in *Critical Essays of the Seventeenth Century*, ed J.E. Spingarn, 3 vols (Indiana University Press, 1963), 2: 54–67.
3. '*Preface to Gondibert*' (1650) in Spingarn, 2: 1–53.
4. *Spectator*, nos. 411–21.
5. *Essay Concerning Preaching*, 2nd edn (1703), p. 72.
6. *A Whip for the Droll* (1700), pp. 4–5.
7. *Spectactor*, no. 253.
8. *Pope's Essay on Criticism 1709: A Study of the Bodleian Manuscript Text with Facsimiles, Transcripts and Variants*, ed Robert M. Schmitz (Washington University Press, 1962), p. 62.
9. 'Answer to Davenant's *Preface to Gondibert*', Spingarn, *op. cit.*
10. Schmitz, *op. cit.*, p. 50.
11. 'Answer to Davenant's *Preface to Gondibert*', Spingarn, *op. cit.*
12. 'On Literary Excellence', in *Literary Criticism: Plato to Dryden*, ed and trans. Allan H. Gilbert (Wayne University Press, 1962), ch. 40: 85.
13. TW. 7: 17.
14. TW. 7: 5.
15. *Op. cit.*, ch. 10: 24.
16. TW. 7: 4–5.
17. Letter to J. Fletcher in *Letters of the Wordsworth Family 1787–1855*, ed W. Knight (London, 1907), 2: 250.
18. Brean Hammond, *Pope* (Harvester New Readings, 1986), p. 31.
19. *Reflections Critical and Satyrical, Upon a Late Rhapsody, Call'd An Essay Upon Criticism* (1711).
20. *Corr.* 1: 128.

CHAPTER SIX

Making Use of 'ev'ry *Friend* – and ev'ry *Foe*'

The first review Pope received was of *An Essay on Criticism*. It showed that his assiduous efforts to win over the literary gatekeepers who direct public taste had – to say the least – not been an unqualified success, and he had only himself to blame, in that he had deliberately provoked the wrath of one of London's established critics, John Dennis. In his *Essay* Pope had included a three-line portrait of Dennis, using him as an example of that literary intemperance which the ideal critic should avoid. The old man's pugnacity was proverbial and he had a persecution mania. Jokes about him had been circulating in the coffee houses for years but no one had gone into print with these until the young tyro Pope wrote:

> But *Appius* reddens at each Word you speak,
> And *stares, Tremendous*! with a *threatening Eye*,
> Like some *fierce Tyrant* in *old Tapestry*! (585–7)

Appius was the name of the hero in Dennis's play *Appius and Virginia* which had failed after four nights a couple of years earlier, while 'tremendous' was a favourite word he overworked in both his conversation and critical writings.

Quite a few readers who knew Dennis raised their eyebrows when they came upon this squib, including Addison. Heaven only knows why Pope made an example of his much older contemporary in this way. As it happened the two of them shared some fundamental critical principles and both of them were passionate about poetry. Perhaps this was part of the trouble. Dennis expressed his opinions in such extreme terms and with so much vehemence that he often hovered on the verge of the ridiculous, so the author of the *Essay* may have been anxious to distance himself. Then again, Pope always had a subversive streak. From the beginning of his career, he felt he had to be circumspect in his dealings with those individuals who wielded political influence or were socially prominent. However, he was not passive by nature and he needed an outlet. So he did not hesitate to speak his mind about members of the literary community, few of whom met with his unqualified approval. He despised many of them and showed it because he did not believe they could do him any real harm.

The *Essay* was published on 15 May 1711. A month or so later the publisher Bernard Lintot sent its author an advance copy of Dennis's commentary on it. It was a thirty-two-page indictment, comprehensively damning the poem and the

poet. On 29 June it would be on sale as *Reflections Critical and Satyrical, Upon a Late Rhapsody, Call'd An Essay Upon Criticism.*

Dennis was a committed Whig and fervent patriot who believed, without question, that English liberty depended on the revolutionary settlement of 1689 and the Act of Settlement of 1701 which ensured the monarchy would remain Protestant. As he also held that nothing could be true poetry which did not support 'the lawful established Government,' he was bound to be suspicious of a writer who was a Papist and who, by the nature of things, was certain to be a Jacobite as well.[1] Sure enough, as Pope sat down to read the manuscript Lintot had sent him, he discovered his *Essay* supposedly contained covert Papist and Jacobite propaganda. What were to prove the lifelong political and religious attacks on him had begun.

[handwritten margin note: Implies these were read in — not intended (directly)]

Then he found that Dennis dismissed ninety per cent of his thoughts on poetry as nonsense. Nor was his character spared. His contemptible and repellent personality was matched only by his contemptible and repellent physique. So he learned he was a stupid, impotent and venomous 'hunch-back'd Toad' who was lucky not to have been put down at birth.[2]

Few young writers can have read such a devastating review as that contained in Dennis's *Reflections*. Yet Pope's reactions were typical of him in that he dismissed it, which says much for his innate self confidence. As he said later, when Lintot told him the review existed, it gave him 'some pain', but that soon passed when he 'came to look into his book' and found the author of it 'was in such a passion.'[3] As he quickly realized, Dennis had killed his case by overstating it, because his dislike of the poem was so obviously founded on his much deeper dislike of him personally. Other readers would also decide that the old man had gone too far, even by the no-holds-barred pamphleteering conventions of the day. In the end this attack won Pope new friends and was one of the reasons why Addison was prompted to write a calm and judicious defence of *An Essay on Criticism* for the *Spectator*, no. 253 in December.

'I can't conceive what ground he has for so excessive a resentment,' Pope wrote Caryll when he sent Dennis's comments on to him.[4] Sitting in the coffee house Pope had observed the Whig critic carefully but hardly knew him personally, as Dennis pointed out when he complained he had been mocked 'by one who is wholly a Stranger to me.'[5] In all probability, on the few occasions when the two of them had found each other in the same company, Pope had been polite and non-committal. He usually was when he was out and about. He was only frank when he was sitting quietly by himself with a quill pen in his hand. So Dennis concluded, on finding himself skewered in the *Essay*, that its author was 'a little affected hypocrite.'[6] It made it worse that Pope was making a name for himself in some quarters and was being 'caress'd and hugg'd' by 'thoughtless Applauders.'[7] Dennis was quick to realize that the 'little Gentleman' was already skilled at the art of career building. Noting how he attached himself to older writers, Dennis would go on to describe him as a

What do the poems of Pope and Keats tell us of the changing role of poetry across the 18th, 19th centuries?

hanger-on, merely endured by the elegant and learned Walsh, for instance, as a 'double Foil to his Person and Capacity.'[8]

Prejudiced as Dennis undoubtedly was, it is still possible to glean from his descriptions some idea of what Pope was like when he first arrived in London and was busy networking, as we now call it. Like his young rival, Dennis had a strong pictorial sense. So his account, already mentioned, of this mere boy haunting the elderly and confused Wycherley, striking him dumb 'by the wonderful' and sinister 'Pow'r of Magick, recreates an unforgettable scene, even if we all put different constructions on what we see.[9] Dennis also bears out statements made by more friendly observers who said Pope was 'full of life and vivacity.'[10] Pope used his hands when he talked, saying himself he was like 'a small windmill.'[11] To Dennis, watching the young poet, at ease and animated in Button's, he appeared 'in shape a Monkey,' adding, he 'is so in his every Action, in his senseless Chattering, and his merry Grimaces.'[12]

Dennis was too furious to write well about the *Essay*. Declaring its author was wrong about almost everything, he hit out wildly and destroyed some of his arguments by misquotation. Interestingly, in view of the fact that Pope would later be accused of being too solicitous of his noble friends, Dennis saw him as a radical and accused him of class bias.[13] His 'particular pique' he declared, 'seems to be at People of Quality, for whom he appears to have a very great Contempt, I mean for Authors of that Rank; as if a Man were to assert his Title to Parnassus, by proving himself a Plebian in Great Britain.'[14] Furthermore, as well as lacking in a 'due sense of Subordination,' he was a political subversive. Noting the *Essay* had nothing in it about the reign of the Papist James II, yet condemned the licence and irreligion presided over by 'our Protestant kings,' Charles II and William III, Dennis concluded the author 'must be by Politicks a Jacobite' who derived his religion from the Catholic seminary of St Omer's' and was 'Politickly setting up for Poet-Laureate against the coming of the Pretender.'[15]

Dennis was obsessive about Jacobite and Papist conspiracies, to the extent that he believed Louis XIV planned to have him assassinated because of his popular play *Liberty Asserted* (1704) which was vehemently anti-French. However, Dennis's political paranoia stood Pope in good stead because few people were likely to take his accusations seriously. One story about him, which had gone the rounds, told how he had been walking on the seashore one day and, sighting a French ship had cried out in panic, 'It has been sent to get me.'[16] Even so, Dennis may not have been far wrong in supposing Pope was a Jacobite, though none of the poems published so far contained more than a hint of this. Apart from the sins of omission which Dennis had noted in the *Essay*, there was the reference to Charles II as a 'sacred monarch' in 'Spring' (86). This could be interpreted as an endorsement of the doctrine of Divine Right, but no one said so in 1709.

Dennis ranted and raved so much that it is easy to underestimate him.

Nevertheless, he could be a perceptive critic. So he was almost the only contemporary reader to pinpoint some of the *Essay*'s ambiguities. Pope noted all he had to say and, deciding he had 'objected to one or two lines with reason,' he told Caryll he would 'alter them in case of another edition,' being willing to 'Make use of ev'ry *Friend –* and ev'ry *Foe.*'[17] He also assured Caryll he would 'never make the least reply' to Dennis, adding loftily 'I've ever been of the opinion that if a book can't answer for its self to the public, 'tis to no sort of purpose for its author to do it.'[18] Actually, Pope would abide by this view, never publishing explicit defences of his own works himself when they came under attack – he got others to do so instead, most notably with *An Essay on Man*.

He would have fewer inhibitions about getting even with the attackers themselves, but as yet had not decided on the best way of doing this. So he accepted Caryll's advice not to retaliate when some Catholics made objections to *An Essay on Criticism*, even though they irritated him more than Dennis had done. These assailants were fretful because Pope admitted Papists had their faults, which he had done because he thought Protestants would be reassured to find he did not approve of the superstitiousness of medieval monks and their neglect of pagan literature. 'Our silence on these points,' he told a sympathetic Caryll, 'may with some reason make our adversaries think we allow and persist in those bigotries, which in reality all good and sensible men despise.'[19] When modern bigots quibbled about the wording of some of his references to religion, he suspected that what they really minded about the poem was his praise in it of the liberal theologian Erasmus, 'whom their tribe oppressed and persecuted.'[20] Thoroughly irritated, he told Caryll to pass the message on to the 'Holy Vandals'[21] that if they did not allow the mention of Erasmus to pass unregarded, he would write a separate, longer and more forceful appreciation of 'that great man and great saint.'[22] And there the matter rested, for the time being.

Nor did Pope react at first when his *Pastorals* were pointedly ignored by Addison's circle, who instead acclaimed those by Ambrose Philips. Richard Steele had praised Philips's poems in *Tatler* no. 12 within a week of their publication in Tonson's *Miscellanies* in May 1709, while they received three further accolades in the *Spectator* between November 1711 and October 1712. In the last of these, *Spectator* 523, Addison wrote that Philips gave 'a new life, and a more natural beauty to this way of writing by substituting, in place of antiquated fables' myths and legends current 'among the shepherds of our own country.' By that time Pope had already realized that one of the reasons his carefully wrought *Pastorals* were not a popular success, was that they were considered old fashioned and remote. Tastes had changed. The large number of men and women who read the *Spectator* had no appetite for exquisite idylls set in the Golden Age, but hungered for what was realistic and familiar. Ever ready to learn from his critics, friend and foe alike, Pope took this lesson to heart. When the two-canto *Rape of the Lock* appeared in May 1712 readers found it was set in modern London, peopled by contemporary English men and women.

Notes

1. *Critical Works of John Dennis*, ed E.N. Hooker, 2 vols (Baltimore: Johns Hopkins University Press, 1939–43), 1: 153.
2. *Reflections Critical and Satyrical, Upon a Late Rhapsody, Call'd, An Essay Upon Criticism* (1711), pp. 26 and 29.
3. Spence, 100.
4. *Corr.* 1: 121.
5. *Reflections*, The Preface.
6. Ibid.
7. Ibid.
8. *Reflections*, p. 28.
9. Ibid., pp. 28–9.
10. Spence, 101.
11. 'The Club of Little Men,' *Prose Works of Alexander Pope 1711–1720*, ed Norman Ault (Oxford: Blackwell, 1936), p. 125.
12. Hooker, *op. cit.*, pp. 103–8.
13. Samuel Johnson, 'Pope,' *Lives of the English Poets*, ed G.B. Hill, 3 vols (Oxford: Clarendon, 1903), 3: 204.
14. *Reflections*, p. 27.
15. Ibid.
16. *Prose Works of Jonathan Swift*, ed Herbert Davis and others, 14 vols (Oxford: Blackwell, 1939–68), 4: 250.
17. *Corr.* 1: 121.
18. *Corr.* 1: 132.
19. *Corr.* 1: 127.
20. Ibid.
21. Ibid., 126.
22. Ibid., 118–19.

CHAPTER SEVEN

On Being Original

The *Rape of the Lock* was a radical new departure for Pope. To begin with it was commissioned, unlike the *Pastorals*, *An Essay on Criticism*, or the various translations which he had already published, without actually knowing whether there was any demand for such works. *An Essay on Criticism* had aroused more widespread interest than the *Pastorals*. It finally received an official seal of approval in *Spectator* no. 253 on 11 December 1711. Yet, as Addison pointed out, when he wrote that review, the *Essay* was just one of three masterpieces 'of the same Nature' which had appeared in the English tongue of late. He would not be able to say that of Pope's next poem.

The *Rape of the Lock* was commissioned in that Caryll had suggested the poet write something to reconcile two Catholic families, the Fermors and Petres, who had not been on speaking terms since the young Lord Petre cut off one of Arabella Fermor's tresses as a trophy.[1] The idea was to 'laugh together' the antagonists by making a joke of the incident. Pope welcomed the suggestion, which he soon realized would give him an opportunity to make an original contribution to English poetry. It would also enable him to use talents for characterization, dramatic presentation and individual comment on the social scene which, so far, he had not employed to any extent.

However, despite Caryll's hope that the poem would reconcile the Papists to its author, Pope did not go out of his way to flatter his co-religionists, so that in the end it annoyed some of them all over again. Yet at first all went well. When the poem was still in manuscript Arabella circulated it among her friends. But by the time it appeared in print Lord Petre had married another girl – a fifteen-year-old heiress and Miss Fermor found she was the subject of gossip which she blamed on Pope. He tried to mollify her in the Preface to the 1714 extended version of his poem, where he assured her that she resembled Belinda 'in nothing but Beauty.'

Nothing could be done to soothe Arabella's relation Sir George Browne, instantly recognizable as Sir Plume, who featured in the poem as a pompous dolt 'With earnest Eyes, and round unthinking Face' (4.125). Sir George was angry for a long time, apparently threatening to lay hands on the poet at one stage, though like others after him, who had the same idea, he thought better of it.[2]

Pope also proved to be independent in the view he gives in his poem of marriage. This is not to say that he questioned the patriarchy. He accepted it as a fact of life. It would have been surprising if he had not done so. A woman's place was pre-ordained in the concept of there being a social hierarchy, sanctioned by both Church and State.

It is generally agreed nowadays that ideas have to await their time. An idea is unrecognized if the public is not ready to accept it. If Pope, or any of his contemporaries, had formulated a theory which said that wives should not be subject to their husbands, it would either have been ignored, or it would have been dismissed as madness, as Lord Monboddo's ideas about our relationship with the other primates were dismissed in Dr Johnson's day.[3] That being said, Pope was sensitive to the plight of women who, in his day, lost all control over their own destiny, once they were married. In 1711, before he began the *Rape of the Lock*, this fact had been brought home to him by the plight of Mrs Weston.

[margin annotation: POPE AS A FEMINIST?]

Mrs Weston, a Catholic and the sister of Viscount Gage, had left her husband and Pope took up her cause with considerable vigour. He was helped at first by Caryll who wrote to her guardian Sir William Goring, asking him to protect her. Pope's view was that the marriage was doomed because ''Tis an easy thing (we daily find) to join two bodies, but in matching minds there lies some difficulty.'[4] From his conversations with the lady, he formed a good opinion of her personality and intelligence. She was one 'whose ill fate it has been to be cast as a pearl before swine.'[5]

No one in the Catholic community, apart from Caryll, took Mrs Weston's side and even Caryll withdrew from the campaign, as soon as he saw the strength of the opposition. Sir William Goring refused to help and when Pope wrote to the victim's aunt asking her to give her shelter, Lady Aston only agreed to take her niece in for a fortnight. In the end the lady had to go back to her husband. The law was all on his side. He could demand, as he had already done, sole custody of their baby daughter. In the unlikely event of Mrs Weston obtaining a judicial separation, she would not necessarily be awarded maintenance. She was not automatically entitled to any money she may have brought to the marriage. According to law she did not own the clothes she stood up in.

It was unconventional of Pope to take the wife's part in a marital dispute and in doing so he antagonized a number of Papists, including his sister Magdalen and his old friends at Whiteknights. Most people believed that if a husband misbehaved a wife should put up with it and him. This remained the standard view of the matter for years. In 1768 Dr Johnson declared that 'a wife ought not greatly to resent it' if her husband 'steals privately to her chamber-maid.' And, he went on, 'I would not receive home a daughter who had run away from her husband on that account. A wife should study to reclaim her husband by more attention to please him.'[6]

The Weston marriage had broken down in a very public way. But even when matters had not reached this point, Pope doubted whether many married couples were happy. Indeed one can search high and low in his poetry and prose without finding a wholehearted endorsement of marriage for either sex. The nearest he got to one was when he contemplated the Carylls, who had the knack of choosing wives they could get on with. In 1711 Pope wished 'ev'ry disagreeing pair might be sent for a while to Ladyholt or Grinstead (the best matrimony-schools in England).' But then he had second thoughts, wishing also 'the blessed example may not prove of ill consequence to many others, as we often see that one person's good luck in a lottery is the cause that twenty venture and lose.'[7] Pope chose to stay unmarried, as did several of his friends who did not have his physical disadvantages – such men as Congreve, Swift, Gay and Kent. For a woman, however, the situation was entirely different. There was no way she could stay single for very long without becoming the object of pity and ridicule.

In the *Rape of the Lock* Pope recognizes that a woman should marry if she has the opportunity, but regards this stage of her personal evolution with something less than enthusiasm. Belinda relishes a degree of freedom and power, which is only hers as long as she is young, beautiful and unattached. She dominates men before they dominate her. By law and convention whoever she marries will become her master. She is waging a war in which the Baron is guilty of an outrage. In a poem that gives us a view of the great and little worlds mirrored in each other, the game of Ombre stands for intellectual endeavour, in which Belinda is superior. She exults vociferously in victory, and the Baron, riled, makes use of that male trump card, physical force. 'What Wonder then, fair Nymph! thy Hairs shou'd feel / The conqu'ring Force of unresisted Steel?' (3.77–8).

Belinda finds herself at the mercy of man because of her sexual instinct. Ariel is powerless to protect her once he discovers 'An Earthly Lover lurking in her Heart' (3.144). Pope took the idea of adding Ariel and the rest of the supernatural machinery to his poem from Philip Ayres's translation of *Le Comte de Gabalis* (1670). This Rosicrucian document is a polemic against marriage. It urges human beings to renounce sexual intercourse with each other and take nymphs or sylphs as their lovers instead. If they do this, they will avoid all the miseries of a mundane union and enjoy an unchanging, ideal amour. When Ariel appears in Belinda's dream, at the beginning of the *Rape of the Lock*, he tells her, 'Whoever fair and chaste / Rejects Mankind, is by some Sylph embrac'd' (ll. 67–8). However Belinda cannot accept this proposal because she is caught in the biological trap.

Furthermore, according to the Rosicrucians, sylphs become immortal if they unite with the daughters of earth but the latter do not. Once Belinda grows old her reign as a belle ends. In a speech Pope added to the *Rape of the Lock* in 1717, Belinda is reminded of the reality of her situation and urged to capitulate gracefully:

> ... since alas! frail Beauty must decay,
> Curl'd or uncurl'd, since Locks will turn to grey,
> Since painted or not painted, all shall fade,
> And she who scorns a Man, must die a Maid (5.25–8)

Clarissa's speech meets with 'no Applause' and Belinda is unconvinced (5.35). So in order to put an end to this particular episode in the battle of the sexes, the poet summons a *deus ex machina*, at the same time ensuring that his heroine's transient beauty will live on in the minds of readers of his verses.

When Belinda's real life counterpart dwindled into Mrs Perkins, Pope was equivocal about the matter, though he wrote her an elaborate letter wishing her every felicity, adding that she was 'in the way to be a great many better things than a fine lady; such as an excellent wife, a faithful friend, a tender parent, and at last, as a consequence of them all, a saint in heaven.'[8] The sting is in that last phrase which hints that marriage is a kind of martyrdom. This letter should be read in conjuction with lines addressed *To Miss Blount with the Works of Voiture*, which Lintot published with the two-canto *Rape of the Lock* in *Miscellaneous Poems and Translations*. In the verse epistle Pope sympathises with a girl who chafes against the restrictions placed on her behaviour while she is single. 'But' he reminds her:

> ... the last Tyrant ever proves the worst.
> Still in Constraint your suff'ring Sex remains,
> Or bound in formal, or in real Chains;
> Whole years neglected for some Months ador'd,
> The fawning Servant turns a haughty Lord.

Therefore, he concludes:

> Ah quit not the free Innocence of Life!
> For the dull Glory of a virtuous Wife!

Arabella Perkins went on to have six children and lived to be fifty. We do not know if she was happy. We do know she looked back nostalgically to the past. According to her niece, the somewhat acerbic Prioress of a French convent, 'Mr. Pope's praise' in the *Rape of the Lock* made her aunt 'very troublesome and conceited.'[9]

One doubts whether the Prioress warmed to Belinda any more than she did to the aunt who inspired her. Opinions about Pope's heroine have always differed, just as they have always differed about the kind of girl she represents, one who is intoxicated by her appearance and its effect on men. John Dennis called her 'an artificial dawbing jilt' and that view has been shared by other readers, well on into the twentieth century.[10] Since the 1980s however, the arguments about Belinda have changed direction with many critics blaming Pope for her vanity and superficiality, accusing him of trivializing her and turning her into a cypher in the male world.[11] It would be unrealistic to suppose one could resolve the debate between those who find Belinda a sympathetic figure and those who find her intolerable, but it is equally unrealistic to expect Pope to share a twentieth-century belief in the equality of the sexes. At best, it is possible to assess the degree of his chauvinism by comparing his attitude to a pretty flirt with that of some of his contemporaries.

Dennis, for instance was far from seeing Belinda as a cypher. He thought she was a self-assertive virago and wondered how Pope could speak of her 'graceful Ease, and Sweetness void of Pride (2.15). As ever Dennis was passionate in his diatribe about anything written by his enemy, and no doubt some of his readers thought he had gone over the top again when he said Pope's heroine was 'an arrant Ramp and a Tomrigg.'[12] For a view of the Belindas of this world, likely to have a more popular appeal, we can turn to the cool and measured Addison.

Some time before the *Rape of the Lock* was first published, Addison wrote *Spectator* no. 73. It appeared on 24 May 1711. In it he described what he called 'idols,' giving the 'Beautiful Clarinda' as an example. Clarinda 'is Worshipped once a Week by Candlelight,' Addison tells us, 'in the midst of a large Congregation generally called an Assembly,' and he goes on, 'To encourage the Zeal of her Idolators, she bestows a Mark of her Favour upon every one of them, before they go out of her Presence. She asks a Question of one, tells a Story to another, glances an Ogle upon a third, takes a pinch of Snuff from a fourth, lets her Fan drop by accident to give a fifth an occasion for taking it up. In short, every one goes away satisfied with his Success, and encouraged to renew his Devotions on the same Canonical Hour that Day Sevennight.' Addison's distaste for Clarinda comes out in every line of his essay. If we wish to see how his attitude to a belle differs from Pope's, we have only to compare his phrase 'glances an Ogle upon a third' with 'Belinda smil'd and all the World was gay' (2.51). Pope admits that Belinda's 'lively Looks a sprightly Mind disclose' (2.9). Addison refuses to give credit where credit is due. Unlike Pope he looks forward with relish to the time when Clarinda will marry, because 'When a Man becomes familiar with his Goddess, she quickly sinks into a Woman.'

Both Addison and Pope know that a belle plays sexual politics, exchanging the joys of falling in love for the joys of power. Addison resents Clarinda because there is no denying she is self-sufficient and independent. Pope, on the other hand, regards Belinda with a mixture of amusement, admiration and sympathy. She is his *alter ego*. Like Flaubert, much later on, speaking of Emma Bovary, he could have said of Belinda, 'She is me.' He knows that, like a poet, a belle has a vocation but beauty alone, like a poet's innate talent, is not enough to win universal admiration. She must also have steady self-possession and judgement. Her natural gift must be maintained and improved by art.[13]

For a while Belinda enjoys an interlude in which she is not a victim and during that time she represents an ideal for the men from whom she withholds herself. But time conquers all. Pope knows that her reign as a goddess is brief. Hence his compassion. Addison and Dennis held conventional opinions about girls who played the field. Pope was unorthodox in the view he took of Belinda, just as he was unorthodox about the joys of marriage.[14]

Even those readers who disapproved of Pope's heroine were fascinated

[Margin notes: Pope sees a beautiful independent woman who must marry) / Addison sees a conceited spoilt child who should grow up / deliberate controversy or just honesty)]

by her and eventually the *Rape of the Lock* became a huge popular success, enjoyed by sempstresses as much as by duchesses.[15] It got off to a slow start though, before Pope expanded it, adding the sylphs and gnomes to the action. When he mentioned to Addison that he had had this inspired notion, Addison advised against changing the 'delicious little thing' in any way but he went ahead regardless.[16] Then, realizing in 1714 that copies of the shorter poem were still unsold, he and his publisher advertised the five-canto version in the *Post Boy* for 26–28 January, as a limited edition on 'fine Paper' with '6 Copper Plates,' urging those who wanted copies to 'send their Names to Bernard Lintott … No more being to be thus printed than are bespoke.' This fiction worked. Lintot was inundated with requests from people who had already heard talk of what was indeed a literary event. When the new *Rape of the Lock* was published in March, three thousand copies were bought in four days. By the time the third edition appeared, late in 1714, six thousand copies were sold. Then, because the society it described was European as much as it was English, the *Rape* was quickly translated into five languages, including Dutch and Polish.[17] Pope had arrived.

He won over his audience with a poem which showed he had solved a question which he had been thinking about from the start of his career. This was the question of whether he dared be original in an era that made a literary virtue out of imitating earlier masterpieces. In July 1706 he asked William Walsh for his views on taking ideas from other writers, assuring his mentor that he had no objection to borrowing, because 'A mutual commerce makes Poetry flourish,' but adding that 'Poets like Merchants, shou'd repay with something of their own what they take from others; not like Pyrates, make prize of all they meet.'[18] Walsh's reply was not encouraging. He said merely, 'The best of the modern Poets in all Languages, are those that have nearest copied the Ancients.'[19] Pope did not argue, but his instinct as a true artist was to add something of his own and, by the time he wrote the *Rape of the Lock*, he had gained sufficiently in confidence to write a poem that was original in more ways than one.

First of all he produced a new synthesis out of his various borrowings – much as Shakespeare did when working on a play. The writers that contributed to his mock epic are many and various. They include Homer, Virgil, Ovid, Boileau, Voiture, Spenser, Milton, Garth and the authors of the *Spectator* and *Tatler* essays. The whole emerges as different from any of the constituent parts.

Second, Pope added something of his own by extending the subject matter of poetry. The idea of writing a burlesque poem set in London had already occurred to Garth when he wrote *The Dispensary* (1699). Pope built on his friend's initial idea when he set his action in the *beau monde*. The *Rape of the Lock* charmed its first readers because it was so up-to-date about a world they either knew, or wished they knew. Many of the latest fads and fashions have a place in the poem: lacquered tables, ornate snuff boxes (snuff taking was relatively new in Queen Anne's reign), and a recent scandalous book, Mrs

Manley's *Secret Memoirs*, which was avidly devoured by young ladies on the quiet. Pope used his eyes as he moved about society. He also kept up with modern publications. The details of that modish ailment, the spleen, came from contemporary medical dissertations, while the footnotes to the Twickenham edition of the poem reveal over thirty references to *Spectator* and *Tatler* papers.

The *Rape of the Lock* was not only in the fashion, it was ahead of it. So it has been called the first rococo work of art to appear in England, its 'memorable imagery' reading 'like an inventory of those small articles by which the French style was first to invade and then occupy whole areas of taste,' such things as the silver vases and tortoiseshell combs on Belinda's dressing table and Sir Plume's clouded cane.[20] There are moments too, when this intensely visual poem anticipates the pleasure laced with melancholy that there is in Watteau. So when Belinda sails with her friends down the river, 'While melting Musick steals upon the Sky, / And Soften'd Sounds along the Waters die' (2.49–50), Pope's words would serve as an epigraph for a picture painted five years after he wrote them – the *Embarcation for Cytherea*.[21]

Pope's growing band of enemies were as quick as anyone else to realize that the *Rape of the Lock* was an innovation. Gildon used the fact as a stick to beat the author with. In his semi-dramatic pamphlet *A New Rehearsal, Or Bays the Younger* (1714), Gildon reinvented Pope as Sawney Dapper, a conceited, young versifier, intent on the main chance who, 'continuing with his art of getting a reputation,' advises other literary aspirants that, if they want to be noticed, they should 'chuse some odd out of the way Subject, some Trifle or other that wou'd surprize the Common Reader that any thing cou'd be written upon it, as a *Fan, a Lock of Hair*, or the like. Then, for good measure, Sawney tells his disciples, 'Besides the newness of the Verse, you must have a new manner of Address; you must make the Ladies speak Bawdy, no matter whether they are Women of Honour or not.'

Gildon was one of the first of a series of critics to accuse Pope of being bawdy, ponderously spelling out the implications of Belinda's anguished cry, 'Oh hadst thou, Cruel! been content to seize / Hairs less in sight, or any Hairs but these! (4: 175–6). He had a point – sexual innuendos abound in the *Rape of the Lock*, beginning with its title. But then, Belinda's story revolves around sex which is the cause of her triumph, as well as her ultimate downfall.

Notes

1.   Spence, 104.
2.   *Corr.* 1: 163.
3.   Mihaly Csikszentmihalyi, *Creativity: Flow and the Psychology of Discovery and Invention* (New York: HarperCollins, 1996), pp. 29–30. When not dismissed as crazy, ideas that appeared before the time was right for them, were ignored. *The Craftsman* no. 38, 17 April 1727 argued clearly and logically against the 'insolent

superiority' of males who decreed women were their inferiors but, as far as I know, this essay produced no printed reaction.

4. *Corr.* 1: 123.
5. Ibid., 132.
6. James Boswell, *Life of Samuel Johnson*, 2 vols (London: Everyman edition, 1906), 1: 347.
7. *Corr.* 1: 123.
8. Ibid., 272.
9. Mrs Hester Piozzi, *Observations and Reflections Made in the Course of a Journey Through France, Italy and Germany* (1789), 1: 20–21.
10. 'Remarks on Mr. Pope's *Rape of the Lock*' (1728), *Critical Works of John Dennis*, ed E.N. Hooker (Baltimore: Johns Hopkins University Press, 1943), 2: 334 and Hugo Reichard, 'The Love Affair in Pope's *Rape of the Lock*', *Publications of the Modern Language Association*, 69 (1954), 887–902.
11. A pioneer in this line of approach was Ellen Pollak, *The Poetics of Sexual Myth: Gender and Ideology in the Verse of Swift and Pope* (University of Chicago Press, 1985). Brean Hammond, *Pope* (Brighton: Harvester Press, 1986) pointed out that the *Rape of the Lock* was hardly a misogynistic satire, when compared with Swift's 'A Beautiful Young Nymph Going to Bed'. While Valerie Rumbold, *Woman's Place in Pope's World* (Cambridge University Press, 1989) maintained that Pope's gallantry was nevertheless sexist, if more subtle than Swift's misogyny. Another line of approach, which has tended to diminish Belinda, has been the neo-Marxist one initiated by Laura Brown, *Alexander Pope* (Oxford: Blackwell, 1985). Laura Brown's thesis, that Pope's mock epic is a celebration of mercantile capitalism, has been refined by Stewart Crehan, 'The *Rape of the Lock* and the Economy of "Trivial Things"', *Eighteenth Century Studies* (31.1, Fall, 1997), 45–68. He argues that Belinda is no more than a commodity, in a poem in which 'things not people are the heroes', p. 47. He concludes that, in showing the destructive values of a bourgeois society, Pope has produced a poem that is especially relevant in our time.
12. 'Remarks on Mr. Pope's *Rape of the Lock*', Hooker, *op. cit.*
13. Helen Deutsch, *Alexander Pope and the Deformation of Culture* (Harvard University Press, 1996). This book also argues Pope identified with Belinda, using her 'to figure his own ambivalent relation to the literary market', p. 46.
14. As time went on Pope's scepticism about marriage would become less and less acceptable as sentimentalism took hold. See Thomas Keymer, 'Reception, and *The Rape of the Lock*, and Richardson', *Alexander Pope: World and Word*, ed Howard Erskine-Hill (Oxford University Press, 1998), pp. 147–75.
15. John Gay, *Trivia*, 2: 262.
16. Samuel Johnson, 'Pope', *Lives of the English Poets* ed G.B. Hill, 3 vols (Oxford: Clarendon, 1903), 3:103.
17. TW. 2: 103–5.
18. *Corr.* 1: 19–20. Pope was more modern than Walsh in wishing to add something of his own. Brean S. Hammond argues that the concept of an author's originality was growing from the seventeenth century onwards. See *Professional Imaginative Writing in England 1670–1740* (Oxford: Clarendon, 1997), pp. 19ff. By the time Johnson wrote his 'Life of Milton' he could regard it as axiomatic that, 'The highest praise of genius is original invention.'
19. Ibid., 1: 20.
20. Joseph Burke, *English Art 1714–1800* (Oxford, 1976), p. 124.
21. Ibid.

CHAPTER EIGHT

Support Groups

When he was in his early twenties Pope spent more time in London, where he was tempted to overdo things, than he did at home. He soon got to know a lot of people in the capital and tried to keep up with them in late-night suppers and sessions in coffee houses and taverns that could go on into the small hours. He went back to Binfield mostly when shortage of cash or sickness forced him to. At the end of 1712 he was at home, 'confind to a narrow Closet', quite seriously ill, a doctor having warned him he would not be 'long above ground' unless he followed his prescriptions minutely.[1]

It was very cold. The world beyond his window was all 'deserts of snow, seas of ice and frozen skies'.[2] He sat by the fire, 'lolling on an Arm Chair ... like a picture of January in an old Salisbury Primer'.[3] Physically inert, he dispelled lethargy and warded off headaches by sniffing sal volatile (ammonium carbonate), as he worked on a revised version of *Windsor Forest*, creating an alternative world of 'woods and forests in verdure and beauty, trees springing, fields flowering, Nature laughing.'[4]

As he described it, he was in a state between sleeping and waking, so utterly absorbed in his task that he could not always tell the difference between what was going on in his mind and what was happening around him, speaking to his family of things as truths and real events, things that he had only dreamed of. Pope's account of the creative process, already quoted earlier, in which he compared himself to a witch, 'whose Carcase lies motionless on the floor, while she keeps her airy Sabbaths,' is a somewhat mysterious, one.[5] Along with Pope, W.B. Yeats found an image for it when he wrote of Michelangelo painting in the Sistine Chapel, 'Like a long-legged fly upon the stream / His mind moves upon silence.'[6] While a psychological term for this experience is 'flow', used to describe the 'almost automatic, effortless, yet highly focused state of consciousness' that creative individuals speak of when their work is going well.[7]

Work on the expanded *Windsor Forest* went on for at least a couple of months and during that time Pope was not in a perpetual state of intense creativity. He needed periodic breathing spaces – maybe while his ideas incubated. In those intervals, when he surfaced, he often wrote letters to friends. One of these was Caryll's son who, like his father, was called John.

The young Caryll was a straightforward, frank and easy extrovert who attracted Pope because he was his opposite. Brimming over with health, John revelled in physical activity. As a lad he had worried his tutors because he would not stick at his books, but he had a generous nature and had little patience with those Papists who carped about things the poet wrote. His support in this way helped his friendship with the poet along.

When Pope wrote him a letter in the glacial December of 1712, part of it, as so often happened with his correspondence, echoed the poem he was working on, which had a passage in it about hunting. He imagined how it was to be a vigorous young man, to whom snow on the ground and crisp air were a challenge. 'You are pursuing the Sprightly Delights of the Field,' he told John:

> springing up with activity at the Dawning day, rouzing a whole Country with Shouts and Horns, & inspiring Animalls & Rationalls with like Fury and Ardor; while your Blood boils high in ev'ry Vein, your Heart bounds in your Breast, & as vigorous Confluence of Spirits rushes to it at the sight of a Fox as cou'd be stirr'd up by that of an Army of Invaders.[8]

But whereas the passage in the letter is as uncomplicated (on the surface) as anything about the same subject by R.S. Surtees, the equivalent lines in the poem present hunting, and its prototype warfare, in depth and with more freedom because Pope is no longer editing his impressions to fit the cast of mind of one particular reader. The poet is more complex than the letter writer and his reactions are multiple. He still conveys the sheer physical pleasure of the chase when 'Earth rolls back beneath the flying Steed,' (158) but now he also empathizes with the victims of the triumphant hunter and warrior, when he imagines how, 'Oft as the mounting Larks their Notes prepare, / They fall, and leave their little Lives in Air' (133–5), or when he conjures up a picture of 'Some thoughtless Town, with Ease and Plenty blest,' taken by surprise and plundered by a triumphant British navy (107ff.).

Pope never forgot that we live in the shadow of death. He got frequent reminders – and not just because of his own chronic ill health. Before the revised *Rape of the Lock* had reached the bookstalls, Lord Petre had died of smallpox at the age of twenty-one. Four years after receiving the poet's letter, the young John Caryll was dead of the same disease.

Windsor Forest was published on 7 March 1713, three weeks before the Good Friday on which a messenger rode down Whitehall, to put a signed Treaty of Utrecht into Bolingbroke's waiting hands, so inaugurating the celebrations of which the poem was a part. It honours England. In it Pope describes an ideal of national harmony, presided over by a just monarch who loves her country and wants her subjects to live in peace and freedom. As a result of her wise policies, including the recent treaty negotiated by her ministers, he predicts that the power and wealth of England will increase, to be a further source of national pride. The Treaty of Utrecht was going to promote the expansion of the British Empire and Pope ends his poem with a vision of *pax Britannica* spreading throughout the world.

Pope's Tory poem is also one in which he expresses his Jacobite convictions with the least equivocation. He dared to do so because, for a brief space, as long as Anne survived, Jacobites could identify with the national interest. Pope dedicated *Windsor Forest* to Lord Lansdowne who exemplified the identification of Tory and Jacobite sympathies at this time. Lansdowne's future as a rebel leader and impoverished exile was still some years off. In 1713 he was a member of the establishment. From 1710 he had served for two years as Secretary at War, while the peerage he had been given in 1712 was one of the dozen created to ensure the safe passage of the Tory Peace through Parliament.

Throughout the poem Anne, a Stuart monarch, is invested with semi-divine status. She rules by hereditary right like the 'sacred Charles' (319). Her fiat 'Let Discord Cease' (327) echoes Genesis, and she is compared to the 'Immortal Huntress' Diana, being 'As bright a Goddess, and as chast a Queen' (160ff.).

Until almost the end of Queen Anne's reign there was less unrest in England than there had been under William who, as well as dragging his adopted country into expensive wars, was personally unpopular. Pope makes the contrast between the peace and liberty a kingdom may expect to enjoy under its rightful and loving Stuart ruler, and the discontent and oppression prevailing under a usurper. When Pope asks 'What wonder then, a Beast or Subject slain / Were equal Crimes in a Despotick Reign?' (57–8) he is supposedly writing about William I. However, it was an easily decoded part of Jacobite rhetoric to equate the Norman king with his later Dutch namesake who, in pro-Stuart eyes, had also gained his throne by conquest.[9]

Pope conveys his partisan account of the state of England after the Treaty of Utrecht in terms of a vision. As it happened Queen Anne was already a sick woman – too ill by 7 July to attend the official performance in St Paul's of Handel's *Te Deum*, giving thanks for the Peace. But if she had lived longer than she did it is doubtful whether Pope's dreams for his native land would have been realized, any more than his dreams for an entirely beneficent British Empire were – perhaps he never seriously imagined they would be. Primarily *Windsor Forest* is not political or social prophecy. It is a poetic re-enactment of an ideal.

When Pope thought about the future, he thought about the past, just as his predecessors in the Renaissance had done. In describing an ideal society he recreated the Golden Age. So his Forest, a microcosm of England, becomes 'The Groves of *Eden* vanish'd now so long' (7). The world had an underlying harmony, broken when the Golden Age came to an end, though vestiges of it remained so that men knew what had been lost. Pope paid Queen Anne a graceful compliment in his poem by imagining the original concord could be restored in her reign.

The harmony Pope is thinking of is dynamic, achieved by the reconciliation of opposites, or *concordia discors*.[10] He shows this metaphysical principle at work in nature and civilization. In the landscape:

> ... Earth and Water seem to strive again,
> Not *Chaos*-like together crush'd and bruis'd,
> But as the World, harmoniously confus'd:
> Where Order in Variety we see,
> And where, tho' all things differ, all agree (12–16).

In society the differing needs of farmers and factory-owners are reconciled and 'Rich Industry sits smiling on the Plains' (41).

The doctrine of *concordia discors* had been widely upheld throughout the ancient world and, in the eighteenth century, it appealed to some political theorists – especially Tory ones, and all educated men were aware of the theory. This familiarity helped Bolingbroke when he argued against the idea of party government, advocating instead the maintenance of a strong monarchy, because a ruler with real power could act as a unifying force, capable of reconciling conflicting interests in the country. A quarter of a century after *Windsor Forest* was published, Bolingbroke described his own unattainable, political ideal in words which read like a gloss of the poem. 'What spectacle can be presented to the view of the mind so rare, so nearly divine,' he wrote:

> as a king possessed of absolute power, neither usurped by fraud, nor maintained by force, but by the genuine effect of esteem of confidence, and affection; the free gift of liberty, who finds her greatest security in this power ... Concord will appear, brooding peace and prosperity on the happy land, joy sitting on every face, content in every heart; a people unoppressed, undisturbed, unalarmed, busy to improve their property and the public stock; fleets covering the ocean, bringing home wealth by the returns of industry, asserting triumphantly ... right and ... honour as far as waters roll and winds can waft them.[11]

If the *Rape of the Lock* made Pope a popular poet, *Windsor Forest* established his reputation as a serious one. After it was published (a year before the expanded *jeu d'esprit* about Belinda), Ralph Bridges wrote to his uncle Sir William Trumbull to report that those in the know were saying that the young man was 'one of the greatest genius's that this nation has bred.'[12] While, within two days of its appearance, Swift, having said that *Windsor Forest* was a 'fine poem,' issued a command to Stella, 'Read it.'[13] He had, as he thought, spotted a new Tory talent.

During Queen Anne's reign, Pope had Tory supporters always to hand, eager to recruit him as their propagandist but, despite having dedicated his poem about the Peace to Lord Lansdowne, he was still hoping to be accepted by the Whigs as well. Rather than signing up with either political party, he was looking for friendship among his fellow artists. He no longer needed mentors but he did hope to find support from other creative people.

In 1713, after he had recovered from his winter illness and was back in London, he found what he was looking for, not with another writer at first but with Charles Jervas who had agreed to give him lessons in painting. Pope spent most of the rest of the year living in his tutor's large, ramshackle house in Cleveland Court, St James's. Jervas was Anglo-Irish, a successful portrait painter who, after Sir Godfrey Kneller's death in 1723, was appointed in his place as King's Painter. His method of teaching Pope was to set him to copy pictures. He had a good collection of these, including Raphaels and Titians, stuffed in cabinets and cupboards around the place.

After drawing in childhood, Pope had begun painting and carried on doing so, on and off, until he was over forty. If he could have painted as well as he wrote, he would have avoided, maybe, some of the religious and political attacks that made him a ready target when he worked in a verbal medium. However, studying with a professional artist quickly showed him that he had no gift for making the 'living image in the Painter's breast' glow on canvas.[14] After a few months toiling away in Jervas's studio he wrote to John Gay in mock despair, giving an account of his progress:

> I have thrown away three Dr. *Swift*'s, each of which was once my Vanity, two Lady *Bridgewaters*, a Dutchesse of *Montague*, besides half a dozen Earls and one Knight of the Garter. I have crucify'd *Christ* over-again in effigie, and made a *Madonna* as old as her mother St. *Anne*. Nay, what is more miraculous, I have rival'd St. *Luke* ... as 'tis said an Angel came and finish'd his Piece, so you would swear a Devil put the last hand to mine, 'tis so begrim'd and smutted.[15]

As he destroyed so much, it is hard to say whether Pope was quite as bad as he made out but when he gave one of his attempts at the Virgin Mary to Caryll's wife, she said, somewhat ambiguously, 'St. Luke himself never drew such a Madonna.'[16] His efforts as a painter's apprentice were not a waste of time however. He claimed they made him even more observant, so that he found himself noticing 'Every Corner of an Eye, or Turn of a Nose, or Ear, the smallest degree of Light or Shade on a Cheek, or in a Dimple.'[17] When one considers Pope's ability to create vivid pictures in words, whether of Belinda's bedroom or the hunting scene at Windsor, it comes as no surprise to learn he was a painter, even if he never graduated beyond the status of being an amateur.

But quite apart from anything Pope learned at Cleveland Court, he enjoyed being there because he got on so well with Jervas. His earlier relationship with Wycherley had brought its problems and he had been in awe of Walsh, but with the painter, who was still in his thirties, he was at ease and did not have to curb, what turned out to be, his varied impulses. If his friend teased him about his amorous yearnings for Teresa and Patty Blount he could retaliate, because the painter adored, from afar, Elizabeth, the Duke of Marlborough's most beautiful daughter. Jervas also had a sense of humour, and what Pope called 'our Fooleries' were part of what he remembered best about his long visit.[18] The two were not working all the time. Jervas must have woken up early, like Pope, for there were morning conferences as they lay in their beds in the same room.

8.1 Alexander Pope, aged about twenty-six years. Charles Jervas

They went for trips on the Thames, walked in the park in the evening, attended lectures and had 'philosophical suppers.'[19]

Among the lectures the two men attended were those given at Button's by the controversial cleric and mathematician William Whiston, after his banishment from Cambridge. Then, after listening intently to arguments about the cosmos, Pope could be found at Will's, regaling Major-General John Tidcombe with 'pretty atheistical jests.'[20] Tidcombe's own blasphemies were so shocking that he was banned from the coffee house for a while but Pope, a practising Catholic, was fascinated by this man whose 'beastly, laughable life' he described as 'not unlike a fart, at once nasty and diverting.'[21] Pope's behaviour while he was staying with Jervas in 1713 is just one instance, among many, of his capacity to identify with contradictory extremes. It was part of his nature as a poet, though he was as puzzled as any less complex onlooker could be by this state of affairs. As he told Caryll:

> Every hour of my life, my mind is strangely divided. This minute, perhaps, I am above the stars, with a thousand systems about me, looking forward into the vast abyss of eternity, and losing my whole comprehension in the boundless space of extended Creation, in dialogues with Whiston and the astronomers; the next moment I am below all trifles, even grovelling with Tidcombe in the very center of nonsense.[22]

Sometimes 'the tumult of acquaintance' became too much for him but then, as he did not have to stand on ceremony with Jervas, he wandered off to another room in Cleveland Court, 'to enjoy the pleasing melancholy of an hour's reflection alone.'[23]

When, in the autumn of 1715, Pope wrote a poem about all his painting year had meant to him, he addressed it to his friend. The 'Epistle to Mr. Jervas' recalls that:

> Smit with the love of Sister-arts we came;
> And met congenial, mingling flame with flame;
> Like friendly colours found them both unite,
> And each from each contract new strength and light.
> How oft' in pleasing tasks we wear the day,
> While summer suns roll unperceiv'd away?
> How oft' our slowly-growing works impart,
> While images reflect from art to art?
> How oft' review, each finding like a friend
> Something to blame, and something to commend? (13–22)

This description of the meeting of the complementary minds of two men, each secure in his possession of a creative gift, so that neither was jealous of the other, represented Pope's ideal of friendship among artists. His best – and worst – relationships were with other writers. He enrolled Jervas, who pursued a sister art, as a member of the same band of brothers he found when he exchanged ideas with Gay and Swift. He would have liked to include Addison in this easy fraternity as well, but his relationship with him was very different from the start.[24]

Since Pope went out of his way to cultivate people who might help him, it is a little strange that he had no more than a nodding acquaintance with such a distinguished and influential writer as Addison until after 20 December 1711, when Addison wrote *Spectator* no. 253 praising *An Essay on Criticism*. Pope supposed at first that Steele had written this review and tried to thank him, whereupon Steele offered to introduce him to its real author.

When they met, Pope was impressed. Nor did he ever lose his admiration entirely, even after he was disappointed. Addison had 'something more charming in his conversation than [he] ever knew in any other man.'[25] Nevertheless they were incompatible. Addison, cool and restrained, was disconcerted by the younger man's jokes. He had begun his comments on the *Essay* by obliquely ticking off its author for his lines on Dennis. A contemporary once described Addison as 'a parson in a tye wig.'[26] Pope was irreverent, bawdy and sometimes bumptious. It was hardly likely that the two of them would get on with each other for long.

Nevertheless, flattered by the older man's notice, Pope made an effort in 1712 and was still in favour when Addison asked him to write the Prologue for *Cato* the following spring. By then Button's was the centre of London literary life. Pope never spent as much time there as other Buttonians, if only because he found it physically exhausting. After dining, Addison reigned daily in the coffee house for 'five or six hours – and sometimes far into the night.'[27] He needed wine to loosen up and was a two-bottle man. Then, as the level in the bottles went down, so the intellectual level of his conversation went up. Until, past midnight, or towards morning, 'warmed with his liquor' and the freedom of being with select friends, he became 'the most entertaining man in the world.'[28]

The select friends, with the exception of Steele, were mediocrities. Addison dominated them, including Steele, who 'had the greatest veneration for him' and showed it 'in a particular manner,'[29] which led Pope to suppose they were lovers.[30] Lesser members of the Addison coterie included fat Charles Johnson, a prolific dramatist who, Pope said, 'Means not, but blunders round a meaning'[31] and Ambrose Philips, a lean dandified poet, burdened with the nickname 'Namby Pamby,' though not devoid of talent. Then there was Henry Davenant (thought to be Shakespeare's great grandson), once described as 'a giddy-headed young fellow with some wit.'[32] On the fringes of the circle there were a few non-literary figures, such as the former Member of Parliament and marital adventurer, Colonel Brett. Brett's good looks, along with a clean shirt borrowed from Colley Cibber, finally won him the hand of the notorious Countess of Macclesfield.[33]

Pope was an outsider at Button's – in, but not of, the circle of writers to be found there. For one thing, although he might forget he was a Roman Catholic, they could not, nor the implication that as a Papist he must have Jacobite leanings. Then again, as well as being Protestants, they were active Whigs and, much as Pope might have wished to be politically neutral, it did not escape their notice that *Windsor Forest* was dedicated to a Tory statesman. Furthermore, the writers among them were professionals for whom the young poet was a rival. Their attitude towards him was bound to be different from that of the gentlemen amateurs, whose encouragement he had sought and got when he first arrived in London. All in all, it is hardly surprising that Pope found he was treated by most of the Buttonians with wary courtesy and little warmth.

He kept his own counsel but, as he sat back and watched them all, the scene brought out the incipient satirist in him. Looking round for someone to share the joke with, he rediscovered Nicholas Rowe, whom he had first met in 1707. Rowe, who became Poet Laureate in 1715, was a pioneer editor of Shakespeare and the dramatist whose play *The Fair Penitent* (1703) gave us the term Lothario. Cultivated, witty and vivacious, he was a man Pope said it was impossible to part from, 'without that uneasiness and chagrin which generally succeeds all great pleasures.'[34] It was a relief to find him at Button's because he turned out to be as sceptical about Addison's little senate as Pope was.

Something of the atmosphere at the coffee house can be sensed from the character sketch Pope wrote of a typical Buttonian whom he called 'Umbra.' He did not publish the piece for about fifteen years, and then, only anonymously. It begins with Umbra, a hanger on, filling in time until Addison appears:

> Close to the best known Author, *Umbra* sits,
> The constant Index of all *Button*'s Wits,
> *Who's here*? cries *Umbra*: 'Only *Johnson*' – Oh!
> *Your Slave*, and exit; but returns with *Rowe*,
> *Dear* Rowe, *lets sit and talk of Tragedies*;
> Not long, *Pope* enters, and to *Pope* he flies.
> Then up comes *Steele*; and he turns upon his *Heel*,
> And in a moment fastens upon *Steele*.
> But cries as soon, *Dear* Dick, *I must be gone*,
> *For if I know his Tread*, here's *Addison*.

But he is doomed to disappointment:

> Says *Addison* to *Steele*, 'Tis time to go.'
> *Pope* to the closet steps aside with *Rowe*,
> Poor *Umbra*, left alone in this abandon'd Pickle,
> E'en sits him down, and writes to honest T[ickell].

This portrait might fit any of several Buttonians, for instance Eustace Budgell, a writer of miscellaneous pieces who once lodged in a room above Addison's. Because Budgell drove him to distraction, walking up and down over his head all the time, Addison had invited him down to supper one night and found he was a distant relative, 'One that calls me Cousin!' as he said disparagingly.[35] He let Budgell write for the *Spectator* and threw other work his way, sometimes revising it for him.

The high point in Addison's literary career, and in the course of Pope's friendship with him, came when *Cato* was put on at Drury Lane on 14 April 1713. The hero of Addison's play was Cato the Younger, the unselfish patriot who had taken Pompey's side against the incipient tyranny of Caesar, ending his life with honourable suicide when Pompey was defeated. The play fired the political imagination which was all too inflammable in the last year of Anne's reign because no one was sure who would sit on the throne after she died. Despite the Act of Settlement Anne was toying with the idea of a Stuart heir; while letters passing between the Pretender and his half brother the Duke of Berwick, show that in 1713 both Bolingbroke and Harley were making overtures, assuring James, that if only he would change his religion, it was feasible to get Parliament to alter the succession arrangements. The Whigs did not know about the secret negotiations but they could see that Bolingbroke was purging the Church and Army of Hanoverians and that, worse still, he was using his influence to bring Jacobites into a reconstructed Ministry.

With the Tories riding high, Addison was nervous about the political implications they might draw from *Cato* but Steele wanted to make 14 April an occasion for the Opposition. He made his preparations and ensured the opening night was an event to remember – for both parties.

The Pit at Drury Lane had been packed by Steele with City Whigs, while the boxes were segregated, supporters of the two political factions facing each other across the theatre. Throughout the play each side applauded anything they thought supported their cause, so that the 'numerous and violent claps' echoed back and forth, beginning during Pope's Prologue when, to his dismay and amusement, he was 'clapped into a staunch Whig sore against his will, at almost every two lines.'[36] The Whigs would have had the best of the evening if it had not been for Bolingbroke who, more than anyone, was responsible for the Tory Peace. At the end of the performance he called Booth, the actor playing Cato, to his box and gave him a purse of fifty guineas for his part in 'defending the cause of liberty so well against a *perpetuall dictator.*'[37] This hit at Marlborough, who had done so much to keep the war going and wanted to be appointed Captain-General for life, evened up the score for the Tories.

Cato continued to play to packed houses night after night. It was such an extraordinary phenomenon that the wits made jokes about it. When the Whigs decided to copy the Tories and bestow guineas on Booth, Dr Garth remarked drily, that 'betwixt them, 'tis probable ... Cato may have something to live upon, after he dies.'[38] It could not escape notice that Mrs Oldfield, who played Cato's virgin daughter, was evermore visibly pregnant – she hired a midwife to stand in the wings, just in case. The inevitable epigrams circulated in the coffee houses, Pope and Rowe contributing a joint effort about Celia who was physically overcome the night she went to the play. They entitled it, 'On the Lady who P–st at the Tragedy of *Cato.*'[39]

Cato turned Addison willy-nilly into a Whig hero overnight. Everyone was forced to take sides whether they wanted to or not, for by now party feeling was carried to such lengths, that the political opinions of a lady of fashion could be seen from where she wore the beauty patches on her face. Button's was rapidly becoming an exclusively Whig club, with Buttonians quick to notice that Pope was seeing a good deal of Swift, the Tories' most able propagandist. By June Ambrose Philips was going around saying that Swift had recruited the young poet to 'write against the *Whig-Interest*.'[40] In these circumstances it was inevitable that the friendship between Addison and Pope – always a sensitive plant – shrivelled in the political scirocco.

When Philips said that Pope had been recruited by Swift to attack the Whigs, he was thinking of the Scriblerians. They were Tories – literary men whom Swift gathered about him, in the hope they would counteract the influence of the Whig writers orbiting round Addison. Towards the end of 1713 Swift's friends became the Scriblerus Club, for which Pope was eligible because *Windsor Forest* had shown his heart was in the right place. Even so, he did not think of himself as a party political writer. His instincts told him it was safer to keep in with both sides if he could. Hence he was so worried when he heard that Philips was trying to turn the members of the Opposition Hanover Club against him, he went to Lord Halifax to assure him he was not anti-Whig.[41]

Nevertheless, Pope turned with understandable relief from Button's to the Scriblerus Club, which developed into the kind of literary support group he had been looking for, made up of men willing to discuss each other's work amiably, who were also capable of offering suggestions for new works.

Pope and John Gay were the youngest members, both of them still in their twenties. The other, older Scriblerians were Swift, Dr Arbuthnot and Thomas Parnell. All of them combined a conservative approach as judges of literature, along with varying degrees of originality in their capacity as authors. John Arbuthnot was the Queen's physician and, like many eighteenth-century medical men, he had time for other interests: science, mathematics, music and writing. He wrote several satirical papers, creating a national archetype in his *History of John Bull*. Parnell, like Swift, was an Anglo-Irish clergyman who, again like Swift, hoped to find a living in England. He was an excellent classical scholar, a fact appreciated by Pope who transported him to Binfield in the summer of 1714 to help him with the *Iliad*. He was also a poet whose 'Night-Piece on Death' was the first example of the kind of poem Thomas Gray was to write with his 'Elegy in a country Churchyard.' The careers of Swift and Gay were to show they were full of new ideas of course, while Pope had already proved himself in this respect with the *Rape of the Lock*.

There was another honorary member of the Scriblerus Club who came whenever he could. This was Robert Harley, Earl of Oxford, whose rooms were in St James's Palace, on the floor below Arbuthnot's, which was where the Club usually met. The Treasurer came mainly to unwind, though he was shrewd enough to realize how useful a good writer could be to a political party. Hence he had already encouraged Swift and Parnell. The Scriblerians were not over-awed by the Queen's leading minister. If he missed a few meetings, they enticed him back with genial invitations, like the following one written 'From the Doctor's Chamber, past eight':

> The Doctor and Dean, Pope, Parnell and Gay
> In manner submissive most humbly do pray,
> That your Lordship would once let your Cares all alone,
> And Climb the dark stairs to your Friends who have none.
> To your Friends who at least have no Cares but to please you.
> To a good honest Junta that never will teaze you.

The atmosphere was both stimulating and free and easy when the Scriblerians met. No one resented Pope though they teased him sometimes. Parnell was given to devising elaborate practical jokes and at least once the joke was on the author of the *Rape of the Lock*. This was when Parnell arrived one evening with the lines describing Belinda at her dressing table which he had translated into Latin. He brandished these, claiming Pope had cribbed his description from some medieval monk's manuscript. Unfortunately, the Club was short lived but, for a few months until the Spring of 1714, it met regularly and Pope was usually present when it did. He felt at home there, not least because Tory fortunes did not feature largely in the group discussions. The bond that united the Scriblerians was a concern for what they saw as a deterioration in English literary life – what has been called 'cultural politics.'[42]

The literary world had been changing ever since the Licensing Act was allowed to lapse in 1695. From that time on the way was open for a whole new breed of editors and publishers to set up in business, without the fear of pre-publication censorship. At the beginning of the reign of Charles II there had been twenty master printers in London. By the 1720s there were more than seventy-five.[43] The Grub Street hack, who relied on his earnings to pay the rent, came into being and, with him or her, the commercialized print world we are familiar with today.

Pope and other Club members had become aware of this phenomenon when newspapers and journals proliferated, in London and then throughout the country. The market for these was huge and growing. In 1715 the editor of the *British Mercury*, eager to increase his advertising revenue, told the public that 'near 4000' copies of his newspaper were 'printed every Time.'[44] In the early decades of the eighteenth century, a fair number of people in all classes of society were literate. By 1714, 45 per cent of the population could and did read – especially in the towns. By the middle of the century this figure had risen to 60 per cent.[45] As well as Gay saying the sempstresses enjoyed the *Rape of the Lock*, the young Swiss de Saussure found that London workmen, including shoeblacks, habitually began the day 'by going to coffee-rooms in order to read the latest news' and added 'You often see an Englishman taking a treaty of peace more to heart than he does his own affairs.'[46] When the Treaty of Utrecht was being negotiated, Pope wondered what journalists would find to write about once they lacked hard news about the war. But then, on 14 August 1712 in *Spectator* no. 457, his prophetic soul enabled him to envisage newspapers filled with details about the 'Sickness of Persons in high Posts, Twilight Visits paid and received by Ministers of State, Clandestine Courtships and Marriages, Secret Amours' and the like. Our modern tabloids were on their way.

Nor was it just newsprint that flourished. A growing readership showed it had an appetite for books and pamphlets – the more sensational the better, such as those provided by the publisher/bookseller Edmund Curll. Curll, who opened his first shop in the Strand in 1706, paid a team of hacks to write the works he sold there, one of his most profitable lines being lurid biographies. He was none too scrupulous about how he obtained the material for these, reputedly infiltrating the homes of the deceased and making off with private papers he found there. Dr Arbuthnot said the 'Lives' sold by Curll added 'a new terror to death.'[47] Curll was sometimes prosecuted for publishing pornography but nothing held him back for long. In 1709 he moved to larger premises in Temple Bar, as well as opening a second shop in Tunbridge Wells.

Of course, not all the new entrepreneurs in publishing were as unscrupulous as Curll. Samuel Richardson was born in the same year as Pope and, well before he became famous as a novelist, he had a career as a printer and publisher that was as respectable and inspiring as that of Hogarth's good apprentice. It was also profitable, his commission to print parliamentary bills and reports bringing in as much as £600 one year, quite apart from what he earned publishing such works as Defoe's *Tour Through the Whole Island of Great Britain* and Thomson's *The Seasons*.[48] One of the few things Richardson and Curll had in common was that they printed and sold books to make money. Otherwise their contrasting careers show that the commercialization of the print world established a gulf between high art and popular culture. With hindsight we can see that this was inevitable.

However, that fact was not obvious at the time to the Scriblerians who fought a rearguard action on behalf of serious writing. With the exception of Pope, they did not think of relying on writing for an income. Swift, Parnell and Arbuthnot had their careers in the Church or Medicine. While Gay, who needed to think about earning money, still hovered on the edge of a dying world in which authors looked for patronage, so he spent some weary years hoping for a Government sinecure. The majority of the Scriblerians therefore could afford to be contemptuous about men and women who were willing to write anything that would pay for bread. Pope, who was determined to make a living as a poet if he could, was also contemptuous of the new journalists and half educated hacks who were invading the literary world. In fact, he was appalled. He had after all caught 'the itch of poetry' from reading Homer and had an exalted idea of his vocation as a writer.[49] Then to complicate matters, he wanted to be considered a gentleman and, in this role, often pretended to an aristocratic indifference to his work as a poet, as if it was nothing more than recreation. For reasons, both solemn and snobbish therefore, he wished to dissociate himself from the vulgar world of time-serving journalists and meretricious publishers, though he was quite willing to make the most of some of the opportunities commercialization offered, contributing over two dozen essays to the new upmarket journals, the *Spectator* and *Guardian* between 1711 and 1713. His feelings about the advent of the professional author were mixed – as were those of a growing number of serious writers as the century wore on.[50]

He had already begun his campaign in defence of high culture when he wrote *Spectator* no. 457. In that essay in 1712 he proposed publishing a monthly journal, 'An Account of the Works of the Unlearned', encouraged in that undertaking, as he said, by 'Several late Productions of [his] own Country-men, who many of them make a very Eminent Figure in the Illiterate World.' He had assured readers that there would be a 'great Variety of Subjects,' including 'Party-Authors ... Editors, Commentators, and others, who are often Men of no Learning, or what is as bad, of no Knowledge.'

Now, a year or so later, realizing there was potential support for his projected burlesque journal among the Scriblerians, he revived the idea, so giving the Club its immediate aim and occupation. The other members agreed to write for the new periodical and did so, Dr Arbuthnot being one of the most active contributors. The periodical itself did not materialize however, because the Club broke up when the Tory party disintegrated in the last months of Anne's reign. Meetings were never resumed after Swift left London at the end of May 1714, disgusted at the inability of the Tory leaders, Bolingbroke and Harley to settle their differences. Pope did not forget about the journal he had wanted though. In 1742 he published the *Memoirs of Scriblerus*, containing some of the papers he and the others had written for it.

In addition, ideas produced during Club discussions inspired his own *Art of Sinking*, the *Dunciad* and Swift's *Gulliver's Travels*.

Notes

1. *Corr.* 1: 163 and 165.
2. *Corr.* 1: 166.
3. *Corr.* 1: 163.
4. *Corr.* 1: 168.
5. *Corr.* 1: 163.
6. 'Long-Legged Fly' – the refrain.
7. M. Csikszentmihalyi, *Creativity: Flow and the Psychology of Discovery and Invention* (New York: HarperCollins, 1996), p. 110.
8. *Corr.* 1: 163.
9. J.R. Moore, '*Windsor Forest* and William III', *Modern Language Notes*, 66 (1951), 451–4. Moore argues that *Windsor Forest* is a full-blown Jacobite poem, 'hardly short of treasonable.' This point of view is endorsed by Pat Rogers, 'The

Enamelled Ground: The Language of Heraldry and Nature Description in *Windsor Forest'*, *Studia Neophilogica*, 45 (1973), 256–71. However, a debate continues over the extent of Pope's Jacobitism. For a sceptic's view see H.T. Dickinson, 'The Politics of Pope', in *Alexander Pope: Essays for the Tercentenary*, ed Colin Nicholson (Aberdeen University Press, 1988), pp. 1–21.

10. Earl R. Wasserman, *The Subtler Language* (Baltimore: Johns Hopkins University Press, 1959).

11. *The Works of Lord Bolingbroke*, 4 vols (Philadelphia: Carey and Hart, 1841) 2: 428–9.

12. George Sherburn, 'New Anecdotes about Alexander Pope', *Notes and Queries*, N.S., 5: 8 (1958), 343–9.

13. *Swift's Journal to Stella*, ed Harold Williams, 2 vols (Oxford: Clarendon, 1948).

14. 'Epistle to Mr. Jervas', l. 42.

15. *Corr.* 1: 187.

16. *Corr.* 1: 115. Pope's copy of Kneller's portrait of Betterton, now owned by the Mansfield family, is competent, to say the least.

17. *Corr.* 1: 187.

18. *Corr.* 2: 24.

19. Ibid.

20. *Corr.* 1: 269.

21. *Corr.* 1: 288 and 71.

22. *Corr.* 1: 185.

23. *Corr.* 1: 172.

24. Arthur S. Williams, 'Pope's "Epistle to Mr. Jervas": The Relevance and its Contexts', *British Journal for Eighteenth-Century Studies*, 8: 1 (Spring, 1985), 51–6.

25. Spence, 148.

26. *Addisoniana* [? by Sir Richard Phillips, 1757–1840], 2 vols (1803), 1: 7.

27. Spence, 181.

28. *Diary of Viscount Percival, afterwards 1st Earl of Egmont*, 3 vols (1920–23), 1: 105.

29. Spence, 189.

30. Spence, 188.

31. TW. 6: 284, ll. 35–6. The verse was later incorporated into the 'Epistle to Dr. Arbuthnot,' without Johnson's name being mentioned.

32. Spence, 183n.

33. Colley Cibber, *An Apology for his Life*, ed R.W. Lowe, 2 vols (1889), ch. 11.

34. *Corr.* 1: 190.

35. Spence, 159.

36. *Corr.* 1: 175.

37. Ibid.

38. Ibid.

39. Pope probably wrote another epigram as well, about Damon who, smitten by Mrs Oldfield, went to see the play every night, to the detriment of both his studies and his health. See TW. 6: 410.

40. *Corr.* 1: 229.

41. Ibid.

42. Brean S. Hammond, *Professional Imaginative Writing in England, 1670–1740: 'Hackney for Bread'* (Oxford: Clarendon, 1997). See discussion of the attitude of Pope and the Scriblerians to professional writing in Chapter 7.

43. John Brewer, *The Pleasures of the Imagination: English Culture in the Eighteenth Century* (New York: Farrar Straus Giroux, 1997), pp. 131 and 137.

44. Michael Harris, 'Print and Politics in the Age of Walpole', *Britain in the Age of Walpole*, ed Jeremy Black (London: Macmillan, 1984), quoted p. 190.

45. R.A. Houston, *Literacy in early Modern Europe: Culture and Education 1500–1800* (London: Longman, 1988) and Keith Thomas, 'The Meaning of Literacy in Early Modern England' in G. Bauman ed, *The Written Word: Literacy in Transition* (Oxford University Press, 1986), pp. 77–131. Also Brewer, *op. cit.*, Chapter 4, 'Readers and the Reading Public'.

46. César de Saussure, *A Foreign View of England in the Reigns of George I and George II*, ed and trans. Madame Van den Muyden (London: John Murray, 1902), p. 162.

47. Jonathan Swift, *Correspondence*, ed Harold Williams, 5 vols (Oxford: Clarendon, 1963–65), 4: 378.

48. Brewer, *op. cit.*, p. 127.

49. *Corr.* 1: 297.

50. As well as telling Boswell that 'No man but a blockhead ever wrote, except for money,' *Life*, ed G.B. Hill and L.F. Powell, 6 vols (Oxford University Press, 1934–50), 3: 19, Dr Johnson also wrote in *The Rambler* about 'drudges of the pen, manufacturers of literature' who wrote worthless ephemera to meet a deadline. Oliver Goldsmith was equally ambivalent about 'the author who draws his quill merely to take a purse.' See Brewer *op. cit.*, pp. 145–9.

PART III

Fighting the Opposition

CHAPTER NINE

Attack – the Best Method of Defence: Strategies

At the same time that Pope was looking for supporters and making friends, he was conducting a campaign against the fair number of enemies he had already made. Quite early on he was slighted or attacked for any number of reasons, literary, religious, political, or just because some people thought he was obnoxious. Whatever the apparent or underlying motive for an attack, Pope was congenitally incapable of not fighting back. Indeed he relished the fact that, as he said himself, 'The life of a Wit is a warfare upon earth'.[1] He was so innately aggressive that, had he been physically able, he would probably have been fighting a duel a week. In which case this world might not have had him as a poet for very long. As it was, a combative spirit has got Pope the man into more trouble than enough, though it prevented the poet from sinking into melancholia or despair when he met with hostility or discouragement.

When Pope wanted to mount a counter attack he rarely acted on impulse. He was willing to wait for the right moment. If friends advised him to ignore his critics, he might acquiesce but, sooner or later an opportunity would arise for going on the offensive which he would find irresistible, whereupon his fertile imagination would suggest appropriate tactics for prevailing over his opponent. There was one constant in all his campaign plans, in that he set out to make his target of the moment look ridiculous. The strategies he used to do so, however, were varied, ranging from finely honed irony in a send up of Ambrose Philips's pastoral verses, to a boisterous treatment of that doyen of the literary world, John Dennis, in hilarious pamphlets, to elaborate ingenuity in a *Key to the Lock*, a parody which he wrote to pre-empt Whig attempts to find Jacobite symbolism in his poem about Belinda. Nor was he above playing crude practical jokes on Edmund Curll, dosing his drink with an emetic on one occasion, as a punishment that most fitted that publisher's crimes. Only when he was criticised by his fellow Catholics, was he willing to exercise restraint.

As we have seen, when some of Pope's more rigid co-religionists objected to his lines about monkish superstition in *An Essay on Criticism*, his first impulse was to retaliate. Then he had second thoughts and wrote the *Messiah*. Even before the poem was written, John Caryll heaved a sigh of relief because his young friend was not going to wage war on his fellow Catholics. He wrote to the poet saying, 'I am satisfy'd 'twill be doubly *Divine* and I shall long to see it.'[2] The key word in that sentence is 'doubly.' Caryll hoped that the work would not only reassure Catholics about the poet's piety but would also give covert cheer to the Jacobites among them, because the subject of the Second Coming had a special significance for those who wanted the Pretender to return.

Pope had to be careful in sending any message to the Jacobites. Until the 1750s men were flogged and imprisoned if convicted of spreading propaganda in support of the Stuart cause, while in 1719, a young printer John Matthews, who published a Jacobite pamphlet, *Vox Populi, Vox Dei*, was hanged.[3] In these circumstances Jacobites learned to write obliquely, or in a code which escaped the notice of all except the initiates. The device was so successful that even to this day not everyone realizes that the English national anthem originally called for God to save the Stuart king, or that the carol, '*O Come all Ye Faithful*' started off as a Jacobite rallying cry.[4]

A code that used religious terminology was one of the most popular, being both adaptable and relatively safe. Hence The *Messiah*, in which Pope described the Second Coming of Christ, an event used by Jacobite journalists and ballad writers to symbolize the return of their absent prince over the water.

The poem appeared in *Spectator* no. 378 on 14 May 1712, two weeks before the anniversary of the Restoration on 29 May, a day which was always celebrated enthusiastically by Jacobites. Since 1689, the return of the divinely sanctioned Charles II had been seen as an event invested with cosmic significance, modelled on the Resurrection.[5] All supporters of the Stuart cause believed in Divine Right, so, in 1712, they regarded James Francis Edward as God's vice regent in England. He could be thought of therefore as a Christ figure. Sometimes he was spoken of as the good Shepherd of his flock whose return to earth would herald a new paradise. This was an especially tempting idea at a time when it was realistic to suppose Anne might yet overthrow the plans for a Hanoverian succession. Jacobites, who believed that the nation fell 'from a pristine, sanctified order into a realm of injustice and depravity'[6] after the monarchy was usurped, could take a special pleasure in Pope's picture of renewal when, 'The Swain in barren Desarts with surprize / See Lillies spring, and sudden Verdure rise' (ll. 67–8) and his assurance that with the Second Coming, 'ancient Fraud shall fail / Returning Justice lift aloft her Scale' (ll. 17–18).

The subtext of the *Messiah* passed non-Jacobites by – as Pope intended it should. The uninitiated read the poem on one level only, as an expression of religious devotion. As such it was admired by Christians of all denominations, with Steele speaking for many readers when he wrote to Pope to congratulate him on the way he had 'preserv'd the sublime, heavenly spirit throughout the whole.'[7]

Pope saw no reason to placate his Protestant rival Ambrose Philips, whose pastoral poems had consistently put his own in the shade ever since both sets were published by Jacob Tonson in 1709. However, he let four years go by before responding to what seems to have been a deliberate policy by the Addisonians to direct public opinion by ignoring his poems while lavishing praise on those of Philips. Soon after the *Poetical Miscellanies* appeared, Steele reviewed the pastorals of Pope's rival in glowing terms in the *Tatler*, and they were lauded again in the *Spectator* no. 223 in 1711 and no. 400 in 1712. None of these essays so much as mentioned Pope's verses which were exquisite but not to the modern taste. The situation was a familiar one, to be found in the literary world in every period, whereby a particular work receives critical accolades, not so much for its intrinsic value but because its subject matter, or the treatment of it, fits in with current trends. No doubt Philips's friends, looking at his good intentions rather than his achievements, genuinely admired his pastorals because they were set in England and peopled by English rustics. At the same time they were not sorry to have an excuse to put a conceited young upstart in his place.

At first Pope hid his disappointment at the reception – or rather lack of it – that his *Pastorals* received. He saw it would do him little good to take the critics to task when his career had barely begun. In the hope maybe of eliciting some reciprocal generosity, he even went out of his way to try and find the good points in Philips's verses. Though he seemed to be pushing the process of fishing for compliments a bit far when he wrote to Cromwell in October 1710, 'On the whole, I agree with the Tatler, that we have no better Eclogs in our Language.'[8] The breaking point came when Thomas Tickell wrote no less than five *Guardian* essays in April 1713 praising Philips's pastorals, again without mentioning Pope's. Before the month was over, Pope sent Steele the essay which he printed as *Guardian*, no. 40. It was a sixth paper (supposedly anonymous as were the previous five) in praise of Philips's eclogues. At least that is what Steele thought it was. Actually it was an accomplished and comprehensive demolition job, in which Pope used his full ironic repertoire to expose the banality of his rival's clumsy verses. There was plenty to work on. Philips's attempts to produce real rustic speech had resulted in such awkward and nearly unintelligible lines as Cicily's exhortation, 'Rager, go vetch the Kee, or else that Zun, / Will quite be go vore c'have half a don.'[9] Philips's shepherds were not just simple men, they were dolts, whose reflections consisted of ruminating in somewhat inaccurate old saws such as, 'He that late lyes down, as late will rise, / And Sluggard-like, till Noon-day snoaring lyes.'[10] Unlike its predecessors, *Guardian* no. 40 mentioned the 'other Pastoral Writer' who had a lamentable tendency to 'deviate into downright Poetry.'[11] Though in a telling phrase that shows Pope was aware of the snobbish nature of some of the prejudice against him, it is admitted that Philips's competitor 'hath imitated some single Thoughts of the Ancient well enough, if we consider he had not the Happiness of an University Education'[12] – The Buttonian was a graduate of St John's College, Cambridge.

Steele may have misread *Guardian* no. 40 but Philips did not. He was furious and the story went round that he brought a rod 'which he stuck up at the bar of Button's Coffee-house' as a warning to Pope, though if he did nothing came of it. The poet told Caryll later, 'he never open'd his lips to my face.'[13] Nevertheless, from that time on he was Pope's implacable foe which, as he was a Whig would prove awkward when the Tories lost power.

Pope's enemies were usually Whigs, including John Dennis, whose *Reflections* on *An Essay on Criticism* he had originally said he would ignore. He did not keep that promise however and, almost immediately pilloried the old man as '*Rinaldo Furioso*, Critick of the Woful Countenance' in a mock prospectus *The Critical Specimin*, supposedly advertising a forthcoming treatise by the Don Quixote of the literary world.

This ingenious spoof made merciless fun of Dennis's extremism, paranoid delusions and violent mannerisms. Yet it was not as harsh as the work which had provoked it. Being compared to Cervantes's hero was less offensive than being called a hunch-backed toad. Pope was relatively good humoured because, whereas the older man loathed him, he enjoyed Dennis's eccentricities, though of course his patronising raillery was galling and did not make his target hate him any the less.

Only at the end of *The Critical Specimin* did Pope show that his opponent's comments on his deformity had lingered in his mind. He concluded his satirical piece with two additional advertisements. The first one was for a work by Dr Bentley in which he argued that Aesop was 'not *Crooked* but *Strait*'. In other words, contrary to legend, the author of the *Fables* was not a cripple and so not Pope's companion in misfortune as he might have hoped. The second advertisement was for a work by Mr Dennis 'making it plain from the late *Essay* upon *Criticisme* that the Author is by no means *Strait* but *Crooked*.'[14] The price was twopence. Of course Pope minded intensely when Dennis and others showed they found him physically repulsive but there was little he could do about this except make a joke of it. It was a case of 'Je me presse de rire de tout, de peur d'être obligé d'en pleurer [I make myself laugh at everything for fear of having to weep].'[15]

The Critical Specimin, crammed with pseudo learning, was over elaborate. It did not sell many copies and apparently escaped comment. It was not Pope's last word on the author of the *Reflections* however. He saw his chance to return to the fray a couple of years later when Dennis amazed everyone by launching a vigorous attack on the play which had recently been such a success at Drury Lane. On 9 July 1713, he published *Remarks on Cato, a Tragedy*. Whereupon Pope, under the cover of defending Addison, seized the opportunity of making it clear just how bizarre he thought its author was. He lost no time. Within three weeks he wrote and published *The Narrative of Dr. Norris*, lamenting the 'strange and deplorable Frenzy' the old critic had fallen into.[16]

The Narrative is a short, semi-dramatic sketch, brimming over with energy. It has a number of characters, including the publisher Bernard Lintot and an unnamed friend of Dennis. It begins when Norris, a well known physician who specializes in the care of lunatics, has been summoned by the Old Woman who 'does for' Dennis because she fears her master has gone mad. The Doctor describes arriving at Dennis's lodging, where he says, 'I observ'd his room was hung with old Tapestry, which had several Holes in it, caus'd, as the Old Woman inform'd me, by his having cut out of it the Heads of divers Tyrants, the Fierceness of whose visages much provok'd him.'[17] Dennis is raving and cries out, 'O I am sick, sick to death.' On being asked what he is sick of, he goes on, 'Of every thing, of every thing ... Alas, what is become of the Drama, Drama?' Whereupon the Old Woman cuts in with, 'The Dram Sir? Mr. Lintot drank up all the Geneva just now, but I'll go fetch more presently.'[18]

The farcical incidents pile up, but Pope lets Dennis win in the end. With the help of his friend (who may have been Cromwell), he resists medical treatment, driving off Norris and Lintot by hurling his library at them. When the Doctor and publisher sit reconstructing a case history for the lost patient afterwards, Pope gets in a riposte for the *Reflections*, as Norris writes down in his notebook, 'That the said Mr. John Dennis on 27 March 1712 finding on the said Mr. Lintot's counter a Book call'd *An Essay on Criticism*, just then publish'd, read a page or two with much Frowning and Gesticulation, till coming on these two lines:

> Some have at first for Wits, then Poets past,
> Turn'd Criticks next, and prov'd plain fools at last,

he flung down the Book in a terrible Fury, and cried out, 'By G___ he means me.'[19]

If Pope supposed he would win the gratitude of *Cato*'s author with this piece, he was mistaken. The correct Addison did not find Pope's rumbustious pamphlet an appropriate defence of himself. However, he took some time to dissociate himself from it and then did so in such an indirect way as to make the possibility of a candid friendship with the young poet seem very unlikely. Pope had offered to show him the *Narrative* before it went to the printer but Addison declined to look at it, though if he had protested at that stage, Pope might well have held the work back, as he did with other pieces he wrote. Nor did Addison say anything to Pope afterwards. Instead a month later, on 4 August, he repudiated the young man's *jeu d'esprit* by telling Steele to tell Lintot to tell Dennis that he wholly disapproved of 'the Manner of Treating Mr. Dennis in a little pamphlet, by way of Dr. Norris's Account', and that when he thought fit to 'take Notice of Mr. Dennis's Objections to his Writings', he would do so 'in a Way Mr. Dennis shall have no just Reason to complain of.'[20]

Pope was not afraid of Dennis. So he was uninhibited when he took him on, giving full rein to his natural high spirits. But he could, on occasion, be circumspect and cautious, particularly if he sensed he was in political danger. This happened after Queen Anne died on 1 August 1714, before she had rescinded the Act of Settlement – if she had ever intended to do so. On 20 October her Hanoverian heir was crowned king as George I. The Whigs swept

9.1   Joseph Addison. Jonathan Richardson

into power, where they would remain for the rest of the poet's lifetime. Pope's Tory friends lost their influence. Dr Arbuthnot was removed from his post as a royal physician. Swift departed for Ireland and would not revisit England for twelve years. In March 1715 Bolingbroke escaped arrest by fleeing to France, where he became Secretary of State to the Pretender. By July Harley was in the Tower, charged with high treason.

Being a Catholic and associated through the Scriblerians with a discredited political party, Pope felt isolated and frightened. Mulling over ways in which his Protestant Whig enemies could harm him, he decided they might try to do so by discovering politically subversive elements and Papist propaganda in his most popular poem, the *Rape of the Lock*. If this sounds far-fetched, one has to remember that, as Pope himself said, it had been the 'Custom of late' for dissidents 'to vent their Political Spleen in Allegory and Fable'.[21] Furthermore, at least two modern critics have argued that the *Rape* is a crypto-Jacobite work.[22] Whatever the truth of the matter, Pope took the threat to his safety seriously and decided to deal with it by making a pre-emptive strike.

Within days of Anne's death, he began writing his own political interpretation of his mock epic in *A Key to the Lock*. He showed it to a friend or two, including Swift before he left for Dublin on 16 August. Then he published it finally in April 1715. The *Flying Post* for 21–23 April advertised the *Key* in a week when there were riots in London to mark the anniversary of Anne's coronation. Most of the newspapers carried alarmist stories about unrest throughout the country and, a few days after advertising the *Key*, the *Flying Post* reported that 'a great number of Jacobites make use of a large room that is over a coffee-house in the Aldersgate Street to meet in on Sundays, and that they have a non-Juring parson, who officiates to them, where they make their boasts that they pray for the right King, as they call the Pretender: the door is carefully kept, and none admitted but such as they think they can trust'.[23] There were plenty of signs that England was on the brink of the 1715 rebellion and plenty of people to suspect a Papist poet of treason.

In *A Key to the Lock* Pope diverted the attention of a politicized readership by reducing to absurdity the idea that his mock epic had any political significance whatsoever. He did this by deconstructing his own text under the name of the non-existent Esdras Barnivelt. In this exegesis Belinda represents England, 'her white breast' (2:7) being the cliffs of Dover. The lock is the Barrier Treaty (a pact to defend Dutch borders) which Lord Oxford (alias the Baron) had broken so as to facilitate the Utrecht peace negotiations. Every character in the poem is identified, down to Belinda's lap dog Shock who, representing the Jacobite preacher Dr Sacheverell, 'leap'd up, that is, into the Pulpit, and awaken'd *Great Britain* with his *Tongue*, that is with his *Sermon*, which made so much *Noise*' in 1709.[24]

The second edition of the *Key*, published at the end of May, was accompanied by an apparatus of prefatory poems, which further spiked Protestant guns with such lines as, 'Can Popish Writings do the Nation good? / Each Drop of Ink demands a Drop of Blood', and 'The *Spaniard* hides his Poynard in his Cloke, / The Papist masques his Treason in a Joke'.[25]

Pope attacked his foes, present or anticipated, for a number of reasons, some of them more obvious than others. In the first place he was getting his own back on those who had slighted or insulted him. All his contemporaries realized that and, as the years went on, they grew to fear him. In the second place, Pope's counter attacks were an aspect of career management. He was protecting his role as a poet, attempting to correct and redirect critical opinion in *Guardian* no. 40 and warding off the political danger that might have put an end to him as a writer in *A Key to the Lock*.

Furthermore, writing in prose provided Pope with yet another way of releasing his creative energy, one that gave him the freedom to be spontaneous, frank and indecorous. He was unbuttoned as a journalist, so we see aspects of him that are not always apparent in his early verses, most notably arrogance. This arrogance sprang from his sure knowledge that most of his contemporaries did not write as well as himself. It is a trait that accounts for some of his unpopularity but one found in other supremely gifted individuals – in Mozart for instance, who was scathing about some of his musical colleagues. In his pamphlet campaigns Pope showed he was an excellent journalist with all the virtues and shortcomings of that breed. He could meet a deadline when he had to. Once he had decided the time was ripe, most of his prose attacks were written within days and printed soon afterwards. He wrote polemics and was therefore one-sided and unfair. Neither Ambrose Philips or John Dennis were as foolish as he made them appear. Philips won praise from Dr Johnson in his *Lives of the Poets* and, as we have seen, Pope himself took notice of some of Dennis's complaints about inconsistencies in *An Essay on Criticism*.

Nevertheless, Pope's partisan pieces convince as well as amuse us while we are reading them because he tells the truth, even if not the whole truth. We recognize that Dennis, forever tilting at literary windmills, was indeed akin to Don Quixote, with whom he is compared in *The Critical Specimin*. While later, in *The Narrative*, we get a complete picture of the old critic in his 'Lodgings near *Charing-cross*, up three Pairs of Stairs,' seated on his bed, unshaven, his eyebrows 'grey, long, and grown together, which he knit with indignation when any thing was spoken.' Unlike some of his contemporaries, Pope has no objection to counting the streaks on the tulip and tells us about the floor 'cover'd with Manuscripts as thick as a Pastry Cook's Shop on a Christmas Eve' and the 'Pot of half-dead Ale cover'd with a Longinus' (pp. 158–9). For the most part Pope makes skilful use of hyperbole to produce his effects in *The Narrative* but sometimes he uses a throw away understatement as well. Almost the only thing we learn about Lintot is when the Old Woman says he has drunk up all Dennis's gin. It is enough to make us wonder about the man.

As well as using a wide range of established literary techniques in his prose attacks, Pope invented a new genre in *A Key to the Lock*. Modern readers may note with surprise that this work is an early example of an exercise in deconstruction, in that it provides 'a reading which analyses the specificity of a text's critical difference from itself.'[26] Well before the twenty-first century, however, its value in providing an additional critical tool was recognized. Soon similar kinds of writing to the *Key* were appearing in Addison's *Freeholder*.[27]

It was fortunate that Pope had so many weapons at his disposal because the hostilities that led to him mounting a campaign over the *Pastorals, An Essay on Criticism* and *The Rape of the Lock* were trifling compared with the war waged against him once he announced his intention of translating Homer.

Notes

1. 'Preface to *The Works* 1717', *The Prose Works of Alexander Pope 1711–1720*, ed Norman Ault (Oxford: Blackwell, 1936), p. 292.
2. *Corr.* 1: 142.
3. R.J. Goulden, '"Vox Populi, Vox Dei", Charles Delafaye's Paper Chase', *The Book Collector* 28 (1979), 368–90.
4. *Oxford Book of Carols*, ed P. Dearmer et al. (Oxford University Press, 1987).
5. Paul Kléber Monod, *Jacobitism and the English People 1688–1788* (Cambridge University Press, 1989), ch. 1.
6. Monod, p. 54.
7. *Corr.* 1: 146.
8. *Corr.* 1: 101.
9. Ault, p. 104.
10. Ault, p. 103.
11. Ault, p. 100.
12. Ault, p. 99.
13. *Corr.* 1: 229.
14. Ault, p. 18 and comment pp. xxx ff.
15. Pierre Augustin Caron de Beaumarchais (1732–99).
16. Ault, p. 155.
17. Ault, p. 158.
18. Ault, pp. 162–3.
19. Ault, p. 166.
20. *Corr.* 1: 184.
21. *A Key to the Lock*, Ault, p. 182.
22. Howard Erskine-Hill, 'Literature and the Jacobite Cause: was there a Rhetoric of Jacobitism?' in *Ideology and Conspiracy: Aspects of Jacobitism 1689–1759*, ed Eveline Cruickshanks (Edinburgh University Press, 1982), pp. 46–99 and Douglas Brooks-Davies, *The Mercurian Monarch: Magical Politics from Spenser to Pope* (Manchester University Press, 1983), ch. 5. For a summary of the debate about Pope's Jacobitism, see also *Alexander Pope: World and Word*, ed Howard Erskine-Hill (Oxford University Press, 1998), pp. 22ff.
23. The *Flying Post*, 5–7 May 1715. Also earlier issues 21–23 and 24–26 April for reports of Jacobite activity.
24. Ault, p. 192.

25.   Ault, pp. 180–81.
26.   Barbara Johnson, *The Critical Difference: Essays in the Contemporary Rhetoric of Reading* (Baltimore: Johns Hopkins University Press, 1980).
27.   Ault, p. lxxv.

CHAPTER TEN

Homer's Pension

When, in October 1713, Pope circulated his Proposals for a new verse translation of the *Iliad*, he amazed and vastly irritated his literary adversaries. Certain he was overreaching himself with this ambitious project, they wondered why he was undertaking it. They decided it must be for the money and they sneered. Oddly enough it was the professionals, not the gentleman amateurs, who said it was unbecoming for a poet to try and make a profit from his work. John Oldmixon, who made his living as a miscellaneous writer and a party political journalist, was typical. 'First take the Gold', he advised Pope. 'So shall thy Father *Homer* smile to see / His Pension pay'd, tho' late, and pay'd to Thee.'[1] Not that this kind of supercilious comment worried Pope. He made no secret of the reason why he embarked on such a laborious and time-consuming task as a reworking of the *Iliad* for a contemporary audience. 'What led me into that', he said when reminiscing to Spence, 'was purely want of money. I had then none – not even to buy books.'[2]

By 1713 Pope had already established a literary reputation but his earnings were small, even though they had increased steadily over the past five years. In 1708 Tonson had paid him a total of ten guineas for his *Pastorals* and his modernization of Chaucer's *Merchant's Tale*, plus a translation of 'The Episode of Sarpedon', the latter being Pope's first published example of what he could do with the *Iliad*. By February 1713, however, Lintot was willing to pay thirty-two pounds and five shillings for *Windsor Forest*. We do not have a record of all the money Pope received for his poems but it is doubtful whether it amounted to more than a hundred pounds in the first five years of his career. The sum he got for *Windsor Forest* was unusually high. The following February Lintot paid no more than fifteen pounds for the five-canto *Rape of the Lock*, after paying seven guineas for the shorter version two years earlier.[3] On the money he was making as a poet, Pope was a long way off from being able to maintain the genteel life to which he aspired. The average of twenty pounds a year which he received for his work equalled the wages of a common seaman at this time.[4] Pope would have been starving in a garret if he had had to keep himself on what he earned between 1708 and 1713. But of course he did not have to do so. Part of the time he was living at home. Otherwise he got free board and lodging, whenever he could, by staying with friends such as the Carylls, Wycherley, Walsh or Jervas. No doubt too, he received some money from his father.

Mr Pope senior, however, was not a rich man. Only a few meagre details have come down to us about his financial affairs, but he gave every indication of living plainly within a circumscribed income, which he tried to augment with high risk investments.[5] William Warburton, who never met him or knew his son until the latter was relatively well off, estimated that Mr Pope had had a capital of between £15–20,000.[6] However, there is no evidence to substantiate this claim. Nor, if it was true, did Mr Pope die worth anywhere near that sum. Patty Blount, who knew the family when they lived in Binfield, believed the poet when he told her his father left him no more than £3–4,000.[7]

Pope had every reason therefore to look round for a way of making serious money from writing – the profession for which he had trained himself and the only one for which he was qualified. The business arrangement he came to with Lintot was meant to be a good one for both men.

The *Iliad* was to be sold initially by subscription. First of all Pope was to get 750 copies to sell to those readers who signed up for them and Lintot was to wait one month before selling copies of his own. Subscribers could collect their copies from Lintot's shop, but where this was inconvenient they were to receive them from Pope, who would despatch them at his own expense. In addition Lintot was to pay the poet 200 guineas for each volume. There were to be six volumes priced at one guinea each, with subscribers paying two guineas as a first instalment, in order to cover the expenses Pope would incur in implementing the scheme.

It comes as a relief to discover that Pope had a good business sense and was not going to be cheated, as some writers before and after him were. At the same time, his publisher stood to benefit as well. In drawing up such a contract, Lintot demonstrated his belief that Pope was capable of producing a work that would have a large sale, which was likely to be all the larger after the poet had generated advance publicity with his subscription list.

Later these arrangements would be modified but that was due to unexpected circumstances, a printer named Johnson having pirated the first volume, sending cut price copies over from the Hague. As this had diminished Lintot's profits, it was agreed that thereafter the publisher was to have the subscription money, and that the poet, keeping only 120 subscribers' copies, would pay him to despatch the rest. In return Pope was to receive an additional 400 guineas for each volume he translated. Again this arrangement suited both men, as well as being a landmark in the history of publishing.[8]

Translating the *Iliad* would dominate Pope's life until 1720 when the final volume was published. Rewriting the epic, however, was only part of the work involved. He also had to make a success of the business arrangement he had come to; his first task being to get subscribers. Naturally enough all his Catholic acquaintances were soon on the list. Characteristically too he was helped by the network of Protestant friends he had built up. Jervas and Congreve were energetic in recruiting a good many Whig readers, while Swift took the campaign to Queen Anne's Court. White Kennett, Bishop of Peterborough, who did not care for Swift very much, described him in action at Windsor in

November 1713. After busying himself giving messages from ministers to other ministers and complaining about a gold watch the courtiers had given him, Swift buttonholed a young nobleman, telling him and everyone else within earshot:

> ... that the best poet in England was Mr. Pope (a Papist) who had begun a translation of Homer into English verse, for which he must have them all subscribe, 'For', says he, 'the author shall not begin to print till *I have* a thousand guineas for him.'[9]

This enthusiastic endorsement of his young friend was typical of Swift and was successful in bringing subscription money in. At the same time it alienated the politically sensitized Buttonians still further, convincing them that Pope's translation was a Tory project, if not worse. Their suspicions were reinforced when the list of subscribers was complete and it was realized that it contained the names of sixty men and women of known Jacobite sympathies.[10] From the end of 1713 the habitués of the coffee house mounted a campaign to undermine the confidence of possible readers of the *Iliad*, with Addison countenancing at least one of the pamphlet attacks.

The battalion of enemies who lined up against Pope at this time all looked forward to his failure. On the grounds that he 'never was at any University,' they insisted he could not possibly know enough Greek to translate Homer.[11] They also spread it around that this 'young Poet of the Modern stamp, an easy Versifyer' was incapable of matching the grandeur of the original epic.[12] In short, they looked forward to the conceited interloper making a fool of himself. Of course these Whig critics were in no way objective in evaluating Pope's chances of success. If they had done more than glance at his 'Episode of Sarpedon' in Tonson's 1709 *Miscellanies* or at 'The Arrival of Ulysses in Ithaca', published more recently by Steele, they might have wondered if their wishful thinking was justified.[13]

Addison, in contrast to some of the other Whig writers, did not underrate Pope and at first he was encouraging. A couple of weeks after seeing the Proposals for the new translation of the *Iliad*, he told the poet, 'I know none of this age that is equal to it besides yourself.' He then went on to invite Pope to stay with him in the country when he began his task, which would require 'solitude and retirement.'[14] The visit never took place. A few months later, as the political infighting intensified, Addison, too, decided he did not want a young Papist, Tory, quasi-Jacobite poet to succeed. Therefore he recruited one of his own circle to become Pope's rival. This was Thomas Tickell, mentioned at the end of the 'Umbra' portrait. Tickell was a Fellow of All Souls who, it was assumed, would show up the self-educated poet's lack of scholarship; especially as Addison, himself a good classicist, was going to revise his protégé's work. Pope signed the final contract for the *Iliad* with Lintot in March 1714. Two months later Tickell signed a contract with Tonson, also to translate the *Iliad*. This contract was kept a secret, and although Pope eventually found out Tickell was working on Book I (all he completed), he never knew his rival had said he would do the whole epic.

Pope had not undertaken the translation of the *Iliad* without receiving the reassurance of classicists that he was capable of it. As early as 3 March 1708 he had arranged to meet one of them, Ralph Bridges, in order to discuss sundry passages from Homer which he had translated.[15] Bridges was a chaplain to the Bishop of London and a nephew of Sir William Trumbull, to whom he sent a copy of his encouraging comments. In the meantime Pope had also given the same passages to Sir William, who had written to say, 'I entirely approve of your Translation of those pieces of Homer, both as to the versification and the true sense that shines thro' the whole.' He then reminded Pope that he had repeatedly urged him to translate all of Homer.[16] The fact that Trumbull pressed his young friend to turn translator, when he knew he had it in him to be an outstanding original poet, suggests he realized that Mr Pope senior was not all that well off and that this was the son's best chance of gaining financial independence.

Towards the end of April 1714 Pope took Parnell home with him to Binfield where the two men worked on the *Iliad* most of the summer. The thought of what lay ahead was intimidating. As Pope began his six-year stint on this 'large work', he said there were times when he wished someone would hang him. Even at the end of his life he was still having dreams 'that he was engaged in a long journey, puzzled which way to take, and full of fears that he should never get to the end of it.'[17] He was oppressed because he was not content with recreating the epic in English verse. He also wanted to provide it with a complete scholarly apparatus, taking into account centuries of commentary. He needed assistants to help him with this side of the work. Over the years he used his contacts to recruit a small team of these. Parnell was the first, followed by William Broome, plus an indigent Oxford don and a brilliant Cambridge student. This last young man, John Jortin, remembered being paid about three or four guineas per book for his work. He had been recruited by his tutor, so he never met Pope who, to his disappointment, never sought him out to thank him for his notes.[18] This insensitivity was to prove part of a pattern of behaviour in which the poet was reluctant to admit to the general public (let alone his enemies) that he was ever helped in his task.

As far as the *Iliad* was concerned, the various scholarly assistants gave Pope summaries of earlier criticism, particularly Eustathius's labyrinthine commentary. He then absorbed these, as well as studying some half dozen previous translations of Homer's poem. The notes Pope eventually wrote for the *Iliad* miss very little of importance said by earlier scholars, including as they do several lengthy essays on particular aspects of the epic, as well as a running commentary on the text. This commentary is very much Pope's own. He uses the material supplied by his assistants as a basis for personal reflections on the

Greek poet and his world. As one might expect, there are detailed analyses of Homer's poetic techniques, plus explanations of ethical attitudes.

We can also discover from these notes what Pope thought about a range of topics: masculinity, female frailty, old age, fashion and herbal medicine, to mention just a few.[19] Furthermore the notes are crammed with factual information. Occasionally Pope surprised even himself with the amount of learned minutiae he collected. Yet he kept his lightness of touch. One example occurs in the later translation he made of the *Odyssey*, where he writes about the age of the hero's dog Argus, who must have been more than twenty years old when he staggered up from a dunghill to greet his returning master. Solemnly, Pope cites the various authorities: Aristotle on dogs that lived to be twenty-two, Eustathius on ones that reached twenty-four years, not forgetting Pliny and Madame Dacier who give further instances of canine longevity. Then he caps the lot with, '... and the Translator, not to fall short in these illustrious examples, has known one that died at twenty-two, big with puppies.'[20]

Pope found writing the actual poem by far the easiest part of his labours. Soon he was composing fifty lines a day, usually in the mornings when he felt freshest. Sometimes he merely wrote down the first half of each line as he sat up in bed, relying on his memory to fill in the rest when he copied out the passage. He wrote on any piece of paper that came to hand, often the backs of earlier poems or of old letters. For a careful man he could be remarkably insouciant about his work as he did it. He once sent the Blount girls some fruit from the Dancastles' garden, explaining they must sent the wrapping back because, written on it, was his only copy of the Homer passage he had just completed.[21]

During the first couple of months or so at Binfield, when the two friends were working intensively on the *Iliad*, the everyday world and its problems receded into the background. Just as Pope had forgotten a frigid winter when raising up the summer scenes of *Windsor Forest*, so now he put the unsettled state of contemporary England out of mind, spending all his waking hours in Troy, or laying siege to its walls. 'While you in the world are concerned about the Protestant Succession,' he wrote Jervas, 'I consider only how Menelaus may recover Helen, and the Trojan war may be put to a speedy conclusion.'[22] Parnell, it seems, was just as lost in the lives of ancient heroes as himself, on the brink of reciting Chryses prayer to Apollo when he should have been saying the 'Our Father.'[23]

Parnell was the best company of any of Pope's assistants on the Greek epics. At Binfield his Irish charm cast its spell on Pope's parents, the neighbours and Nurse Beach, who was so taken with him she was 'in danger of being in Love in her old Age.'[24] By midsummer, as the work was going so well, both men felt they could afford to relax a little. Looking back to the cheerful Scriblerian sessions, they had already tried to revive some of the atmosphere of those occasions by inviting Gay to join them for a working holiday. Gay, however, had succeeded in obtaining one of those government posts he was hoping for.

He was off to Hanover as a secretary to Lord Clarendon's diplomatic mission. So in July Pope and Parnell took a break from their labours to visit Swift.

Swift, in despair over the Tory quarrels, had gone some sixty miles from London to stay with a colleague, the Rector of Letcombe Bassett. As it was the time of the divine service when the travellers arrived, the Rector and his guest were in church. Pope and Parnell found their way round to the back door, where they were eventually discovered by Swift, who first scolded them, then plied them with hospitality. They sat drinking the health of absent friends with some of Lord Bolingbroke's wine and, when that was gone, with the local cider. Then Swift made them coffee, roasting the beans himself, talking about the political situation as he did so. Nothing his friends said could lighten his gloom on this topic. As Pope described the scene, 'When we mentioned the wellfare of England he laughed at us, & said Muscovy would become a flourishing Empire very shortly.'[25]

Swift was right to be pessimistic. Time had run out for his Tory friends. Shortly after his melancholy prognostications, Queen Anne died on 1 August and he left for Dublin, without saying goodbye to any of his Scriblerian friends, who would not see him again in England for twelve years. Before the end of the year Parnell also went back to Ireland, as there was no longer any chance of him being given preferment in England. Meanwhile, the new administration recalled the embassy that Gay was part of, so he was soon in London again, trying to live by literature alone. In contrast the Buttonians flourished. As soon as George I bestowed power on the Whigs, they rewarded their supporters. Steele received a knighthood, Addison was made Chief Secretary for Ireland and then, a Secretary of State. He, in his turn, found Government jobs for Budgell and Tickell.

For a few weeks after the visit to Letcombe Pope and Parnell were in Binfield again, completing work on the first volume of the *Iliad*. Busy as he was, Pope nevertheless made a quick visit to London after the Queen's death to hear what everyone was saying. What he found was not personally reassuring. Hence his decision to go ahead with *A Key to the Lock*, in an effort to neutralize questions that might be raised about his loyalty to the Crown by his now influential enemies. It had soon become clear to Pope, as he moved around the capital, that a cheerful acceptance of a Hanoverian king was more an appearance than a reality. The Stuart alternative was too vivid to too many people for them to dismiss it so lightly. For years senior politicians, including Whigs, had played safe by keeping in touch with the Pretender. As for the Tories, on the day Anne died their most prominent leaders: the Duke of Ormonde, Lord Bolingbroke, Lord Bathurst, Sir William Wyndham and Atterbury, the Bishop of Rochester met at Lord Harcourt's house to consider what to do next. It was alleged that Atterbury wished to declare for James at once, placing him on the throne with French help. 'He would' he said, 'at the Royal Exchange read, in his lawn sleeves, the Proclamation.' Bolingbroke said if he did, they would all get their throats cut. There was a violent quarrel between the two men which ended in Atterbury storming out, saying 'This pusillanimous fellow will ruin our country.'[26]

During this anxious period Pope was 'perpetually afflicted with headaches', which were probably migraines as they affected his vision.[27] He was urged to take a holiday and decided to do so – as soon as the verses and notes for the first volume of the *Iliad* were finished and could be left with his neighbour and friend Thomas Dancastle, who had volunteered to make fair copies.

At the beginning of September Pope went to visit the Blounts at Mapledurham, where he was touched to find the deposed 'Great Ones of the Earth' toasted daily for, as he assured Teresa and Patty, these men were grateful if anyone still favoured them with 'a visit by Daylight.'[28] From there he went to Bath, accompanied by Parnell. Flush with subscription money, he invited Gay to join them, promising him that if he was short of cash, 'Homer's shall support her Children', but Gay was too disconsolate to reply.[29] The doctors had told Pope to go to Bath to take the waters. Drinking these made him feel dizzy but nevertheless, once he found his way around the spa, his health and spirits revived. Soon he was taking part in all the amusements the place had to offer, 'the Pump-Assemblies, the Walkes, the Chocolate Houses, Raffling Shops, Plays, Medleys etc.'[30]

After Bath it was back to London again for the coronation of George I on 20 October. Town was crammed with families who had come especially for the occasion, so once again Pope plunged into the social whirl, going from one assembly and diversion to another, still relieved to be on remand from a translator's prison and also sounding out the general mood.

It was probably during this visit that he ran into Addison one evening at Button's. Since the beginning of the year the two had done no more than nod to each other on the few occasions they had met, so Pope was surprised when Addison called him to one side and asked him to stay until 'those people', meaning Philips and Budgell, had gone because he wanted to take him to a tavern to dine. Pope had known for months that he could expect little help from Addison but, over an amiable dinner, he tried again. He asked his host if he would look over his *Iliad* Book I and let him know what he thought of it. Addison said he could not because Tickell was engaged on the same book and, as he had promised to read that, it would have the 'air of double dealing' if he looked at Pope's as well. However, no doubt filled with curiosity, he asked to look at Book II and, having done so, returned it after a few days 'with very high recommendations.'[31] Apparently Addison wanted to distance himself from the behaviour of some of his followers. Yet he can hardly have felt very comfortable that evening at the tavern. For even as he held forth on double dealing, he kept quiet about the extent of Tickell's commitment to Tonson, letting Pope go away with a fraction of the truth.

Pope kept in touch with political events during the last months of 1714, promising Caryll 'the secret story of states and poets intermixed' when he visited him before Christmas.[32] In the New Year he went to stay with Bolingbroke, who had taken refuge with his unbeloved wife at Bucklebury. The story he heard there was hardly a soothing one. Bolingbroke told him that, during his stay in the country, he had 'felt the general disposition to Jacobitism increase daily among people of all ranks; among several who had been constantly distinguished by their aversion to that course.'[33] He was beginning to wonder if had made a mistake in refusing to back Atterbury's idea for a Jacobite coup that Sunday morning when Anne died.

While sympathetic to the Jacobite cause, Pope knew that an abortive rebellion, or a continuing atmosphere of unrest, would do him no good at all personally. Fear about the instability of the Hanoverian regime would make him, along with all his Catholic friends, the object of suspicious attention and, very probably, punitive measures. Not least, he feared that sales of his Homer would suffer in the current situation. After his return from Bucklebury he told Congreve, 'I am in the fairest way of being not worth a groat, being born both a *Papist* and a *Poet*.'[34]

The winter of 1715 was not, however, all gloom and uncertainty for Pope and his friends. On 23 February Gay's *The What D'Ye Call It* was put on at Drury Lane. Like much of Gay's work, it gave the public something new. It took a cheerfully disrespectful look at life among the bucolic squirearchy and their tenants and was interlaced with literary jokes, sending up the sort of sentimental, moralistic comedy that writers such as Richard Estcourt and Richard Steele were establishing as the norm. Cromwell was bewildered when he went to see the play because, being deaf, he could not hear the dialogue and, seeing the hero facing a firing squad and the girls all in tears on the stage, he wondered why the audience was laughing so much. For the audience, having got over its initial surprise, enjoyed the farce immensely. *The What D'Ye Call It* was attacked by the critics at Buttons's, partly for its irreverence, partly because Gay was Pope's friend and they believed Pope had helped write it. Their somewhat pompous objections did not put the general public off. As Pope told Caryll, even those that came to hiss 'were forced to laugh so much they forgot the design they came with.'[35]

The Buttonians did not give up. Soon afterwards a couple of Whig hacks, Thomas Burnet and George Duckett, made a last ditch attempt to sabotage Pope's Homer. Their pamphlet, which they wanted to call *The Hump Conference*, made even more of Pope's physical disabilities than usual. However, when they showed it to Addison he winced at the title, so they changed that to a more long-winded one and, on his advice, cut out the direct references to the poet's deformity. Otherwise, Addison did not, or could not, stop his coffee house colleagues going ahead with their all-too-familiar predictions that the English *Iliad* would be a vulgar travesty of the original and Papist propaganda to boot. Then, as Pope's flair for salesmanship had not escaped them (it being the talk of the literary world) they suggested he went a stage further and used 'his friendship with Robin Powell, the puppet-showman at Bath, to get him to do a puppet-show of the Siege of Troy,' pointing out that this would be a good idea, because 'Powell is a favourite of the Beaux and Ladies,' and they supposed, 'it was only for such as them, who do not understand *Greek*,' that the author intended his translation.[36] The pamphlet, now called *Homerides: Or, A Letter to Mr. Pope, Occasion'd by his intended Translation of Homer. By Sir Iliad Doggerel*, was printed on 7 March 1715 and reprinted on 30 May. Between those two dates Jervas tried to bring Addison and Pope together again, by inviting them both to his studio one day in April. The meeting was not a success.

Pope spent most of the first five months of 1715 in the capital, before returning home at the end of May to work, as he would do every summer for the next five years, on another volume of the *Iliad*. On leaving town he circulated the poem 'Farewell to London' amongst his friends. London was that 'dear, damned, distracting town' where despite the bitter battles between Whigs and Tories, mirrored in the 'envious Feuds' of wits, he had enjoyed himself with an ever-increasing circle of acquaintances which, as well as painters and poets, included peers, politicians (of both parties) and actresses from *The What D'Ye Call It*.

No longer short of ready money, he had been living it up. Not everything Pope says about his life in town, however, is to be taken literally in a poem where he would have us believe he spent 'Seven Hours in Eight' chasing girls. He dearly wanted to be thought a rake. He spoke of – boasted about – being clapped, once telling Teresa Blount that if he was, it was her fault because she resisted him.[37] Exchanging irreligious and scurrilous jokes with that old reprobate General Tidcombe also contributed to his reinvention of himself as a latter day Lord Rochester. No doubt there were several reasons for this endeavour. In one way he was displaying the familiar reaction of a spirited young man to a pious, somewhat straitlaced upbringing, as well as an understandable relief at being temporarily released from his bondage as a translator. In addition, he was reluctant to admit (as yet) that his stunted, crippled body prevented him pursuing the primrose path of the libertine. Never lacking in determination, he tried. Later, when Colley Cibber published a story about these early days, Pope did not deny having gone with him and Lord Warwick to a bawdy-house near the Haymarket one evening.[38] In any case, for many of his enemies his words, whether or not they were matched by deeds, were enough to give him a growing reputation for indecency and blasphemy. Describing the London self he wanted to create in his 'Farewell', Pope put a gloss on his so-called debauchery, calling himself 'The gayest Valetudinaire, Most Thinking Rake alive', who must now say goodbye to 'nymphs', actresses, delicious lobster suppers, and sitting up with Rowe, Garth and Arbuthnot till the third watchman made his rounds, for as he lamented, 'Homer (damn him!) calls.'

Anyone writing about Pope in the twenty-first century knows that the debonair man about town was just one of the roles he enjoyed playing. However it would not have been apparent to many of his contemporaries that this was a single aspect of a complex personality. Up to a point therefore, we can sympathize with critics who refused to believe that the bawdy, light-hearted young man they saw was capable of doing justice to the mighty Homer, particularly as he made no secret of the fact that he found the work of translation such a chore. But as they were to discover, now and in the years to come, this protean human being was always capable of springing surprises on people.

Pope made sure he was out of London when the first volume (Books I–IV) of his version of the *Iliad* was published on 6 June. This was followed two days later by Tickell's Book I. Gay wrote to give his friend the town's reaction to the two translations:

> I have just set down Sir *Samuel Garth* at the Opera. He bids me tell you, that everybody is pleas'd with your Translation, but a few at *Button*'s; and that *Sir Richard Steele* told him that Mr. *Addison* said *Tickel*'s translation was the best that ever was in any language. He treated me with extream civility, and out of kindness gave me a squeeze by the Sore finger – I am inform'd at *Button*'s your character is made free as to morals etc. and that Mr. A_____ says, that your translation and *Tickel*'s are both very well done, but that the latter has more of *Homer*.[39]

Richard Bentley echoed Addison when he uttered his scholarly judgement, saying 'It is a very pretty poem, Mr. Pope, but you must not call it Homer.'[40] Dennis would take the same line, declaring 'The Homer which Lintot prints does not talk like Homer, but like Pope.'[41] Fair enough – Homer talks like his translator and this was deliberate. Pope had begun his work in the belief that 'It is the first grand Duty of an Interpreter to give his Author entire and unmaim'd; and for the rest, the *Diction* and *Versification* only are his proper Province; since these must be his own.'[42] As he well knew, 'It is certain no literal Translation can be just to an excellent Original.'[43] So, for example, he did not attempt to render Homer's compound epithets and repetitions exactly into English because this would have destroyed 'the Purity of our Language.'[44]

Addison, Bentley and Dennis had concentrated on Pope's diction as they read his version of the *Iliad* and not at all on whether he had conveyed the spirit of the epic. As Pope admitted (regarding the diction as his own province) he had modernized this so that his contemporaries would find it easy on the ear. At the same time he had been intent on conveying the poetic soul of Homer, his 'Fire and Rapture', that is his emotional power. For Pope, Homer surpassed every other poet because he had 'the greatest Invention of any Writer whatever.'[45] This he displayed in his creation of stirring scenes, as well as in his ability to portray subtly differentiated characters and in writing natural description. Pope used the word 'invention' when we (since the Romantic period) would use the word 'imagination', and he regarded it as 'the very foundation of Poetry.'[46]

Homer had been the writer who had shown Pope what poetry was at its noblest. In his translation we miss nothing of Homer's grandeur and expansive sympathy which encompassed both the glory and pity of war. Pope could recreate these things because, as well as having the technical skill, he himself entered fully into the emotions he was describing, whether it be Sarpedon's wish for magnificence when he decides to give up his life in battle, or Priam's despair on learning of the death of Hector. When Pope himself was a boy dreaming of glory, he had translated Sarpedon's rallying cry and, forty years later, when he read Homer's account of an anguished father's grief, it still moved him to tears.[47]

Pope recreated a work that had been written in about the 8th century BC, when the times and manners were wholly different from those in the England of his day and he succeeded in his aim of making the epic live for the majority of his Augustan readers. His translation was a poem in its own right. The extent to which it met the needs of his century can be judged by Dr Johnson's pronouncement, made over sixty years later, 'It is certainly the noblest version of poetry which the world has ever seen.'[48]

Notes

1. *Poems and Translations By Several Hands. To which is Added. The Hospital of Fools; A Dialogue by the Late William Walsh Esq.* (London, 7 April 1714), p. 245.
2. Spence, 192.
3. Reginal Berry, *A Pope Chronology* (London: Macmillan, 1988), p. 20. This book gives details of all the known sums paid to Pope by his publishers.
4. Gregory King, *Natural and Political Observations and Conclusions upon the State and Condition of England* (1696). See also Roy Porter, *English Society in the Eighteenth Century* (Harmondsworth: Penguin Books, 1982), p. 57. Porter estimates that London labourers earned about £25 p.a. in 1700.
5. Spence, 13n.
6. Pope, *Works*, 9 vols (1751), 4: 212n.
7. Spence, 13.
8. Details given of Pope's contract with Lintot are taken from David Foxon, *Pope and the Eighteenth-Century Book Trade. The Lyell Lectures*, ed James MacLaverty (Oxford, 1991), ch. 2 and George Sherburn, *The Early Career of Alexander Pope* (Oxford, 1934), pp. 188–9.
9. John Nichols, *Swift's Works* (1801), 19 vols, 19: 22.
10. Matthew Hodgart, 'The Subscription List for Pope's *Iliad*, 1715', *The Dress of Words* (University of Kansas Libraries, 1978), pp. 25–34.
11. John Oldmixon, *The Catholick Poet: Or, Protestant Barnaby's Sorrowful Lamentation* (1716), p. 5.
12. Charles Gildon, *A New Rehearsal* (1714), p. 8.
13. *Poetical Miscellanies, Consisting of Original Poems and Translations. By the best Hands ... Publish'd by Mr. Steele* (29 December 1713).
14. *Corr.* 1: 196.
15. *Corr.* 1: 41.

16. *Corr.* 1: 45–6.
17. Spence, 197.
18. John Nichols, *Literary Anecdotes of the Eighteenth Century,* 9 vols (1812–15), 2: 556–7.
19. There is an interesting study of Pope's view of masculinity in Carolyn D. Williams, *Pope, Homer and Manliness: Some Aspects of Eighteenth-Century Classical Learning* (London and New York: Routledge, 1993).
20. *Iliad,* Book 18: 399n.
21. *Corr.* 1: 317.
22. *Corr.* 1: 240.
23. *Corr.* 1: 223.
24. *Corr.* 1: 255.
25. *Corr.* 1: 234.
26. Add MS. 35837 f. 509. See also the discussion of this episode by G.V. Bennett, *The Tory Crisis in Church and State 1688–1730* (Oxford: Clarendon, 1975), p. 182.
27. *Corr.* 1: 238.
28. *Corr.* 1: 252.
29. *Corr.* 1: 255.
30. *Corr.* 1: 260.
31. Spence, 162.
32. *Corr.* 1: 266.
33. *A Letter to Sir William Wyndham* (1717).
34. *Corr.* 1: 275.
35. *Corr.* 1: 282–3.
36. *Homerides* (30 May 1715), p. 7.
37. TW. 6: 232, 'Lines Supressed at the End of the Epistle to Miss Blount.'
38. Spence, 251.
39. *Corr.* 1: 305.
40. Johnson, *Lives of the Poets,* ed G.B. Hill, 3 vols (Oxford, 1905), 3: 213n.
41. *Remarks Upon Mr. Pope's Translation of Homer* (1717), p. 12.
42. 'Preface to the *Iliad*', TW. 7: 17.
43. Ibid.
44. Ibid., p. 19.
45. Ibid., p. 3.
46. Ibid.
47. Spence, 529.
48. *Lives of the Poets,* 3: 119.

CHAPTER ELEVEN

A Poet and War

Even before Volume I of the *Iliad* was published on 6 June 1715, Pope was hard at work on the second volume. Despite suffering from a recurrent fever, he completed 'several hundreds of verses', within two weeks of reaching Binfield.[1] However, by the time he was finishing that year's assignment in July, Greek and Trojan battles were eclipsed by what was going on in England. The Jacobite invasion was now expected daily.

During the summer civil unrest had accelerated rapidly. On 29 May, the anniversary of Charles II's restoration, Stuart supporters staged riots in London and Oxford and by the Pretender's birthday on 10 June, there were violent demonstrations throughout the land, from Leeds in Yorkshire to Frome in Somerset. On 15 July the Government met to discuss the crisis, ordering the mobilization of troops and the arrest of potential leaders of a forthcoming insurrection. These included some of Pope's Tory friends, who reacted variously to the crisis. Bolingbroke fled to France after Marlborough hinted that his life was in danger. He was soon joined at James's court in exile by the Duke of Ormonde, who abandoned his task of organizing an uprising in the West Country, leaving it to Lord Lansdowne. The Earl of Oxford was impeached in June but decided to sit it out. Although there was no evidence he had been involved in recent Jacobite plans, he was one of those arrested in July.

Pope was in London again in time for Oxford's trial. On 23 July he was trying to write a letter to Teresa and Patty Blount, who were clamorous for news. As he pointed out, there was too much news to write down. In any case it was dangerous to do so but he did his best to give them some idea of what was going on, without compromising himself. He started off by telling them about the Earl of Oxford. This slow, somewhat unimaginative man was at his best in adversity. Suffering severe physical pain because of a stone in the kidney, he surprised his critics with the resolute speech he made in the House of Lords on 8 July, when charged with high treason and other crimes. The charges would be dropped eventually, but not before Oxford had spent two years in the Tower, where he was sent on 16 July, a week before Pope wrote his letter. Pope, who admired heroic behaviour in others, glowed at the thought of him and told the girls, 'The utmost Weight of Affliction from Princely Power and Popular Hatred, were almost worth bearing for the Glory of such dauntless Conduct as he has shown under it.'[2]

Pope was not tempted to play the hero himself, however, in a situation that he knew was perilous for Catholics. Back in Binfield the Dancastles feared a house search by Government officers looking for weapons. They also stood to lose all their best horses. Pope was distinctly apprehensive and when he wrote to the Blount girls, he wanted to satisfy their curiosity but did not want to display obvious Jacobite sympathies because there was always a possibility his letter would be intercepted or stolen. So he resorted to irony, finding no shortage of subjects.

The real possibility of another civil war had been brought home to him that morning, as he watched the tents being put up in Hyde Park to accommodate the hastily recruited regiments. Half London turned out to view this spectacle. There were so many fashionable coaches, latecomers were turned back. Most people thought it a pretty sight. Pope was more ambivalent. Looking at the stalwart young men, resplendent in new uniforms, he wryly supposed it was a show to give infinite delight to female eyes, 'So many thousand gallant Fellows, with all the Pomp and Glare of Warr, yet undeformed with Battle.' At Court, the Prince's secretary had been so busy writing despatches, 'his weary hand could hardly shake the Box and Dice afterwards.' Catholic drawing rooms were rife with gossip and rumour. Mrs Nelson was optimistic. Looking forward to entertaining the Pretender in her lodgings within the week, she had 'bought a Picture of Madame Maintenon to sett her features by.' Thomas Gage, brother of the unhappy Mrs Weston, unable to endure the confiscation of his Flanders mares, had suddenly seen the errors of Popish superstition, and had become an Anglican. Pope was thinking of following suit, so that he could 'be chosen City-poet.'[3]

A few days after he had sent his letter, the Ten Mile rule was re-imposed, requiring all Papists to leave London. Pope wrote again, asking if he could take 'Sanctuary for a day or two' at Mapledurham. The Riot Act had just been passed and Pope mused over the question of 'whether the Meeting of Two Toasts and a Poet may not be as great a Riot, as can be made by any five in the Kingdome?'[4]

Whenever there was any attempt to bring back the Stuarts, Pope was cautious, thinking primarily of how an abortive uprising would affect his family and himself as a Papist poet. Unlike Mrs Nelson and other enthusiasts, he was pessimistic about the Jacobites bringing off a successful coup, though naturally he did not rule out the possibility of a second restoration – no one in the first half of the eighteenth century did that, whichever side they supported. Yet while Pope was circumspect, he had every reason to be deeply sympathetic to the Stuart cause and often his actions and silences tell us more about his feelings than his words.

So, between 19 August and 7 October 1715 there are no Pope letters, either because he did not commit his thoughts to paper, or because he made sure later that his correspondence for those seven weeks was destroyed. During that time he was making a tour of rebel strongholds. In August he set off for the West Country with Dr Arbuthnot. He could be candid in expressing his political opinions with his fellow Scriblerian because Arbuthnot came from a family of

Stuart supporters, one of them, his brother Robert, being James's agent, as well as the Jacobites' banker, in Paris.

The two friends had hoped to visit Sir William Wyndham, who was deeply involved with the rebels in Somerset, but they were forestalled at Orchard Wyndham by soldiers, coming at dawn to take Sir William. With the help of his wife he tricked them, escaping through a bedroom window, only to be arrested soon afterwards, as was Lord Lansdowne. Pope and Arbuthnot then moved on to Bath and were probably there on 21 September, when Government troops moved in and garrisoned that disaffected town. During the last part of their tour, the two travellers were in Oxford which they found was in a high state of Jacobite euphoria, though it too would be garrisoned before the end of October.[5] No doubt one of the reasons Pope took this journey with the Doctor was a wish to see for himself how it was with the Jacobites. Having done so, he can only have concluded that his initial doubts about there being a successful insurrection had been justified.

By autumn the Government had the situation under control. Through their agents in France, ministers knew about James's plans well in advance and took all necessary steps to deal with these. The Jacobites quarrelled among themselves and were inept. They were also unlucky because they lost French support after the death of Louis XIV on 1 September. Then bad weather delayed their ships, so the invasion scheme failed. Without help from outside, the rebels at home could not succeed. On 13 November there was a simultaneous defeat of the Scottish Jacobites at Sheriffmuir and the English ones at Preston.

With the rebellion all but over, the Ten Mile rule was forgotten and Pope was able to return to London where, on 9 December, his boyhood friend Charles Wogan was paraded with other prisoners from Preston through cold grey streets lined with jeering crowds. As Pope had written to Caryll in October, 'If expectation is a jilt, experience is a downright whore.'[6]

To add to the misery of fugitives who were still being rounded up, a Great Frost set in at the end of November. Over the next three months the temperature stayed well below zero, until trees at Binfield split open as the sap froze, while in London a canvas city appeared on the ice-bound Thames.

During this winter Pope made no explicit references to the Jacobite disasters in his letters, though he was haunted by the spectre of the rebellion, in both his professional and domestic life. The volume of Homer he was working on consisted entirely of battles, so that he wondered whether to publish it, lest it be thought an incitement to violence. Lintot was in no hurry, as he had done well out of the rebellion. Busily printing accounts of trials, he boasted he had got 'much more this year by politics' than he could 'lose by poetry.'[7] Lord Burlington, a Whig, pleaded for leniency towards the convicted rebels but was unable to save the lives of Lord Kenmure and the Earl of Derwentwater. They were condemned to be hanged, drawn and quartered. A huge crowd stood listening to a brave speech made by the young Catholic Derwentwater, as he stood on the scaffold on 24 February 1716. By now the sympathies of his volatile audience had swung his way. He told them, 'I only wish now, that the laying down of my life might contribute to the service of my King and country, and the re-establishment of the ancient and fundamental Constitution of these Kingdoms, without which no lasting peace can attend them. Then I should indeed part my life with pleasure. As it is, I can only pray that these blessings may be bestowed upon my dear country; and since I can do no more, I beseech God to accept my life as a small sacrifice towards it.'[8]

Afterwards his speech was copied down and printed on 3 March in the Jacobite newspaper *Robin's Last Shift*, which the Papist George Flint began in 1716. Pope was grateful to Lord Burlington for trying to intercede but, deciding that any public word of thanks from a Catholic poet was unwise and could only embarrass the recipient, he wrote a few lines anonymously about Burlington's generosity towards his foes. Then he asked Richard Graham to include them in the dedication to his edition of Du Fresnoy's *Art of Painting*, written for the Earl.[9]

As well as being anxious about his future as a poet at this time, Pope worried about his family and whether they would be victimized in days when hostility towards Papists was more intense than usual. On 29 November he wrote to Sir William Trumbull, now well on into his seventies, afflicted by the intense cold and soon to die. Pope wanted his help one last time. 'I am afraid Innocence will be no security to some People of my Persuasion,' he began. He was particularly concerned about his father, whom he feared might become a target, probably because, as was suggested earlier, Mr Pope senior had been in trouble with the authorities before – soon after the poet's birth. Writing about him, Pope assured Sir William, he 'will be as quiet himself as he would suffer others to be. If not I flatter myself the little Malignities of ill Neighbours may be soften'd by your Mediation and good offices.'[10]

Pope's fears were not misplaced. The Government decided to make Catholics pay the cost of suppressing the rebellion. An Act was introduced, calling for the appointment of 'Commissioners to inquire of the estates of certain traitors, and of Popish recusants, and of estates given to superstitious uses in order to raise money out of them severally for the use of the public.'[11] As a result Catholic landowners were faced with a choice of either having two-thirds of their estates confiscated, or of paying a tax in lieu. Aware of what was to come, Pope's father sold his place at Binfield two months before the Act received royal assent on 26 June 1716. In April the family moved to Mawson's New Buildings in Chiswick, under the protection of Lord Burlington, whose villa was nearby. The poet continued to pull whatever strings he could to save his parents from further persecution, and the new house had a garden where his father decided to grow white strawberries. Even so it was yet another personal frustration for Mr Pope to have his fifteen years of independence as a modest country gentleman arbitrarily brought to an end.

As for his son, although he had spent so much time in London in recent years, there is no doubt that having to abandon his home in Binfield, where he had spent his happiest years, was a sad affair. At the end of March he went with his parents to say goodbye to their Papist neighbours, 'much as those who go to be hanged do their fellow prisoners, who are condemn'd to follow 'em a few weeks after.'[12] All Catholics had their problems. Some of them, like Pope's friend Edward Blount (not one of the Mapledurham Blounts) went into voluntary exile. If Catholic landowners stayed on the Continent for a few years, they might be able to avoid paying the new tax. There was also talk of the poet and his family leaving England. Writing to Caryll in March 1716 about the fate of their mutual friends, Pope added, 'the next day may be – nos patriam fugimus [we will flee from our country].'[13]

Pope's family did not go abroad. Nor did the Blounts in Mapledurham who were in financial difficulties. From now on the poet's letters show that Patty and Teresa were short of money, all the more so because in 1716 their brother Michael decided to marry and asked his mother and sisters to leave the family home. Henceforth we find Pope looking for various ways of investing money for the girls in order to increase their income. Michael paid his sisters an allowance but he could not provide a dowry for either of them, which considerably reduced their chances of marriage. Despite their many attractions we never hear of them receiving any offers. They stayed single though they did the social round in London, where they went to live, shortly before Pope and his parents moved to Chiswick at the invitation of Lord Burlington.

Richard Boyle, the third Earl of Burlington, was twenty-one in 1716 when he offered his protection to Pope's family. He was already a discriminating patron of the arts. In about 1714 he invited Handel to become his resident musician. Within a few years he would provide a permanent home in Burlington House for the versatile Willim Kent, currently in Italy choosing paintings for him. He probably met Pope for the first time at Jervas's studio in 1713 and promptly invited him home. Pope thoroughly enjoyed the 'high luxury' he discovered at Burlington's villa in Chiswick where, as he told Patty Blount, his host's gardens were 'delightful, his musick ravishing.'[14] The food was good too. It was there and at the house in Piccadilly that Pope developed his taste for lobster suppers. Being a rather austere young man, Burlington was attracted by vivacious people and found Pope amusing company. Much later he and his wife took up the charming, voluble David Garrick. Dorothy Savile, whom Burlington married in 1721, complemented his personality well, being an out-going, quick-witted woman. She had a gift for making lightning caricatures and sometimes drew Pope. He, in his turn made a lifelong friend of this high spirited, satirical lady – as well as recruiting her, along with Dancastle and others, into his team of manuscript copiers.

Not everyone liked Burlington, still less admired him. Johnson was particularly scathing. He was one of those splendid acquaintances Pope assiduously courted, despite a 'good man' deriving 'little honour' from the notice of most of them.[15] It is true that unlike Johnson, who put Lord Chesterfield in his place, Pope was one of those Englishmen who loved a lord. He would like to have been an aristocrat himself and once tried to trace a non-existent connection between his family and the Popes in Oxfordshire, 'the Head of which was the Earl of Downe.'[16] Pope was also aware that his noble friends were influential and made full use of this fact of life. Burlington was one of several titled individuals who gave the poet practical assistance, of one kind or another, during the course of his life.

As far as the friendship with Burlington was concerned, one other factor came into play. Burlington was one of the first of several men who became Pope's heroes. For him the earl became a model for the responsible aristocrat. First of all because, quite early, he showed he had the courage of his convictions and magnanimity when he argued with his fellow Whigs about the Jacobite executions. Later on, because he employed his considerable wealth to enhance, not just his own life, but the lives of his countrymen, using his money and influence to see that public buildings were put up which were a credit to the nation. For Burlington was more than a collector of art and artists; he was an architect of professional distinction, responsible for popularizing the Palladian style in England, and so promoting the elegant, well-proportioned simplicity we associate with Georgian houses.

When Pope was living in Chiswick he often spent summer afternoons in the gardens of the villa nearby. Sometimes he went with Gay, who noted how his friend usually sat down under a fruit tree, devouring any peaches or plums he could reach.

Pope also went with Gay to Hampton Court, where both of them amused, and were amused by, the Maids of Honour – a title considered by some a misnomer. Actually the girls made a varied group. Some were ebullient – bonny Madge Bellenden for instance, who bounded down the stairs of the palace singing 'Over the Hills and Far Away,' or the ill-fated Sophie Howe, given to giggling noisily in church. Others were more sedate and a few were gifted, such as Anne, Countess of Winchilsea who wrote plays and poems.[17] And then there was the bookish Molly Lepell who knew more Latin than Lord Chesterfield thought it was good for a woman to know.

Pope composed verses for the younger girls and listened sympathetically when they complained of their lot. Outsiders, particularly if they were female, might envy them their supposedly ceaseless round of gaiety, the balls and assemblies which offered marital, and extra-marital, opportunities. But the Maids of Honour did not see it like that. As they talked, Pope learned just how circumscribed the life of a young woman at Court could be. 'To eat Westphalia Ham in a morning, ride over Hedges and Ditches on borrowed Hacks, come home in the Heat of the day with a Feavor, and what is worse a hundred times, a red Mark in the forehead with a Beavor Hatt; all this may qualify them to bear

oratorical flourish, as Curll exclaims, 'Why flutter ye your Leaves, and flap your Covers, at me? *Damn ye Wolves in Sheeps Cloathing; Rags ye were, and to Rags ye shall return* ... To my Shop in Tunbridge Wells ye shall go',[35] and so on.

Before, during and immediately after the 1715 Jacobite rebellion, Pope worried about his professional career. Yet, as has already been mentioned, he knew he could do little about the madness and violence of modern heroes. At his most pessimistic, he feared he might have to go abroad with his family, in which case it was hard to see how he would have got his verses published. Even if he stayed at home it was possible that there might be official objections to a translation of Homer by a Papist. Contemplating a doubtful future he consoled himself with the thought that, if the worst came to the worst, he could always earn his living as a writing master.[36] These fears receded and he realized he could go on pursuing his vocation as a poet, albeit at one remove because he was still saddled with the chore of translation. So he turned his thoughts to the reading public again, this time by attempting to regulate conduct in the literary world.

Engaging in literary battles served Pope's purpose in several ways. In the first place, it was psychologically satisfying. It meant he was no longer a passive onlooker. Not being a man to turn the other cheek, taking action always came more easily to him than Christian resignation. He obviously enjoyed himself making a fool of Curll and he felt justified in doing so because that opportunistic publisher demeaned the profession of writing. As for Addison, Pope's portrait of Atticus was the equivalent of those letters that a modern author sometimes writes to a newspaper or magazine about unfair treatment of their work by a critic. There is one crucial difference however. Whereas the modern author's letter seldom does any good and is soon forgotten, Pope lines had the desired result in silencing Addison and have endured as a masterpiece in their own right. When faced with hostile criticism, Pope was one of a very few writers who have been able to turn their ripostes into works of art.

Furthermore, even while he was employing his verbal skills with such bravura in waging war on paper, he was using his creative gifts in conducting an affair of the heart, having fallen passionately in love with Lady Mary Wortley Montagu.

Notes

1.   *Corr.* 1: 292.
2.   *Corr.* 1: 307.
3.   *Corr.* 1: 308. Pope sold his own horse, a good one given him earlier by Caryll, rather than have it confiscated. Another friend, William Fortescue, then found him a horse for 5 guineas, which he could keep without breaking the law. See *Corr.* 1: 341.

4.   *Corr.* 1: 311.
5.   *Corr.* 1: 317 and 315.
6.   *Corr.* 1: 318.
7.   Ibid.
8.   F.J.A. Skeet, *The Life of James, third Earl of Derwentwater*, quoted by Sir Charles Petrie, *The Four Georges* (London: Collins, 1936), p. 48.
9.   *Corr.* 1: 334. The lines Pope wrote for insertion were probably those that spoke of 'that exemplary Moderation and Generosity, which mov'd You to intercede for the *Lives of Those*, against whom You stood prepar'd to hazard *Your Own*.'
10.   The complete text of this letter is reprinted in Maynard Mack, *Collected in Himself* (London & Toronto: University of Delaware Press, 1982), p. 467.
11.   1 Geo. I, st. 2, c 50, 55.
12.   *Corr.* 1: 337.
13.   Ibid.
14.   *Corr.* 1: 338.
15.   *Lives of the Poets*, 3:206.
16.   Epistle to Dr Arbuthnot, l. 381n.
17.   *The Anne Finch Wellesley manuscript poems: a critical edition*, eds Barbara McGovern and Charles H. Hinnant (Athens: University of Georgia Press, 1998).
18.   *Corr.* 1: 427.
19.   *Corr.* 1: 351.
20.   Ibid.
21.   *Corr.* 1: 343.
22.   *Diary of Dudley Ryder 1715–1716*, ed William Matthews (London: Methuen, 1939), p. 255.
23.   Letter to Sir William Trumbull, 29 November 1716 in *Collected in Himself, op. cit.*, p. 467.
24.   *Letter of Advice to a Young Poet* (1720).
25.   Epistle to Dr Arbuthnot, l. 196.
26.   Letter of 1 June 1716, quoted in J.V. Guerinot, *Pamphlet Attacks on Alexander Pope 1711–1744* (London: Methuen, 1969), p. 36.
27.   Both men referred to Eastern kings who, 'to secure their reign' have their heirs slain. See *Spectator* no. 253 and Epistle to Dr Arbuthnot, l. 198.
28.   Epistle to Dr Arbuthnot, ll. 209–10.
29.   Spence, 166.
30.   Shakespeare's *Winter's Tale*, 4.2.26 and Curll's statement on the title page of *Court Poems* – he was lying as he had bought the poems from John Oldmixon.
31.   J. Baker, Kt., *A Letter from Sir J_____ B_____ to Mr P_____* (1716).
32.   *Prose Works of Alexander Pope 1711–1720*, ed Norman Ault (Oxford: Blackwell, 1936), pp. 262–3.
33.   'A Roman Catholick Version of the First Psalm', TW. 6: 164.
34.   Oldmixon's *The Catholick Poet* and Dennis's *A True Character of Mr Pope* (31 May 1716).
35.   *Prose Works*, pp. 284–5.
36.   *Corr.* 1: 242.

CHAPTER TWELVE

The Art of Love

Pope first met Lady Mary Wortley Montagu at the beginning of 1715 when she was already well known in Whig circles as a beauty and a wit. She was by far the most intellectual woman Pope had encountered. Living when she did, she often chafed against the social routine imposed on her; that endless round of tea and card parties, punctuated with visits to the opera and playhouse. She had wanted something more than the cursory feminine education available. So from the age of thirteen to fifteen she shut herself up in the library at home for five or six hours each day to master the Greek and Latin classics. She once dreamed of founding a women's college, with herself at the head of it. She fought prejudice and suspicion when she publicized inoculation for smallpox in England. She was tough, practical and had a firm grasp of finance. Finding few outlets for her talents, she read widely and learned seven languages. She also wrote verse and essays, but as she usually circulated her work privately, much of it was forgotten until it was edited recently.[1] The letters she wrote from Turkey however, escaped into print and were soon considered masterpieces. In her lifetime she was admired as a practised conversationalist, one who had learned the art of listening as well as talking when, as a young girl, she had acted as her father's hostess, entertaining statesmen and wits who included Walpole, Addison, Steele and Congreve.

In Pope's eyes Lady Mary's ability to express herself was a cardinal point in her favour. She had ruined him for 'all the Conversation of one Sex,' he told her.[2] At first he was dazzled by a bravura performance and, even when he came to see her plain, he never saw her whole. Early on he did not realize that her cool head ruled her cool heart. She enjoyed being surrounded by admirers, but it was not until she was middle aged that she became sentimental about any of them, when she and Lord Hervey both fell in love with the same handsome and opportunistic Italian.

Impressed as Pope was by his new friend, he might not have singled her out from a fair number of aristocratic hostesses with whom he flirted, if she had not gone away on 1 August 1716 with her husband Edward Wortley, who had been appointed England's ambassador in Constantinople. No sooner had she left these shores than Pope recreated her in his mind as an object of courtly love. He became a cenobite in a religion of love in which, as he said of himself, he was imitating in his 'ravings the dreams of Spleenatic Enthusiasts and Solitaires, who fall in love with Saints, and fancy themselves in the favour of Angels, and Spirits, whom they can never see, or touch.'[3] Her beauty, marred in any case by

12.1 Lady Mary Wortley Montagu. Godfrey Kneller, 1720

an attack of smallpox the previous December, was of far less importance than her 'Reason and Virtue.'[4] In the first letter he sent after her as she began her travels, he told her he was different from the 'Fops,' who admired her for her 'fair Face,' because he could discern those qualities which they 'pretend to no acquaintance with.'[5]

His devotion fed on a meagre diet; the memory of passing friendly glances and casual expressions of regard. At their last meeting before her departure, she had waited until the end of a crowded assembly to exchange a few words with him. This made him think she was especially perceptive. 'I would fain imagine,' he said, 'this was not accidental, but proceeded from a Penetration which I know you have in finding out the truth of people's Sentiments, and that you were not unwilling, the last man that would have parted with you, should be the last that did.'[6]

Supposing that Lady Mary had singled him out encouraged him to think he could be completely frank, revealing his deeper feelings to another human being. He promised his letters would be 'the most impartial Representations of a free heart.' He would be 'Thinking aloud ... or Talking upon paper.'[7] Talking on paper to a woman he adored, who was absent for over two years, had distinct advantages. It was something in which he could employ all his considerable powers of eloquence, and he could show her his mind and heart without his incongruous 'crazy Carcase' getting in the way.[8] Not that he ever forgot his appearance but, to someone who was not physically in front of him, he could present an edited version of it. So, when he sent Lady Mary a copy of his 1717 *Works* it had, as a frontispiece, an engraving of the portrait Jervas had made of him three years before. In the picture he appears elegant and engaging. Jervas had brought to life on canvas Pope's own image of himself as a thinking rake.

With the help of maps Pope traced Lady Mary's itinerary across Europe, from Paris to Vienna, to embattled Hungary and on into a semi-barbarous Middle East. He trembled at the hazards before her, though she did not and went calmly on her way after her coach nearly toppled over into the Hebrus. Pope hoped to persuade her not to proceed to Turkey and offered, more than once, to meet her in Italy, if she would go there instead. He tried to imagine a place or situation in which she might return his feelings, if not in Lombardy then India or, more likely still, in the life after death.[9]

Death is a recurrent theme in the letters to Lady Mary. Pope thought she might not survive her journey, while he himself was seriously ill several times during her absence, in January 1717, again in the summer and also the following winter. He identified with the Provençal troubadour Jeffrey Rudel, who followed the Countess of Tripoli to Jerusalem. The journey killed him, as Pope probably imagined any journey across the Continent would kill himself. However, as he reminded Lady Mary, when Jeffrey lay expiring, the Countess came to the ship. There she took him by the hand and, 'having been blest with a sight of her, he was satisfied; and so departed this life.'[10]

Lady Mary's letters were resolutely impersonal. At first Pope feared she might not send him any at all and wrote, 'For God's sake Madam, let not my correspondence be like a Traffic with the Grave.'[11] Then, when she did write, she covered page after page with a detailed description of the Emperor's art collection. This elicited a desperate response, 'The Shrines and Reliques you tell me of, in no way engage my curiosity.' 'When you write to me,' he told her, 'talk of your self, there is nothing I so much desire to hear of; talk a great deal of your self, that She who I always thought talk'd best, may speak upon the best subject.'[12] Lady Mary was not introspective but, the further east she went, the better her letters became. She was the best kind of tourist, curious and observant. She studied Turkish and found her way into a harem, where she questioned the women about their life. She had literary discussions with a local scholar and sent Pope her own rendering of a lengthy Turkish love poem, which she said she found difficult to translate, because English was not designed 'to express such violence of passion, which is very seldom felt among us.'[13] Pope did not comment on that statement but, when he sent her his *Works*, he drew her attention to 'Eloisa to Abelard' – one of the most erotic poems in the language. In writing of his sexually obsessed heroine, Pope had found an objective correlative for the physical desire he felt, which he knew he could never speak of openly to the woman who had aroused it.

Lady Mary wrote to Pope because he was a poet. She shared a taste for the company of literary men with her father who, as Marquess of Dorchester, had been one of the select dozen to read the *Pastorals* before they were published. In the whole course of their correspondence the most handsome thing she said to Pope was when she complimented him on his poetic achievements. She thought Pope's translation of the *Iliad* was a literary triumph and was equally impressed by the fact it made money. 'You ... have found the *Philosophers stone*,' she told him, 'since by making the Iliad pass through your poetical crucible into an English form without losing aught of its original beauty, you have drawn the golden current of Pactolus to Twickenham.'[14]

All the time Pope was addressing himself to his *princesse lontaine*, life at home was as harassing as ever. He and Dr Arbuthnot had helped to write a farce, most of which was the work of Gay. *Three Hours after Marriage* opened to a full house at the Theatre Royal, Drury Lane on 16 January 1717. The hero of the play is the elderly Dr Fossile, who marries the young and sprightly Mistress Townley – with predictable results. Her lovers take bets on who can cuckold him first. Fossile was based on the actual John Woodward, a medical man renowned for his passionate espousal of modern scientific theories, some of them better than others. The story of January wedded to May (a familiar staple of Restoration comedy) was updated therefore with Scriblerian satire about the vagaries of contemporary learning.

The work amused audiences when it was performed by the Royal Shakespeare Company a few years ago and it ought to have been a hit in 1717.[15]

It was not because a cabal decided to wreck it.[16] Orchestrated catcalls, which began in one part of the house on the first night, spread and increased in volume the next. The popular actor Colley Cibber, who was in the piece was dismayed. Such a thing had never happened to him before. The actresses, Mrs Bicknell and Mrs Oldfield, were so upset by the continuing uproar that they refused to go on. Gay's friends did their best to help. They too tried to pack the house and some of the Maids of Honour bribed the actresses to continue. But it was no use. The play was driven off the boards at the end of seven nights by what Pope called 'a tide of malice and party.'[17]

Gay, on his own, would never have incurred such enmity. It was Pope's association with *Three Hours* that caused it to be attacked so viciously. The war which began in the theatre was carried on later in pamphlets, with Pope as the target. Buttonians, who were still irritated by the success of the Homer translations, were joined by hacks summoned up by Curll – still getting his own back for the episode with the emetic. The campaign however was caused only in part by anything Pope had done. As much as anything it was due to the resentment felt by a few Whigs and Protestants because so many readers praised a writer who was politically unacceptable. Attacking Pope needed no excuse; it was a patriotic duty. As usual, it was Dennis who expressed this point of view most forcibly. 'I regard him as an Enemy,' he wrote in February 1717, 'not so much to me, as to my KING, to my COUNTRY, to my RELIGION, and to that LIBERTY which has been the sole Felicity of my life.'[18]

The political climate was hardly more temperate in 1717 than it had been just after the Rebellion. The Government was justifiably nervous about fresh Jacobite plots. The year had begun dramatically with a pre-emptive strike on 29 January, when infantry surrounded the Swedish embassy in London and arrested the ambassador, after it was discovered the Pretender was seeking help from Charles XII for another invasion attempt. One of Pope's friends, Charles Caesar, was also arrested at this time. So, even though Pope stayed in the background when it came to Jacobite activity, in the eyes of some men he was guilty by association, as were all Papists. The hostility towards Catholics found expression in December, when Colley Cibber's *Non-Juror* played to enthusiastic audiences at Drury Lane. Cibber was a man who liked to keep in with the authorities and the *Non-Juror* was his way of making it clear he had nothing to do with subversives. Pope, who was by now one of the best known Papists in London, merited three references in this adaptation of Moliere's *Tartuffe*, which the adapter dedicated to George I. Pope tried to neutralize the anti-Papist impact of Cibber's play by publishing another of his exercises in deconstruction in February. In *A Clue to the Non-Juror* he set out to ridicule mob hysteria by making a selective use of chapter and verse from the work to 'prove' that, far from being a defence of the constitution, it was the product of a double agent penning a Jacobite libel against the Government. The pamphlet satisfied Pope's need to answer back but did nothing to diminish Cibber's theatrical triumph.

Pope was so taken up with extraneous activities that he got behind with Homer in 1717. On 7 June he wrote to Caryll asking if he could come to Ladyholt because if he stayed at home he could not work. 'Not a line of my next year's task is writ,' he told his friend. 'I am really in St. Paul's condition, distracted with many businesses.'[19] In addition to defending himself against his enemies, he had more social engagements now he was famous including one, probably, when he joined a party on a Thames barge to listen to the first performance of Handel's *Water Music* in July. Then although he had not written much original verse since embarking on Homer, he made sure his reading public did not forget him. He saw his *Works* as well as the third volume of the *Iliad* through the press, both of them being published in June. He also worked on an anthology, containing some of his juvenilia and verse by other writers, which Lintot printed in July as *Poems on Several Occasions*. Apart from 'Eloisa to Abelard', a short new poem included in the *Works* was the controversial 'Elegy to the Memory of an Unfortunate young Lady', celebrating a girl who kills herself rather than marry the man chosen for her by her guardian. Once again Pope had taken an unconventional view of marriage. In the 1760s James Boswell echoed the orthodox opinion of the majority when he said that any young lady who ignored her parents' choice of a husband 'ought to suffer.' Otherwise the example 'gives encouragement to girls of impressionable hearts and light heads to forget the weakness of their sex, to scorn the sage maxims of prudence, and to disturb the settled order of Society.'[20]

Once Pope got away from London, he applied himself with his customary diligence to translating the fourth volume of the *Iliad*. By September he was at liberty again and set off on a ramble to see his friends in Oxford and elsewhere. At the start of his journey he called on the Maids of Honour. Some of the time over the next few weeks he spent on his own, even at Hampton Court, where in the deserted, moonlit gardens he saw no one but the King, 'giving Audience all alone, to the Birds under a Garden-Wall.'[21] From there he went to Binfield, spending all one afternoon walking in the woods and taking stock of his life. He was now nearly thirty and, as he strolled under the trees where he had spent so much time as a boy, he thought of the dreams he had had then and of what had happened since; how he had become a literary celebrity and how he had tried to construct a love life for himself. He put his reflections down in a 'Hymn Written in Windsor Forest', recalling how he was chosen to be a poet:

> All Hail! once pleasing, once inspiring Shade,
> Scene of my youthful Loves and happier hours!
> Where the kind Muses met me as I stray'd
> And gently pressed my hand, and said, Be Ours!
> Take all thou e'er shalt have, a constant Muse:

> At Court thou may'st be lik'd, but nothing gain;
> Stocks thou may'st buy and sell, but always lose;
> And love the brightest eyes, but love in vain.

In these elegiac verses Pope is saying goodbye to his youth. He knows now that even if his genteel ambitions have been amply fulfilled in that he is welcomed by Society, he can hope for no honours from a Hanoverian king, though under a Stuart one, he and others (including Dennis) supposed he could have become the Laureate. He has made money but prophetically, in view of the fact that he is writing three years before the South Sea Bubble disaster, he fears he might lose it again. Lastly, although he has been falling in love since he was sixteen, he despairs of being loved in return. The one constant thing in his life is poetry. He still belongs to the muses – as yet.

Pope had still more time to reflect on age and change as he made his way on horseback to Oxford. The leisurely ride took him over wooded hills and along winding rivers. The moon came up in a clear sky as he approached the town. When he was about a mile away he heard the clocks in every college tell him it was eleven. He went to St John's where he was staying with the chaplain, Dr Abel Evans. Surrounded by 'old Walls, venerable Galleries, stone Portico's, studious walks and solitary scenes' where he was treated with great respect, he felt far more at ease than he had done in London of late.[22] Still thinking about his non-existent love life, he wrote to Teresa and Patty Blount, whose faithful courtier he had been for ten years. 'Methinks I do very ill' he told them, 'to return to the world again, to leave the only place where I make a good figure, and from seeing myself seated with dignity on the most conspicuous Shelves of a Library, go to contemplate this wretched person in the abject condition of lying at a lady's feet in Bolton Street' – Bolton Street being where the girls and their mother now lived.[23]

He had no sooner decided his muse was his only mistress, than he was offered a wife. On his way home he stayed for a while with Lord Harcourt, who had the idea of marrying him off to a young relation of his, Miss Jenings, whom Pope admitted was 'nearer an Angel than a Woman.' Apparently the girl had very little money and so might consent to marry a crippled poet she hardly knew. He rejected the proposal straightaway, in words that show his dread of becoming a laughing stock, if Miss Jennnings should turn out to be more of a woman than an angel after all. 'I told him his Lordship could never have thought of such a thing,' he said, 'but for his misfortune in being blind, and that I never cou'd till I was so. But that as matters now were, I did not care to force so fine a woman to give the finishing stroke to all my deformities, by the last mark of a Beast, horns.'[24]

Notes

1. Isobel Grundy, *Lady Mary Wortley Montagu* (Oxford University Press, 1999). Grundy assesses Lady Mary's notable achievements, including five volumes of writings, of which she was also one of the editors.
2. *Corr.* 1: 354.
3. *Corr.* 1: 389–90.
4. *Corr.* 1: 354.
4. Ibid.
6. *Corr.* 1: 355.
7. *Corr.* 1: 352–3.
8. *Corr.* 1: 55.
9. *Corr.* 1: 369.
10. *Corr.* 1: 441.
11. *Corr.* 1: 363.
12. *Corr.* 1: 368.
13. *Corr.* 1: 402.
14. *Corr.* 1: 423.
15. Performed at the Swan Theatre, Stratford-upon-Avon, May 1996, then transferred to The Pit, London in January 1997.
16. George Sherburn, *The Early Career of Alexander Pope* (Oxford: Clarendon, 1934), p. 193.
17. *Corr.* 1: 395.
18. *Remarks Upon Mr. Pope's Translation of Homer. With Two Letters, concerning Windsor Forest, and the Temple of Fame*, by Mr. Dennis. Printed for E. Curll, in Fleet Street, 1717.
19. *Corr.* 1: 411.
20. *Boswell in Holland, 1763–64*, ed F.A. Pottle (London: Heinemann, 1952), p. 327.
21. *Corr.* 1: 470.
22. *Corr.* 1: 430.
23. Ibid.
24. *Corr.* 1: 431.

PART IV

The Wrong Place at the Wrong Time

CHAPTER THIRTEEN

Loss

For his thirty-sixth birthday Pope wrote a poem which ran:

> With added Days, if Life brings nothing new,
> But, like a Sieve, lets ev'ry Pleasure thro';
> Some Joy still lost, as each vain Year runs o'er,
> And all we gain, some pensive Notion more!
> Is this a Birth-day? Ah! 'tis sadly clear,
> 'Tis but the Fun'ral of the former Year.
> If there's no Hope, with kind, tho' fainter ray
> To gild the Evening of our Future Day;
> If ev'ry Page of Life's long Volume tell
> The same dull story – Mordaunt thou did'st well.[1]

Harry Mordaunt, a young Guards officer, was not a man Pope knew well. He is applauded in the birthday poem because two weeks earlier he had shot himself. Pope's commendation of Mordaunt's suicide, which he did not publish, is a startling, but by no means unique, manifestation of his, by then, settled melancholy. When, after nine years separation, Pope wrote to Swift, he warned him, 'The merry vein you knew me in, is sunk into a Turn of Reflection, that has made the world pretty indifferent to me.'[2]

Once Pope was in his thirties melancholy events and situations mounted up. To begin with, a number of men closest to him died, pre-eminently his father. Others, on whom he relied, joined friends who had already left the country. Then his fragile relationship with Lady Mary Wortley Montagu disintegrated and he quarrelled with the Blount sisters. Furthermore, despite making a sizeable sum from his translation of the *Iliad*, he ran short of money and, when he became infected with the speculation fever produced by the South Sea Bubble phenomenon, he was not one of the winners. So he turned unwillingly to yet another Homer translation and the even more uncongenial task of editing other men's work. Some of these projects landed him in yet more trouble – partly of his own making. Worse still, against all his instincts, he found himself publicly involved with the Jacobites, who devised one of their most spectacular plots in 1722.

Finally, he came to the conclusion he was finished as a poet. When asked about his work he said ruefully, 'I have wholly given over scribbling, at least anything of my own, but am become, by due gradation of dullness, from a poet a translator, and from a translator, a mere editor',[3] adding on one occasion, 'I am apprehensive I shall be nothing of value.'[4]

If the Muses no longer claimed Pope, it was not because he was any less creative than he had ever been. The plans he made for the garden at his Twickenham villa showed that. Nor was he suffering from writers' block – he still wrote short poems on personal themes, as well as the occasional, strictly anonymous, political ballad.[5] The reasons for the hiatus in his career as an original writer were complex – one of the most important being that he had lost his support group.

For a long time he had been a social poet, who had taken ideas for poems from suggestions made by sympathetic friends and allies, such as Trumbull, Lansdowne and Caryll, as well as comfort from the knowledge they were on his side. Trumbull had died in 1716. Lansdowne was now an exile, while Caryll was an embattled Catholic like himself. Those Tory allies who remained in England were disorganized as well as powerless, whereas the Jacobites were embarrassingly active. Pope felt isolated and afraid. This inhibited him from embarking on any significant work, which would certainly come under attack from his Whig and Protestant enemies, scrutinizing whatever he wrote for Papist and Stuart propaganda.

In addition, as Pope entered his thirties, he lost his personal myth – the character he had created for himself as a debonair man about town and rake. He no longer felt able to play that part before an audience of men and women who believed, and did not hesitate to say, he was a physical freak. In attempting to live that role, he decided he was making himself ridiculous. However, bereft of his chosen image, he had yet to find a new one.

As we have already seen, this low period in Pope's life as a man and a poet, first became apparent at about the time he composed the 'Hymn Written in Windsor Forest' in 1717. Soon after that came a series of deaths to make him feel lonely and bereft. On 23 October Mr Pope died suddenly of a heart attack. He was seventy-one and had survived his expulsion from Binfield by just under eighteen months. After his funeral Pope said, 'I have lost one whom I was even more obliged to as a friend, than as a father.'[6] This was no more than the truth as Mr Pope had been an exemplary parent and ally of his volatile and gifted son.

The loss of his father was followed by the deaths of his friends Parnell, Rowe and Garth, all within the space of four months at the end of 1718. Nor did the dismal roll call end there. The year 1718 was when John Caryll's high spirited son succumbed to smallpox, while in 1720 Lord Harcourt also lost his son and heir. Less unexpectedly, the poet's older allies, Wycherley and the Duke of Buckingham (in addition to Trumbull) were all gone by 1721, while in 1719 Addison had died at the age of forty-seven. Pope was outliving the men with whom he had spent his youth.

The personal crisis Pope underwent after 1717 was accompanied by deterior-ating health, and may have helped precipitate it or, perhaps, been provoked by it. Some of the ailments he spoke of, he was mentioning for the first time, such as the neuralgia that kept him in bed, banked round with hot bricks and tiles, in October 1719. Three months later he was too ill, even to translate Homer, because for weeks he had been afflicted with 'perpetual vomiting and nervous distemper', which produced a 'dejection of spirits' that had 'totally taken away everything which could be called vivacity or cheerfulness.'[7] And so it went on until, by the autumn of 1722, he was writing to Gay, 'I have never been in a worse state in my life.'[8] Even before he reached that stage, he also announced that he had 'utterly left off' his 'amours.'[9] This suggests that he may have become sexually impotent, which he probably was not in those early days in London. Whatever the truth of the matter, over the next few years, he would give up paying racy court to Teresa Blount, as well as his attempt to construct a one-sided romance with Lady Mary.

The first sign of a change in his relationship with the Blount girls came at the end of 1717, when he told them he would not be calling at Bolton Street so often in future. Apparently he had been spending a good deal of time there since the death of his father. Earlier Teresa had been his favourite and he had entertained her with bawdy jokes. But, when he was in low spirits, he found Patty more sympathetic, especially as she was willing to protect him from other visitors who came to the house. Now he sensed he had outworn his welcome, so he promised, 'I will not bring myself to you at all hours, like a Skeleton, to come across your diversions and dash your pleasures.'[10]

Teresa, the more forthright of the sisters, found Pope's decision surprising and exasperating. She questioned him closely. In another letter to the girls, in the New Year, he defended his action. 'I scarce ever come but one of two things happens, which equally afflicts me to the Soul. Either I make her Uneasy, or I see her Unkind. If she has any Tenderness, I can only give her every day Trouble and Melancholy. If she has none, the daily sight of so undeserved a coldness must wound me to death.'[11] Taken on its own, this letter is puzzling, because it is not clear who 'she' is. It could be either sister. But once again, it was Teresa who questioned Pope, forcing him to confide in her. He seems to have told her something about his feelings for the absent Lady Mary. She did not take his secret very seriously, and what she did next made Pope write an angry letter, addressed to her alone. 'You pretended so much generosity, as to offer your Services on my behalf; the minute after, you did me as ill an office as you could, in telling the party concerned, it was all but an amusement occasion'd by the Loss of another Lady.'[12] Piecing this together, it would appear that even if Teresa had once been the sister he preferred, it was now the fear of losing Patty's friendship that was causing him distress. In mentioning his passion for Lady Mary, he hoped to make it plain that all he wanted was Patty's goodwill and kindness. However Pope had once been Teresa's. It was humiliating to lose a beau – even an undesirable one. So she betrayed his confidence and, at the same time, kept her sister in her place by saying Patty meant little to Pope, because he was languishing with unrequited love for Lady Mary. Patty and Pope patched up their quarrel and their relationship would eventually enter a new phase, but disagreements with Teresa continued to surface periodically.

Pope did not always parade his melancholy. In March 1719 he moved to the riverside villa he had rented in Twickenham and there he kept depression at bay to some extent, as he busied himself with plans for the house and garden. The money which enabled him to establish himself as a gentleman in a rural, yet highly fashionable area, came from his translation of the *Iliad*, which was now almost completed – Lintot would pay him a final instalment of £210 for the sixth and final volume the following February. Altogether Pope had made over £5000, a larger sum than anyone before him had earned from writing. He promptly began spending it.

Soon after arriving in Twickenham, Pope called on the architect James Gibbs to submit plans for enlarging and embellishing the house and, from then on, monitored every stage of Gibbs's work. In July 1720, when he was ill again, he was poring over blueprints and spoke of living on a 'diet of Water-gruel and *Palladio.*'[13] Pope, a disciple of Lord Burlington, was in the architectural vanguard. He was so modern he was not at all sure whether curious passengers on the Thames, watching his house rising that summer, would like what they saw, 'whatever delight the true, unseen poetical Gods of the River' might take 'in reflecting on their Streams' his '*Tuscan* Porticos, or *Ionic* Pilasters.'[14] By the end of the year most of the rebuilding was done. His house now had some ten or twelve rooms on three storeys and was a northern Italian villa with an English accent.

Pope was also in the vanguard when he created the garden at Twickenham. At the beginning, instead of drawing up one of those formal designs with straight lines and clipped shrubs, still favoured by some of his contemporaries, he decided art must imitate nature, in the newer style promoted by his friend William Kent. Pope's name for this was 'landscape painting', with 'clumps of trees' that, as he was to say, were 'like groups in pictures.'[15]

The garden took Pope the rest of his life to create. He had five acres and, according to his gardener John Searle, 'There were not Ten Sticks in the Ground when his Master took the House.'[16] Yet before too many years elapsed, visitors strolled along winding paths under limes and elms, continued down a fir grove, their gaze directed towards the bust of Isaac Newton, lingered in a leafy recess to contemplate the statue of a dancing Venus, and so on to the orangery and bowling green. They rested in a stone summer house, presided over by another bust of Dryden and surveyed the vaguely oriental Shell Temple, which collapsed in 1735 but was speedily rebuilt. Pope helped his gout-plagued friend Atterbury up one of the two mounts he had built, from the top of which they could see Sheen, Richmond. Edward Blount's two little girls, when they climbed the mount, showed Pope the quickest way to descend from its heights by rolling down its grassy banks. There was also a vineyard, a kitchen garden where you could find some fairly out-of-the-way vegetables, such as fennel and broccoli and eventually, hot houses for pineapples.

When drawing up plans for his garden, Pope followed certain principles. The

13.1 An exact draught and view of Mr Pope's house, Twickenham, c. 1735. Engraved by N. Parr after Peter Andreas Rysbrack

first of these was to consider 'the Genius of the Place.'[17] This meant taking into account the physical limitations of the terrain and its imaginative potential, the ultimate aim being to bring fallen nature to perfection. How this worked can be seen by considering the grotto. The grotto started off as an underground passage, necessary to connect the two parts of the garden, which were separated by the main road going from Hampton Court to London. Then, as Swift put it, Pope 'turned a blunder into a beauty which is a Piece of Ars Poetica.'[18] For in becoming a grotto, the passage became a cave of the Muses, where the poet was sketched, working at his table under an alabaster lamp. Pope entertained his friends in the grotto. There he invited the Duchess of Marlborough to a moonlight supper and discussed tactics with Bolingbroke and other members of a revived Opposition. In developing the 'Genius of the Place' Pope had added two more rills to the single spring he found when opening up the cavern. So his meditations and conversations were accompanied by the sound of falling water. Finally, as well as being a literary nymphaeum, a campaign headquarters and a dining room, the grotto was a geological museum. Its walls were embedded with fragments of minerals which Pope solicited from all over the country.[19]

When he was working on his garden Pope used his wide ranging creative powers to the full. It was a place where he could express his varied interests and the diverse aspects of his personality: his need for solitude and for friendship, his love of the classical past, his scientific curiosity and his admiration for great thinkers and poets. The garden also expressed his belief in the unity of all life which, as *An Essay on Man* would show, was fundamental in his philosophy.

This philosophic concept is the theme of the allegorical illustration Kent made of his friend's garden.[20] The drawing shows an expanse of grass, trees and sky. In the centre is the fragile Shell Temple in which a brazier is burning. The temple stands in front of the grotto, through the entrance to which we can see the river. So the four elements – earth, air, fire and water – are represented. A rainbow links heaven to a group of divine figures, seated on the ground to the left. On the right stand Kent and Pope, representatives of the sister arts. Behind Pope there is a bust of Homer. Kent holds a palette in one hand and his other hand is on Pope's shoulder, indicating friendship. Man's relationship with the animals is shown by the poet's Great Dane. Bounce is looking up at her master hopefully. There is also an improbable dolphin basking in a small font in the foreground, which reminds us of further friendly relationships between other of God's creatures and men – especially poets.

In short, Kent reveals the garden to be a manifestation of the harmony of all things, physical, intellectual and spiritual. It is a paradise, but not cut off from the world outside. Through the entrance to the grotto we glimpse a boat sailing down the Thames from London.

While he was still settling in at Twickenham, Pope was trying to find a house there for Lady Mary and her husband, who had arrived back in England the previous October. Eventually, in 1720, they bought one about a third of a mile

13.2 Alexander Pope's garden at Twickenham. William Kent, c. 1725–30

from the poet's villa, but before that they rented a place nearby from Sir Godfrey Kneller. Whereupon Pope busied himself ensuring that the landlord provided the house with beds and other necessary furniture – one of Pope's ways of trying to win the regard of women he was interested in, was to make himself useful.[21] He also commissioned Sir Godfrey to paint a picture of Lady Mary in Turkish dress, even persuading the artist to go to her house to make a preliminary drawing of her face, instead of insisting she come to his studio – a thing he rarely did for 'any but Crown'd Heads.'[22]

Pope was delighted by the finished portrait, which showed Lady Mary with dark searching eyes and a dimpled chin in her voluptuous prime. He wrote a poem about the picture as soon as he received it, despairing of his ability to match the painter's work by conveying in words his subject's 'Heavenly Mind', her 'Learning not vain, and Wisdom not severe.' The Turkish costume helped to keep alive the romantic vision he had of her as his princess.

The real Lady Mary was soon acclaimed as a leader of cultivated society in Twickenham. She was probably the hostess Edward Young was thinking of in his poem, 'On Women' (1725) – 'With legs tost high on her Sophee she sits / Vouchsafing audience to contending Wits.' The contending wits included her old friend Congreve, the brilliant, erratic Duke of Wharton and the entertaining, handsome Lord Hervey, who had recently married Molly Lepell. For a couple of years or so Pope was one of this circle, lending Lady Mary books, helping her to arrange musical evenings. When Gay wrote to congratulate him on finishing his house in 1720, he replied in verses, which showed that architecture and gardening were only partly successful as therapy. 'In vain my structures rise, my gardens grow', he began. 'Joy lives not here, to happier seats it flies, / And only dwells where WORTLEY casts her eyes.' It would appear from the rest of this mournful poem that Pope had not achieved the special relationship he had once hoped to enjoy with his feminine ideal. 'What are the gay parterre,' he went on:

> The chequer'd shade,
> The morning bower, the ev'ning colonnade,
> But soft recesses of uneasy minds,
> To sigh unheard in, to the passing winds.
> So the struck deer, in some sequester'd part
> Lies down to die, the arrow in his heart.[23]

One of Pope's many rivals, the Duke of Wharton, bought a house in Twickenham, the fashionable tone of society there being enhanced by the presence of the Prince of Wales at Richmond Lodge, across the river, and by Mrs Howard, the Prince of Wales's mistress, who came to live at Marble Hill. William Fortescue, private secretary to Robert Walpole, also had a house within walking distance. He was one of the few close friends in the political establishment that Pope had and, sometimes in the evenings, he took Bounce and crossed the fields to visit him.

Another well-disposed neighbour, whom Pope had met when he was in Chiswick, was the young Secretary of State James Craggs. In 1719 Craggs was working behind the scenes in a quixotic attempt to get relief for Papists from the Penal Laws.[24] At about the same time he offered Pope a pension of £300 a year, which he was going to pay out of the Secret Service funds he controlled, so that no one need know anything about it. This was not the first time Pope had been offered a pension. He refused Craggs's offer because he did not want to get used to an income he would lose if the giver lost office and also because he did not want to be the paid dependant of the Whigs.

He had no inhibitions about receiving, and even soliciting, less momentous gifts, especially presents in kind such as plants, trees and ornaments for his garden, or building materials for his house. Even so, he found the creation of his home at Twickenham an expensive business. John Searle reckoned Pope spent about £5000 on the garden over the years – that is all the money he made from translating the *Iliad*, while when Patty Blount said he spent a further £1000 on the grotto, she was probably underestimating the cost.[25]

The final volumes of the *Iliad* were published in May 1720 and by that time Pope had dreams of becoming seriously rich through his investments in the South Sea Company. The man in the street had discovered the theory of credit, whereby he realized a fortune could be made by putting his name to pieces of paper. Suddenly hundreds of people burned with investment fever, from the Prince of Wales to the porter in Exchange Alley. The latter made £2000 in a day, bought himself a coach, and was henceforth dubbed 'the Duke.'[26]

Although Pope expressed reservations about the whole extraordinary phenomenon, he asked James Eckersall to buy stock for him in February 1720, because it was 'ignominious not venture.'[27] He also urged Lady Mary to buy shares and bought some for Patty and Teresa. Then he tried unsuccessfully to raise more money to invest by cashing in lottery tickets. His carefully cultivated façade of indifference barely concealed the fact that, by the Spring, he was in and out of Exchange Alley continually. On 21 March we find him writing to Eckersall, having already called at his house before the man was up. In this letter he admitted to being 'alarm'd and vex'd' because, no sooner had he sold some of his shares to make a quick profit, than there was 'a prodigious and unexpected rise.'[28] Nevertheless, by 3 July he and Gay were so rich on paper, they were talking of buying an estate in Devon. On 22 August Pope assured Lady Mary the value of her shares was sure to keep on rising. He was wrong. The value of the stock, which stood at nearly 1000 at the end of June, had already fallen to 900 by 17 August. On 28 September it stood at 190. The bubble had burst. Hundreds of people lost everything and a score of Government officials were due for investigation.[29]

It is not certain how hard Pope was hit. He said he salvaged half the sum he imagined he would have, but as he had also said to Eckersall, when he first told him to go ahead, 'If we fail, let's e'en keep the mishap to ourselves,' he may have underplayed his losses.[30] Unlike many less cautious folk however, he was not ruined, nor were the friends he advised.

Nevertheless he still needed money so, having failed to get rich quick, he turned again to literary work. For reasons already explained, he was disorientated and could not see his way forward to writing poetry of his own, so he decided to translate some more of Homer's. He also turned himself into an editor. Over the next few years he worked, part of the time simultaneously, on the *Odyssey*, a prestigious edition of Shakespeare's plays, and the writings of the Duke of Buckingham, which the Duchess had asked him to get ready for the press. He thought of these tasks as routine chores which would not get him into trouble, even if he did not enjoy doing them. However, his lack of enthusiasm was in itself dangerous. Boredom and a wish to get this new work over and done with as soon as possible made him careless and worse. By the time he had finished his reputation was in shreds.

The *Iliad* had been an incubus but profitable, so translation was the first thing he thought of. Atterbury parcelled up Chapman's Homer to send him in August 1720, which suggests Pope was contemplating the *Odyssey* then, though the first volumes did not appear in print until shortly after the edition of Shakespeare plays in the spring of 1725. Before he got properly started on either Homer or Shakespeare, the Duke of Buckingham died on 24 February 1721 and Pope agreed to edit his writings because he felt he owed him a debt of gratitude.

Pope had known John Sheffield, Duke of Buckingham, since boyhood, looking upon him as a literary mentor from the time he had shown him the manuscript of the *Pastorals*. Later, when the *Iliad* translation was under way, Pope asked Buckingham for his critical opinion. Gradually the relationship between the two of them developed into one of 'familiar esteem.'[31] They exchanged complimentary verses about each other and Pope contributed two Choruses to his friend's play *Brutus*. This tragedy was not performed during the Duke's lifetime, but his widow Katherine arranged for it to be given a lavish production during a grand ball to mark her son's seventh birthday on 10 January 1723. Pope's Choruses were sung to music composed by Handel's rival Bononcini. Two weeks after this glittering celebration, held in what is now Buckingham Palace, the elegant edition of the Duke's *Works* was published.

Three days later, on Sunday 27 January, the King's Messengers raided Jacob Tonson's shop and seized all the copies, because one or two pages the Duke had written were thought to be Jacobite propaganda.[32] During his lifetime the Hanoverians had believed Buckingham shared his wife's sympathies, Katherine being a very indiscreet supporter of her half-brother, the Pretender. Nothing much was likely to happen to the Duchess but Pope, as editor of the offending volume, might well be held chiefly responsible for it now that the author was dead.

Only the year before the Reverend Lawrence Howell had died in gaol, where he had been serving a three-year sentence for writing a subversive pamphlet.[33] Pope was seriously worried. He knew Tickell and other Buttonians were now ensconced in the Secretary of State's office which had authorized confiscation of the Duke's *Works*. Furthermore, because of his association with Atterbury, he was suspected of taking part in the latest Jacobite plot, which Walpole was already investigating. Before we see how Pope extricated himself from this predicament, it is time to say something about his dangerous friend.

Notes

1. TW. 6: 247.
2. *Corr.* 2: 185.
3. *Corr.* 2: 140.
4. *Corr.* 2: 142.
5. For example, the ballad 'Duke upon Duke' (1720) TW. 6: 217–24 which attacked the Attorney General Nicholas Lechmere, who after the 1715 Rebellion spearheaded the attack in the House of Commons on Non-Jurors and Papists and was partly responsible for the punitive taxation, which disrupted the lives of the Popes and other Catholics.
6. *Corr.* 1: 448.
7. *Corr.* 2: 31.
8. *Corr.* 2: 137.
9. *Corr.* 2: 3.
10. *Corr.* 1: 456.
11. *Corr.* 1: 460.
12. *Corr.* 1: 468. Another interpretation of this letter assumes that 'another lady' was Teresa herself. See Valerie Rumbold, *Women's Place in Pope's World* (Cambridge University Press, 1989), ch. 4.
13. *Corr.* 2: 50.
14. *Corr.* 2: 44.
15. Spence, 606 and 607.
16. Interview with Edmund Curll 1735 in *Mr. Pope's Literary Correspondence*, 2: 79.
17. Spence, 609. Also *An Epistle to Burlington*, l. 57.
18. *Corr.* 2: 326.
19. The grotto is recently being restored under the direction of Nicholas Debenham. For accounts of the house and garden see Maynard Mack, *The Garden and the City* (Oxford University Press, 1969), Morris R. Brownell, *Alexander Pope and the Arts of Georgian England* (Oxford: Clarendon, 1978) and John Dixon Hunt, *Garden and Grove: the Italian Renaissance Garden in the English Imagination 1600–1700* (London: Dent, 1986). Mavis Batey, *Alexander Pope: Poetry and Landscape* (London: Barn Elms, 1999), shows how innovative Pope was when he created his garden and grotto.
20. The drawing which Kent made *c.* 1725–30 is in the British Museum.
21. Rumbold, *op. cit.*, ch. 4.
22. *Corr.* 2: 22.
23. 'To Mr. Gay', TW. 6: 225–6.
24. Charles Butler, *Historical Memoirs of the English, Irish and Scottish Catholics*, 4 vols, 3rd edition (London, 1822), 3: 170–8.

25. Spence, 355 and note.
26. For an account of the South Sea Bubble fiasco see J. Carswell, *The South Sea Bubble*, rev. edition (Stroud: Alan Sutton, 1993).
27. *Corr.* 2: 33–4. For the speculations of Pope in the South Sea Company, see Colin Nicholson, *Writing and the Rise of Finance: Capital Satires of the Early Eighteenth Century* (Cambridge University Press, 1994).
28. Ibid.
29. Carswell, *op. cit.*
30. *Corr.* 2: 33.
31. Warburton's note to *An Essay on Criticism*, l. 724. Quoted TW. 1: 323–4.
32. *The British Journal*, 2 February 1723, p. 5.
33. J.C.D. Clark, *English Society 1688–1832* (Cambridge University Press, 1985), p. 144.

14.1 Francis Atterbury. Godfrey Kneller, *c.* 1713

give him the hard evidence on which to convict Atterbury, he had the Bishop closely watched in the Tower. ''Tis the first time dead Pigeons have been suspected of carrying intelligence,' was Pope's comment when pies and puddings sent to the prisoner were inspected for messages.[7] Nevertheless, Atterbury managed to smuggle out a letter to Pope in April, thanking him for his friendship. Realizing he might never be permitted to see either Pope or Arbuthnot again, he prayed, 'God bless you both! May no part of the ill fortune that attends me, ever pursue either of you!' Then he suggested a way in which Pope might help him. 'I know not but I may call upon you at my Hearing, to say some what about my way of Spending my Time at the Deanery, which did not seem calculated towards managing Plots and Conspiracys.'[8] In conclusion he hinted at the line Pope might take by reminding him of their pleasant literary discussions.

So Pope appeared as a character witness at Atterbury's trial in the House of Lords. He worried considerably about his testimony beforehand and, once again, wrote to Lord Harcourt, this time because he wanted to be coached on what to say. He was particularly concerned about how he should reply if he was asked about being a Papist. He rehearsed a careful answer to this question which would show that, contrary to popular opinion, it was possible to be a Catholic and a loyal subject of a Protestant king.

The trial began on 6 May 1723. Walpole and Atterbury were evenly matched in forensic debate, both of them vigorous and clear-headed, but Walpole had not been able to find the conclusive evidence he needed. So the Bishop fended him off adroitly in a speech that lasted two hours. One of the surprises of the trial was provided, characteristically, by the young Duke of Wharton. He offered to speak for the prosecution and went one evening to Walpole's Chelsea home to be briefed. Having got the information he wanted, he spoke brilliantly the next day – for the defence!

Pope was called early in the trial. Later he described what happened, when he stood up to give his evidence and peered short-sightedly at the serried ranks of noblemen before him. 'Though I had but ten words to say, and that on a plain easy point (how the Bishop spent his time whilst I was with him at Bromley), I made two or three blunders in it, and notwithstanding the first row of Lords (which was all I could see) were mostly my acquaintance.'[9] Pope stumbled when he gave his evidence because he was frightened. All his life he had tried to keep out of the Jacobite limelight. Now he was thrust into it for the second time in four months. Actually, although he was dissatisfied with the way he delivered his testimony, an unofficial summary of it, printed later, shows he answered the questions asked without hedging. He told the court how much time he had spent with Atterbury over the past two or three years and how 'he was admitted to him at all Hours, and into all Companies, and never found the Discourse change at his coming in.' He was determined to do the best he could for his friend, even if it meant committing perjury and went on, 'His Lordship never in the least discover'd any Thought or Intentions like those charged upon him.'[10]

After the trial Pope wrote to his mother from his friend Lord Peterborough's London house, saying he would be home as soon as the Lords gave their verdict. This they did on Thursday, 16 May. The vote having gone against Atterbury by eighty-three to forty-three, he was to be sent into exile. The next morning Layer was hanged at Tyburn, his execution having been postponed several times, in the hope that he might produce more information that would take Atterbury to the scaffold with him.

Pope had been back in Twickenham barely twenty-four hours when he learned that his brother-in-law had been arrested. Charles Rackett and his eldest son Michael were charged with deer stealing. They belonged to an organized group known as the Berkshire Blacks, so called because the members of it went out at night with blackened faces, hunting deer in Windsor Forest. There were several groups of Blacks operating in the South of England. They were socially mixed, including farm workers and minor tradesmen as well as the local gentry. The motives of those joining were mixed as well. Some members were just poachers and others were social bandits who resented the stringent game laws imposed, in recent years, by the Whig Government. There is also evidence that the Hampshire Blacks, among others, had clear Jacobite connections and that their gang had recruited conspirators for the Atterbury plot.[11] In 1723 the Waltham Black Act appeared on the Statute Book, whereby any man found disguised, or with his face blackened, in woodlands was guilty of a felony and liable to be put to death. Walpole went to some trouble to get prosecutions under this Act, not just because the Blacks were lawless, but because he was determined to crush anyone who helped the rebels.

While Pope was growing up, Charles Rackett lived the life of a well-to-do country squire but we know nothing of where he came from, or what he had been doing, before he married Magdalen. One thing is clear however – he was far less cautious than the poet. As a Papist it was assumed he would be a supporter of the Stuarts and joining a subversive organization set the seal on the matter. Captain Brereton, the officer who drew up a list of the Berkshire Blacks, did not doubt it. He put Charles Rackett's name in the column headed 'Jacobites.'[12]

It did not take long for the *London Journal* to realize that the Racketts were related to the poet. A piece appeared in that newspaper making the connection on 25 May, a few days after the accused were summoned to appear at Westminster. By then Michael had fled to the Continent, where he was to stay at least sixteen years. Pope turned again to Lord Harcourt and asked him to intercede for Charles. Harcourt was particularly useful to the Tories because, while he was one of them, he was a moderate, who could act as an intermediary with the Whigs, especially as he had become a member of the Privy Council by 1723.

Harcourt approached Walpole, who may well have seen the advantage of having Pope in his debt. Something was arranged and Charles never stood trial. He too went abroad and we hear nothing further of him until his death in 1728. It looks as if he had had to pay a high price for his liberty. The house in Bagshot had to be mortgaged and he left his family in severe financial difficulties.[13] This is hardly surprising. Paying a fine, or bribing his way out of trouble, would have been all the more difficult in 1723 because, as happened before when there was trouble with the Jacobites, an extra tax was levied on Catholics to make them pay for dealing with it.

The new tax received royal assent on 27 May. It was set at five shillings in the pound, but Papists feared they would find themselves paying nine shillings if the new levy was added to the double taxes they were already subject to.[14] Pope thought so, and shortly before the new tax became law he wrote to Caryll, 'If this Bill passes I shall lose a good part of my income.'[15] If he was to safeguard his standard of living, it was now all the more important to make as much money as he could from his various literary projects.

Notes

1. G.V. Bennett, *The Tory Crisis in Church and State 1688–1730* (Oxford University Press, 1975) gives the life and career of Atterbury. P.S. Fritz, *The English Ministers and Jacobitism between the Rebellions of 1715 and 1745* (Toronto University Press, 1975) discusses Atterbury's work for the Stuarts. The evidence Fritz provides suggests that Atterbury was a Jacobite well before Bennett said he was.
2. *Corr.* 1: 451.
3. *Corr.* 1: 454.
4. *Corr.* 2: 104–5.
5. Details of Robert Harley's involvement with the Jacobites, including his fund raising activities, are given by Fritz, *op. cit.*
6. *Corr.* 2: 161. In 1726 the *Works* were reprinted, unabridged.
7. *Corr.* 2: 133–4.
8. *Corr.* 2: 165.
9. Spence, 234.
10. William Wynne, *Defense of Francis, late Lord Bishop of Rochester* (1723).
11. R.A. Stuart, 67/17. See also B.L. Add. MS, 17, 677, kkk, vol. 5, fos 548–9. For a summary of various theories about the significance of the Blacks, see Paul Kléber Monod, *Jacobitism and the English People 1688–1788* (Cambridge University Press, 1989), pp. 114–18.
12. Light was thrown on the Rackett case by E.P. Thompson in Appendix 2, 'Alexander Pope and the Blacks', in *Whigs and Hunters: The Origin of the Black Act* (Harmondsworth: Penguin, 1975). See also, Eveline Cruickshanks and Howard Erskine-Hill, 'The Waltham Black Act and Jacobitism', *Journal of British Studies*, 24, no. 3 (1985), 358–65. For an appraisal of the differing points of view of these writers see J.C.D. Clark, *Revolution and Rebellion: State and society in England in the seventeenth and eighteenth centuries* (Cambridge University Press, 1986), pp. 48–50.

13. *Corr.* 4: 160. For an account of the Rackett affair see Pat Rogers, 'Blacks, Poetry and Pope' in *Essays on Pope* (Cambridge University Press, 1993), pp. 168–83.
14. Hist. MSS. Comm. Polwarth MSS. 3: 202–3.
15. *Corr.* 2: 173.

CHAPTER FIFTEEN

Failure all Round

The new edition of Shakespeare was the young Jacob Tonson's idea. He rightly supposed that with Pope's name on the title page the six *de luxe* volumes of the plays would be in great demand, even at the price he was asking for them – five guineas. Accordingly an advertisement appeared in the *Weekly Journal or Saturday's Post* on 18 November 1721, announcing the 'Celebrated Mr. Pope is preparing a correct Edition of Shakespear's Works.' Unfortunately this good intention paved the way, if not to Hell, to literary Purgatory.

Pope already had some editing experience, having prepared the poems of Parnell as well as those of Buckingham for the press and he began his new task well. He advertised for early copies of the plays and soon had a collection of quartos, as well as access to the first folio. In his 'Preface to Shakespeare' he also proved he had sound ideas on how to treat the different texts. 'The various Readings are fairly put in the margin,' he declared, 'so that everyone may compare 'em: and those I have preferred into the texts are constantly upon authority.' Then he concluded, 'I have discharged the dull duty of an Editor, to the best of my judgement ... with a religious abhorrence of innovation and without any indulgence to my private sense or conjecture.'[1]

All would have been well if Pope had put these principles into practice but instead, in his marginal notes, he ignored some of the texts he had. Nor did he abhor innovation, or fail to indulge in highly idiosyncratic conjecture. Part of the reason for this dereliction is hinted at in the phrase 'the dull duty of an Editor.' Furthermore, as well as not having his heart in his work, he had a natural horror of pedantry. Nor were the editorial assistants he recruited any better than he was in this respect.

From the beginning it had been understood that Pope would not do all the work needed to edit the plays by himself. To help him, he paid £100 out of the £217 12s. he received from Tonson to Elijah Fenton, John Gay and a couple of men from Oxford. Also, working for the love of it, were William Broome and the distinguished physician Dr Cheselden. Pope sought out William Cheselden because he was known to take an amateur interest in Shakespeare studies. However, all these men had other work in hand. Broome and Fenton, for instance, were engaged on the *Odyssey*, while none of them had the editorial temperament. The person who would have been a useful addition to the team was Lewis Theobald. He was known to be interested in Shakespeare and was an admirer of Richard Bentley, the pioneer in modern methods of textual analysis. Theobald, however, was no friend of Pope. The two had been at odds since 1715 and in 1723 Theobald had a particular grievance. He had written a life of Buckingham for an edition of the Duke's poems Curll had hoped to publish, before being prevented from doing so by Pope's friends in the House of Lords.

When Pope's edition of Shakespeare was published in March 1725, Theobald was not displeased to note that many people said it was ill done and over priced. Exactly a year later he decided to show how the work ought to be carried out and published his *SHAKESPEARE restored: or, a SPECIMIN of the Many ERRORS, as well Committed, as Unamended by Mr. POPE In his Late EDITION of this Poet. DESIGNED not only to correct the said Edition, but to restore the True READING of SHAKESPEARE in all the Editions ever yet publish'd.*

Theobald's triumphalist title was not wholly justified. Not all his corrections have been judged valid, while some of Pope's amendments, such as his metrical improvements have lasted into modern editions of the plays. Also, when Pope did fulfil his promise to compare the texts he had, he was able to restore missing words and half lines, so making passages fully comprehensible again. When the poet fell short, it was due to artistic arrogance as much as to carelessness. This led him sometimes (though not often) to change Shakespeare's language, for no other reason than a belief that his choice of word was the better one. However, there were occasions when Theobald was equally guilty of this sin, with the result that some twenty of his unsubstantiated conjectures in *Hamlet* have since been thrown out. Furthermore, a good proportion of Theobald's alterations were to the punctuation. Much to Pope's scorn, his rival was obsessed by the lack of commas in the early texts.

Nevertheless, Theobald collated these texts more thoroughly than Pope had done. So this, together with his extensive reading of Elizabethan drama, which enabled him to find parallel uses of language, meant he solved several linguistic problems satisfactorily. Overall therefore, it was generally agreed that his Shakespeare was better than Pope's.[2]

Whatever discomfort Pope may have felt on reading *Shakespeare Restored*, he did not show it. As usual, he counter attacked, characteristically after some delay. In 1728 Theobald found he was the hero of the *Dunciad*.

Pope's literary reputation was dented when he published his edition of Shakespeare. Next it was the turn of his moral reputation when, six weeks later, the three first volumes of the *Odyssey* appeared in print, on 23 April 1725. Pope had asked Broome and Fenton to be his assistants again and, determined to reduce the labour involved, he invited them to help with the actual verse translation, as well as with the notes. Broome did eight books, Fenton four and Pope the other twelve. This meant the whole epic was completed in a little over three years, half the time the *Iliad* had taken. Broome and Fenton proved to be good at matching the style of Pope, who carefully revised the whole work. Readers liked what they read and all three men made money. Pope made £5,000 again, as much as he had made on the *Iliad*, even though Lintot's contract was less favourable than the one he had offered in 1714.

Trouble arose because Pope had been afraid subscribers would not be so ready to buy the *Odyssey* if they realized beforehand he was not going to do all the translation himself. Fenton and Broome agreed, not just because the better the work sold the more they would gain financially, but because they believed that their literary standing would be enhanced when the truth was finally revealed. Certainly Broome, who had a comfortable private income, was more interested in public esteem than in cash. For that reason, he could not resist telling his friends what he was doing, and, long before the first volumes of the *Odyssey* appeared, those friends had told half literary London.

As a result Pope's enemies had a field day, beginning with George Duckett, whose letter quickly appeared in the *London Journal* on 17 July 1725. Writing as 'Homerides,' Duckett was merciful to Broome and Fenton, excoriating Pope in the following terms:

> I shall not say anything concerning the Persons who are supposed to be our Poetical Undertaker's Deputies in this Affair, because were they as able to translate Homer as even their Taskmaster himself, yet to have one or more Authors obtruded upon us, without our Knowledge or Consent, under the Name and Character of another to whom we have subscribed, is *Quackery* and C—licism in the greatest perfection.

No one has ever attempted to defend Pope's double dealing over the second Homer translation. The use of ghost writers was not unheard of in the eighteenth century, but was frowned upon then – as it often is nowadays. Yet Pope himself expressed no shame. He attempted instead, not very successfully, to brazen the matter out, arguing that he had done no more than Kneller did every week when he used his assistants to complete portraits. He made Broome express this point of view in a note for Book XXIV of the *Odyssey* wherein his co-translator, speaking for himself and Fenton obediently wrote:

> It was our particular request, that our several parts might not be made known to the world till the end of the work; and if they have had the good fortune not to be distinguished from His [Pope's], we ought to be less vain of it, since the resemblance proceeds much less from our diligence and study to copy his manner, than from his own daily revision and correction. The most experienced Painters will not wonder at this, who very well know, that no Critic can pronounce even of the pieces of *Raphael* or *Titian*, which have, or which have not, been worked upon by those of their school? When The same Master's hand has directed the execution of the whole.[3]

Nor did Broome's penance for having given the game away end there. He was made to write a concluding note to Homer's epic, which was deliberately vague about how many books he and Fenton had translated, leaving the unwary reader to suppose it could have been as few as seven.

This whole episode is as good an example as any of the way in which Pope put whatever he believed might be an advantage to him in his professional career before every other consideration.

Some time before the first volumes of the *Odyssey* appeared in print, Pope's attempt to find a role for himself as Lady Mary's courtly lover, ended in failure and his adoration turned to hatred. He was the only person who ever knew why or, precisely when, his feelings changed so dramatically. In 1721 he admired her as much as ever, saying how much it pleased him that Broome wished to immortalize her in verse, commending as a particularly good idea the mention of her campaign to promote inoculation for smallpox, because this was 'an action which all posterity may feel the advantage of.'[4] That summer Bononcini, with the opera stars Anastasia Robinson and Senesino, all had lodgings in Twickenham. Lady Mary melted her time away 'in almost perpetual concerts,' some of which were held in the gallery at Pope's villa.[5]

The first hint of a rift came the following year when Lady Mary wrote to her sister in Paris, 'I see sometimes Mr. Congreve, and very seldom Mr. Pope who continues to embellish his garden at Twickenham.'[6] The last known letter in her correspondence with the poet came at the end of 1723. She sent him a brief note, offering to come over to the villa if he was ill because she had 'something particular to say to him.'[7]

Eventually Lady Mary got 'a third person to ask why Mr. Pope had left off visiting her', and he answered 'negligently that he went as often as he used to.' Then she sent Dr Arbuthnot to make enquiries, whereupon Pope said that she 'and Lord Hervey had pressed him once together ... to write a satire on some certain persons, that he refused it, and that this had occasioned the breach.'[8] Lady Mary could not recall the episode. Years later her granddaughter spread the story that Pope had made Lady Mary a declaration of love, which she had greeted with gales of laughter.[9] It is unlikely that there was ever such a spectacular scene as this. If there had been, Lady Mary need not have wondered why she no longer saw her admirer. Nevertheless, it could well be true that there was a sexual crisis in their relationship.

It is sometimes said that Pope's was a romantic and 'imaginary passion.'[10] But it is more likely that he really had fallen in love with this brilliant and beautiful woman. In which case she would certainly have known. Pope wore a mask, and the mask he chose to wear was that of the cultivated, literary lover, playing a game of love according to the conventions of stylized romance. Sometimes, however, he invited Lady Mary to look beyond the mask and glimpse the face of a man who was consumed with longing for her. So he gave her a copy of the unprinted verses (already quoted in chapter 13), in which he said 'Joy ... dwells only where WORTLEY casts her eyes' and compared himself to a stricken deer that lies bleeding, 'the arrow at his heart' (TW. 6:225–6). Lady Mary 'stifled' these lines but not before she had sent a copy to the Countess of Mar, with strict instructions to her sister not to let them go further than her closet.[11] She was flattered to receive a love poem from a distinguished literary figure but had no intention of responding.

Ever since she had known Pope, she had resisted any attempt by him to wax romantic and was brutal if he tried to play upon her feelings. For instance, while she was on her travels, he had written to her about two village lovers who were struck dead by lightning while haymaking at Stanton Harcourt – just a week before they were to marry. When the bodies were found, the young man had one arm round his girl, while with the other he had tried to shield her face from the storm. Pope was touched, and, identifying with the pair, wrote that, 'the greatest happiness, next to living as they would have done, was to dye as they did'.[12] He hoped Lady Mary would shed tears when she read the sad story of John Hewet and Sarah Drew. He was wrong. She implied he was being maudlin. She told him that John's attempt to protect his girl was no more than he would have done for his horse. Then, to drive her point home, she predicted that had the couple survived their wedding day, within a year, 'A Beaten Wife and Cuckold Swain / Had jointly curs'd the marriage chain'.[13]

During the early years of her own disappointing marriage, Lady Mary was relentlessly unsentimental, though Pope refused to believe that this was more than a pretence. After she came to live in Twickenham, he sought her out so often that folk began to gossip. In July 1722, one of her female neighbours wrote, 'She and Pope keep so close yonder that they are talk to the whole town'.[14]

Scandal mongering of this kind (if she heard it) could only have irritated Lady Mary. As it was, the assiduous attentions of a middle class, physically repellent, would-be lover must have struck her as both misguided and silly. So maybe, in a fit of impatience one day, she tried to bring him to his senses. Pope was eventually to say she had '*too much wit*' for him.[15] She had a very cutting wit, which she used at the expense of friend and foe alike. Her letters to her sister in the early 1720s are punctuated with caustic comments about mutual acquaintances who fancied themselves to be in love. It is not hard to imagine a situation therefore in which she made a man who adored her the butt of a devastating joke. She would then have forgotten about it in a few minutes – but it would have been quite enough to turn the ever sensitive Pope's love into loathing.

Lord Bathurst who, like Pope, had been one of Lady Mary's 'humble Admirers', reproached him mildly for his change of attitude saying, 'I think of her as I always did.'[16] But then he had no illusions about women. He asked no more 'Than not to wait too long, nor pay too dear.'[17] Pope idealized the women he fell in love with. Now he awoke from his dream of a fair lady in whom he saw nothing but virtues, to see nothing but faults. Lady Mary had plenty of them, being for instance arrogant and demanding. Whether she actually told Pope who, or what, to write about, she was capable of doing so. Ever since the publication of the *Court Poems*, she had been suspected of pretending her writings were the work of others.

When Pope fired the salvo that began their celebrated feud, he wrote 'The Capon's Tale', dedicated to her as 'A Lady who Father'd her Lampoons upon her Acquaintance.' To this day no one has identified the precise occasion for this satire. There may not have been one. Pope could well have been using this plausible excuse as a face-saving device, rather than admit that he was waging war on a woman because she had humiliated him.

As the years went on his attacks became more outrageous. He said she was obsessed by money and men, adding she had syphilis. This last was common gossip, if untrue. Then as she grew older, she became careless of her appearance and he recorded, with mordant satisfaction, her dirty linen and greying hair.

Lady Mary, in her turn, gave as good as she got. She also invented slanders, including a farcical account of how the poet was stripped naked and whipped on his way home one night, only to be found by Arbuthnot and the fond Patty Blount, who gathered him up in her apron. She jeered at him for his 'Birth obscure' and harped continually on the subject of his deformity.[18]

Neither Lady Mary nor Pope could forget each other. Two years before his death the poet wrote to Hugh Bethel, who had mentioned that Lady Mary was famous throughout Italy, 'I wish you had told me if the Character be more Avaricious, or Amatory? And which Passion got the better at last.'[19] Fifteen years later, when Lady Mary showed a visitor in Venice a commode decorated with emblems of Swift, Bolingbroke and Pope, she expressed her satisfaction in 'shitting on them every day.'[20] Yet she kept Pope's letters, copying them into a diary which her prudish daughter destroyed, while Pope kept a portrait of her in his bedroom till the day he died.

Writing in a feminist era, it is tempting to imagine that Pope had fallen out with Lady Mary because she was intelligent and forceful and did not conform to the feminine stereotype. Certainly the average eighteenth-century gentleman did not want women to be clever or well-informed. Instead he expected them to be sentimental and self-effacing. It does Pope a disservice however to suppose he was as pompous and insecure as Richard Steele who, in *Spectator* no. 342, admitted he would rather a woman be 'less entertaining than she could be to please Company,' than have her outshine her male partner. For one thing, it is doubtful whether Pope ever supposed anyone, male or female, would outshine him when it came to the use of words.

There is evidence Pope was at ease with intelligent and articulate women throughout his life. Indeed, he sought them out. As a young man he made a lasting friendship with the vociferous and satirical Countess of Burlington. She enjoyed good conversation and he made a point of saying he liked to hear her talk.[21] When he was an older man he made a new friend of Ann Arbuthnot, saying he liked her because she had her father's sense of humour – a humour that could be quite acerbic on occasion.[22] Furthermore, none of his female contemporaries was more self-assertive than the old Duchess of Marlborough, with whom he got on famously. On the other hand a tentative relationship with a young admirer Judith Cowper never matured, in part because she lacked a sense of humour and was given to the vapours.

Judith Cowper, who was an aspiring writer as well as a young lady of fashion turned out not to be Pope's type, even though he had been enchanted by her appearance when he first saw her in Jervas's studio. Added to which she came into his life when his relationship with Patty Blount was more intimate and relaxed than it had been earlier. Like himself, Patty was now over thirty. With each year that went by she saw her chance of marriage receding. But whereas the prospect of staying single made Teresa desperate and bad tempered, her good humoured sister decided to make the most of whatever life had to offer, including her friendship with Pope. There was much to build a friendship on. They had in common a beleaguered Papist background and shared memories from the Binfield days onwards. Patty, though her eyes were as blue as ever, found it harder to play the belle, while Pope was as helpful as before, but kept his vow to stop playing the artificial gallant. The new system worked. A letter he received in 1723 shows Patty welcomed Pope's company and took 'it a little ill' if he had not been to see her for a while.[23]

They were often seen together and people talked. In 1722 Broome wrote to ask Pope if the rumours about his impending marriage were true? Pope said they were not. He did not contemplate getting married. For one thing, to do so would have exposed both Patty and him to ridicule – we can imagine what Lady Mary would have made of it! But apart from that, he had always been dubious about marriage. As a young man Pope had dreamed of a grand romance, now he found satisfaction in a loving friendship. He assured Caryll in 1725 the relationship was no more than that. Caryll was anxious because it was rumoured that Patty (his goddaughter) had been Pope's mistress for two or three years. Naturally Pope denied this, though many people believed she was. However, Pope made sure that neither his contemporaries, nor his future biographers, could prove it.

Unlike Lady Mary, whose deeds and words speak for her, we see Martha Blount through other people's eyes, mainly Pope's. According to Magdalen Rackett, however, her brother had no idea what his friend was really like. Jonathan Richardson recorded Magdalen's opinion that 'Miss Patty Blount was the very reverse in her Conduct to what Pope took her to be, that she was indeed a great Romp and by no means a Prude, but that she would change Carriage, whatever Company was there, and however she had behav'd, as soon as ever Mr Pope came into the Room.[24] This view raises the possibility that Patty, like her lover, was a role player and a social chameleon, though one has to remember that Magdalen uttered her strictures after she knew that her brother had left most of his estate to his female friend.

Perhaps it was jealousy that made Magdalen Rackett as well as William Warburton resent Patty's presence in Pope's life, but she also encountered hostility in Ralph Allen's house and was not always welcome at Caryll's. As

Pope paints her, she appears good tempered and unselfish, a view borne out by one of her maids, whom she had taken round London, sightseeing. This girl said her 'mistress was one of the best natured and kindest persons possible.'[25] She was also better than most of Pope's friends at dispelling the clouds of gloom when he was depressed. In his most extended tribute to her, he implied he felt better in her company because she was blessed with a temperament 'whose unclouded ray / Can make to morrow cheerful as to day.'[26]

More than ten years before Pope wrote those lines in *An Epistle to a Lady*, he wrote some verses for Patty's birthday in 1723, which give us some idea of how he had come to regard the woman he had known since she was a school girl:

> Oh be thou blest with all that Heav'n can send!
> Long Health, long Youth, long Pleasure – and a Friend.
> Not with those Toys the Woman-world admire,
> Riches that vex, and Vanities that tire:
> Let Joy, or Ease; let Affluence or Content;
> And the glad Conscience of a Life well-spent,
> Calm ev'ry Thought, inspirit ev'ry Grace,
> Glow in thy Heart, and smile upon thy Face!
> Let Day improve on Day; and Year on Year,
> Without a Pain, a Trouble or a Fear!
> And ah! Since Death must that dear Frame destroy,
> Die by a sudden Extacy of Joy!
> In some soft Dream may thy mild Soul remove,
> And be thy latest Gasp a Sigh of Love![27]

In these lines he assumes that Patty, like himself, has realized she will not find ecstatic love in the waking world. Mutual disappointment has brought them closer together.

Notes

1. *Prose Works of Alexander Pope: Volume II 1725–1744*, ed Rosemary Cowler (Oxford: Blackwell, 1986), pp. 24–5.
2. For comments on the editions of Shakespeare by Pope and Theobald see E.G. Fogel, *Shakespeare Quarterly*, 9 (1958), 485–92; Maynard Mack, *Alexander Pope: A Life* (Yale University Press, 1985), pp.426–33; George Sherburn, *The Early Career of Alexander Pope* (Oxford: Clarendon Press, 1934), pp. 244–7 and Nicol Smith, *Eighteenth-Century Essays on Shakespeare* (Oxford: Clarendon Press, 1963).
3. TW. 10: 378.
4. *Corr.* 2: 77. In 1724 Pope lent his house to Fortescue's family as a sanatorium when they had their smallpox inoculations.
5. Robert Halsband, *Life of Lady Mary Wortley Montagu* (Oxford: Clarendon, 1956), quoted p. 106.
6. Quoted TW. 6: 204.
7. *Corr.* 2: 204.
8. Spence, 751.

9. Lady Louisa Stuart, 'Introductory Anecdotes', *Lady Mary Wortley Montagu: Letters and Works* (1861), 1: 92. Most of the reasons ever suggested for the quarrel are discussed by Isobel Grundy, *Lady Mary Wortley Montagu* (Oxford University Press, 1999), pp. 270–4 and as she concludes, there is, to date, no way of proving any of them.

10. TW. 4: xv.

11. *Complete Letters of Lady Mary Wortley Montagu*, ed Robert Halsband, 3 vols (Oxford: Clarendon, 1965), 2: 15.

12. *Corr.* 1: 494–6.

13. *Complete Letters of Lady Mary Wortley Montagu*, 1: 445–6.

14. Ibid., 2: 15n. The writer was Griselda Murray's mother.

15. 'Letter to a Noble Lord', Cowler, *op. cit.*, p. 444.

16. *Corr.* 3: 134.

17. 'Sober Advice from Horace', l. 160.

18. *Verses address'd to the Imitator of the First Satire of the Second Book of Horace. By a Lady* (1733).

19. *Corr.* 4: 377.

20. Robert Halsband, 'New Anecdotes of Lady Mary Wortley Montagu', in *Evidence in Literary Scholarship*, eds Rene Wellek and Alvaro Riberio (Oxford, 1979), p. 245.

21. TW. 6: 336–8. For an earlier version of 'On the Countess of B_____ Cutting Paper' and Pope's Foreword to the poem, see James M. Osborn, 'Pope, the "Apollo of the Arts," and his Countess', *England in the Restoration and Early Eighteenth Century*, ed H.T. Swedenberg (University of California Press, 1972), pp. 102–43.

22. *Corr.* 4: 177 and Spence, 649.

23. *Corr.* 2: 191.

24. 'New Anecdotes about Alexander Pope', *Notes and Queries* (August, 1958), p. 349.

25. Samuel Rogers, *Reminiscences and Table Talk*, ed G.H. Powell (London, 1903), p. 12.

26. 'An Epistle to a Lady', ll. 257–8.

27. Reprinted in Norman Ault, *New Light on Pope* (London: Methuen, 1949), p. 196. Later versions of the poem emphasise that ecstasy is not to be had in this world. Instead Pope concludes by hoping Patty will 'wake to Raptures in the Life to come'.

PART V

Pope Recreates Himself

CHAPTER SIXTEEN

The Return

In his early thirties Pope said so often that he was no longer a poet, his friends might have been forgiven if they had believed him. However, two men, Bolingbroke and Swift refused to listen to his lamentations when he said he would never write anything of his own again. Encouraging and occasionally hectoring, they suggested a way forward that led to poems different from those with which he had made his name. Their confidence was stimulating. Their efforts were successful because the time was right. By the mid-1720s the Tories had regrouped and become an effective Opposition. In this changed political climate Pope remained wary but he was not as apprehensive as he had been in the years of intense Jacobite activity. Nor did he feel so alone. He had a support group again.

In June 1723, as Atterbury stepped ashore at Calais, he heard that the newly pardoned Bolingbroke was at an inn nearby, waiting for a boat to take him to his native land. Whereupon he is supposed to have said drily, 'Then I am exchanged.'[1] Even if this story is an invention, it is true that Bolingbroke replaced Atterbury as an Opposition leader, albeit with a different manifesto. When the Bishop faded from the English scene, the hopes of many of his countrymen for a Stuart restoration faded with him. It would be more than twenty years before Jacobitism at home produced another rebellion. In the meantime attention was focused on Walpole who, far more than a Hanoverian monarch, was seen by his varied opponents as the main thing wrong with England. Bolingbroke came home to unite Tories, disillusioned Jacobites and disappointed Whigs into a movement capable of overthrowing the first minister.

As a glance at the newspapers and journals of the day shows, the Opposition took as their own those popular rallying cries of Patriotism, Liberty and Virtue. By the last term they meant civic virtue; a combination of probity and public spiritedness. Walpole, who lacked parliamentary whips to keep his supporters in line, bribed them instead. Then, not unnaturally, he despised those sycophants whose price he knew. As his opponents saw it, the first minister was corrupt, while his unprecedented efficiency in controlling his political pensioners meant the country was evolving from a one-party to a one-man state.

Bolingbroke stayed in England less than two months in 1723. In August he returned to France because, although he had been pardoned, his property was still forfeited. It took another two years, much lobbying by his French wife and a bribe of £11,000 to a mistress of George I, before he was given back his property rights. Walpole was successful in keeping Bolingbroke out of the House of Lords and would have liked to have kept him out of England altogether. Nevertheless, in 1725, his rival from their schooldays at Eton settled at Dawley Farm, across the fields from Pope's house in Twickenham and, even if his voice was not to be heard in the Upper Chamber, he had no intention of remaining silent.

In the months before that Bolingbroke wrote to Pope regularly from France, waging a campaign to get him to write verse again. In one of Pope's replies (now lost) he appears not to have said anything about his work, which made Bolingbroke admonish – and flatter – him by saying, 'If you imagine the matter dropp'd you are mistaken. I shall attack you once again upon the same Subject. Are you composing? … after translating what was writ 3000 years ago it is incumbent upon you that you write, what will deserve to be translated 3000 years hence into Languages as yet unform'd.'[2]

Then Swift added his voice. In September 1725 he wrote, 'I am exceedingly pleased you have done with Translations. Lord Treasurer Oxford often lamented that a rascally World should put you under a Necessity of Misemploying your Genius so long a time. But since you will be so much better employed, when you think of the World give it one more lash at my Request.'[3]

Like Pope, Swift had been slow to write anything of his own in the early years of the Hanoverian reign. After leaving St James's for a deanery in Dublin it had taken him some time to reconcile himself to the 'Scene and Business' he was condemned to.[4] He awoke from what he called a 'Scurvey Sleep' in 1722.[5] This was when William Wood of Birmingham was granted a patent by the English Government to mint copper coins for use in Ireland. Since the total currency of the country was worth less than the projected coinage, it was possible all the remaining gold and silver would be driven overseas and an already impoverished land plunged into utter destitution. Swift's *Drapier's Letters*, more than any other protest, put a stop to the scheme. As Walpole had been determined to 'pour the coins down the throats of the people,' it was a rare victory for Ireland when the patent was revoked in 1724 – and a triumph for Swift.[6] Recharged with energy, he finished *Gulliver's Travels* the following year and got ready to visit England again. By the autumn of 1725, having heard quite a bit about Gulliver, Pope was promising, 'My own … shall never more be in a strange land, but a diligent, I hope useful, investigation of my own Territories. I mean no more Translations, but something domestic, fit for my own country, and for my own time.'[7] The way was already opening up for *An Essay on Man*, or perhaps the *Dunciad*.

'A person was come to London who demanded my immediate repair thither,' wrote Pope to Edward Harley, the new Lord Oxford in March 1726. He was announcing the arrival of Swift whom, to his delight, he found 'in perfect health and spirits' at lodgings in his old haunt, Bury Street, already surrounded with friends.[8] Many people, including members of Bolingbroke's entourage, were eager to meet Swift. Dr Arbuthnot, Lord Chesterfield and William

Pulteney took him through the town. At Dawley, the Opposition's country headquarters, Bolingbroke briefed him politically, outlining plans for the future and telling him about a newspaper, *The Craftsman*, that he and Pulteney intended to launch later that year.

As well as the week at Dawley Swift was invited to the Opposition's base in town, Leicester House. Here the Prince of Wales, on bad terms with his father (as behoved a Hanoverian) kept a rival court. Above all, however, Swift wanted to meet Walpole, in the hope of persuading the 'Great Man' to do something about the 'scene of misery and desolation' in Ireland.[9] Harcourt and Peterborough smoothed the way, and Walpole invited Swift to one of his dinners, where the guests were 'up to the Chin in Beef ... over the Chin in Claret' and their host talked bawdy so that everyone could join in.[10] So the first minister, uninterested in Irish problems, made sure that he would not have to hear about them, on that evening at least, while Swift realized that he had no alternative but to oppose Walpole as best he could.

After a few weeks the ever eager Pope transported Swift to Twickenham, along with Gay. They were both his house guests and Arbuthnot joined them whenever he could. Throughout the summer the four used Twickenham as a base. They missed Parnell's elaborate jokes and the occasional incursions of the Lord Treasurer, both of whom were dead. Even so, this Scriblerian quorum succeeded in recreating the camaraderie and atmosphere of those meetings, more than a decade earlier, in the Doctor's rooms in St James's Palace. In Pope's villa and garden they read and discussed their current works and gave each other ideas for new ones just as they used to do.

They were all busy. Gay was writing his *Fables* for the amusement of the four-year-old Prince William, hoping thereby to win the favour of the boy's mother, Princess Caroline. Arbuthnot was putting the finishing touches to a scholarly dissertation on ancient coins. Swift and Pope sorted through their earlier verse and prose pieces and would eventually publish four volumes of these *Miscellanies*. One reason for revising and publishing their minor pieces was to circumvent Curll, who if they did not, certainly would, given the chance. As Swift told Pope soon after the *First Psalm* escaped into print, 'I think the frolicks of merry hours, even when we are guilty, should not be left to the mercy of our best friends, till Curll and his resemblers are hanged.'[11] Swift's good sense in this matter was underlined in July when the enterprising Curll once more embarrassed the poet by publishing some of the letters Pope and Cromwell had written to each other – sexual innuendoes and all.

Pope was also smarting because, soon after Swift's arrival, Theobald had published his indictment of the poet's editorial shortcomings, *Shakespeare Restored*. But this event gave Swift an idea. Among Pope's sundry papers was a preliminary sketch of a poem on Dulness, probably with Elkanah Settle as the protagonist. Settle had died in 1724 and Pope thought he might as well send the verses into oblivion after him. Swift snatched the pages from the fire, and it was probably he who suggested how Theobald could replace Settle as the hero. The conscientious Theobald, agonizing over punctuation in the plays, qualified for this honour because of what both men considered was his pettifogging, sterile approach to literature.

So the *Dunciad* was not aborted. It was a productive summer even though Pope kept open house. When there seemed to be no end to the visitors, he complained he felt like one of those patriarchs 'in the Old Testament, receiving all comers,' but actually he was enjoying every minute of it.[12] He was emerging from the literary wilderness. It was his guest of honour who found the social programme a trifle wearing. 'Mr Gay and I find ourselves often engaged for three or four days to come,' Swift wrote Lord Oxford about his host, 'and neither of us dare dispute his Pleasure.'[13]

In July Pope took Swift and the other two Scriblerians on a ramble for a few weeks. They were going to pay visits to various friends, including Bathurst and Cobham. Pope also wanted to see Binfield again, so they went via Windsor Forest. It was a cheerful expedition. The friends were certainly in good spirits when they stopped at The Rose in Wokingham where, as they sat outside in the sun, they soon noticed that the girl who brought them their drinks was a true English beauty – well worth making a song about. She was called Molly Mog, so they decided on a crambo, in which every verse had to have a rhyme on her name. Gay wrote most of it, with the others making contributions, a typical verse being:

> Will-a-wisp leads the Trav'ler a-gadding
> Thro' Ditch and thro' Quagmire and Bog,
> But no Light can set me a-madding
> Like the Eyes of my sweet Molly Mog.

The ballad was printed in *Mist's Weekly Journal* on 27 August, whereupon readers sent in extra verses, with more and more outlandish rhymes. When it was set to music, the song became popular and was sung for years. It made Molly famous – to this day there is a pub named after her in the Charing Cross Road.

After the ramble to Cirencester and Stowe, Pope went back to Twickenham and Swift went to London, to see about getting *Gulliver's Travels* published. He stayed in the Whitehall lodgings of Gay, who borrowed bed linen from Jervas for his guest. As the *Travels* was partly a political allegory, it seemed best not to bring it out under the author's own name. Swift sent the first volume of it to Benjamin Motte, as if it had come from one, Richard Sympson, Gulliver's cousin. Motte liked what he read and agreed to publish the whole book for £200. The story from there is taken up by Pope, who described how the bookseller received, 'he knew not from whence,' nor from whom the rest of the manuscript 'dropp'd at his house in the dark, from a Hackney-coach.'[14]

It could have been Pope who was in the hackney coach but perhaps it was not for, much as he would have enjoyed such an assignment, he was far from well at the time. His health had been better than usual during Swift's visit, partly because he was feeling cheerful, but throughout the summer he had lived, as he often did when the pace of life quickened, on his nerves and by August he was exhausted. He was ill the day Peterborough gave a farewell dinner for their friend. Afterwards Swift, who was gathering up his luggage to return to Dublin, wrote him a solicitous letter, 'I had rather live in forty Islands than be under the frequent disquiets of hearing you are out of order ... Pray let me have three lines under any hand or pothook that will give me a better account of your health; which concerns me more than others, because I love and esteem you for reasons that most others have little to do with.'[15]

On 15 August, a broiling hot day, the Scriblerians said goodbye to Swift as he made his way to the coach station, on the first stage of his journey to Ireland. He forgot his spectacles. They were sent after him, as well as the printed copies of *Gulliver's Travels*, published on 28 October.

By the beginning of November Gay and Pope were able to tell Swift how London received *Gulliver's Travels*. Gay informed him all the copies were sold out in a week. It was 'universally read, from the Cabinet-council to the Nursery.' Lord Harcourt thought 'in some places the matter is carried too far'; the old Duchess of Marlborough had no such reservations and was 'in raptures.'[16] A few took fiction for fact and claimed to have met Captain Gulliver but most people knew who the author of this anonymous work really was. The ever wary Pope spent a fortnight in London, especially to observe how men regarded the *Travels* and sought to reassure his friend when he wrote, 'I find no considerable man very angry at the book: some indeed think it rather too bold, and too general a Satire: but none I hear accuse it of particular reflections. I mean no persons of consequence.'[17] Nevertheless, in its indictment of contemporary society, it was the first blast of the Opposition trumpet.

The Opposition campaign was officially inaugurated on 6 December 1726 when the first number of *The Craftsman* appeared. It was to become the best-written, most-discussed political journal of the next decade. It claimed to be non-partisan, its aim being to 'reconcile all Parties to one another; to unite them in their common interest and Cause of their country.'[18] It would defend liberty, including liberty of the press.

Walpole was its main target, the man of craft of the journal's title, who featured in the opening number as Robin the rascally coachman. In the years to come he would make many appearances: as a Persian Grand Vizier, Cardinal Wolseley, Queen Elizabeth's Leicester, Harlequin or, more simply, as the Robinarch. Bolingbroke and Pulteney wrote some of the papers and, as time went on, there were those who were convinced Pope contributed a few of them, in particular an allegory entitled 'The Norfolk Steward' which appeared in September 1727.[19]

In April 1727 Swift arrived in England again but this time the busy timetable that Pope drew up for his friend and the other Scriblerians was soon in ruins, partly because of illness. First, Mrs Pope was sick and needed her solicitous son's constant attention, while he himself was in poor health for much of the summer. Then, toward the end of his stay Swift was both physically afflicted and deeply depressed. As well as suffering these personal troubles, Pope and all his Tory friends were disappointed because, although they got a new king they did not get a new regime.

The main event of 1727 was the death on 11 June of George I at Osnabruck, in the same room where he was born. Everyone was taken by surprise, not least Walpole. He hardly expected to be employed in the new reign because he was not liked by George II who, when Sir Robert woke him up to tell him of his father's demise, told him to take his orders from the Speaker of the House of Commons, Sir Spencer Compton. However, Sir Spencer was in Lord Hervey's words, 'a plodding, heavy fellow' whose 'only pleasures were money and eating; his only knowledge forms and precedents.'[20] As he could not even write the first speech which the King had to make to his Cabinet but asked Walpole to write it for him, George soon realized how useless he was. Sir Robert took charge again and watched sardonically as courtiers and ministers, who had been avoiding him during the previous weeks, now waylaid him in every antechamber.

Even though the first minister remained, the Opposition still hoped, that things would change under the new king who, as Prince of Wales, had encouraged some of them. Swift expressed their feelings when he trusted that henceforth, 'nobody shall be used better or worse for being call'd Whig or Tory.'[21] Walpole soon made it clear however that he had no need of help from the Tories and intended to carry on exactly as before.

He made a minor exception of Pope. In 1725 he had paid the poet £200 out of Treasury funds to help him while he was translating the *Odyssey* and, over the next five years or so he invited him, at fairly regular intervals, to dine with him. Pope was gratified to be 'civilly treated by Sir Robert.'[22] Ever since he was a young man he had tried to protect himself by keeping on good terms with the leaders of both political parties. Occasionally he extracted favours from the 'Great Man', as when he won his support to have Southcote appointed the Abbé at Avignon. Nor was it hard to like Walpole. He could be most affable and was a man of taste, as well as a shrewd operator, who saw no reason to antagonize the finest living poet if it could be avoided. However, he knew exactly how much he was prepared to pay for a writer's good will. Despite a success in the matter of Southcote, Pope would find it impossible to get the first minister to extend his patronage to other friends, such as Gay, let alone Swift.

By the beginning of July, as Mrs Pope had recovered and the poet was well enough to suggest a ramble, he and Swift went to stay with Lord Oxford at Wimpole. They had no sooner returned to Twickenham than Swift was afflicted with one of his recurrent fits of deafness. He had Ménière's Disease, though neither he nor anyone else knew this. He imagined its various symptoms, including the spells of dizziness, were something to do with eating fruit. Whenever he had an attack he was too embarrassed to meet people because he could not hear anything they said. So he sat down now in the corner of a room at the villa, waiting for the ringing in his ears to stop, while his friend paced up and down, composing aloud verses for the work on Dulness which was well under way, Pope having made a triumphant return to poetry.

In between times Pope, who tended to fuss over people when they were unwell, hovered anxiously round Swift who preferred to be left alone. The Dean's attack was aggravated by depression. It was already dispiriting enough to realize that the new reign would bring no change for the better but, in addition he had a more immediate reason to be melancholy. In mid-August a letter had arrived from Dublin to tell him that his close friend Esther Johnson (Stella) was dying. He was afraid to go home yet could bear it no longer at Twickenham where, even if Pope tried, he could not keep out callers. Complaining there were too many visitors and that his host was 'too sickly and complaisant,' Swift went to stay with a cousin in Greenwich.[23] Then, on 18 September Pope and Gay found he had set off for Ireland. He left kind messages for his friends but was never to return to England. Nor, though he tried repeatedly, could he ever persuade Pope, afraid of crossing the Irish Sea, to visit him at the Deanery. The two of them continued to write long letters to each other but did not meet again.

The new king's coronation in October was more magnificent than any previously held in Westminster Abbey. George was glorified in a ceremony in which 160 players and nearly fifty singers performed the four anthems Handel composed for the occasion. Blonde, pink, plump Caroline was covered in jewels, public, personal and borrowed. At the rehearsal on 7 October the Abbey was filled with the greatest concourse of people ever seen there. Later, many of them flocked to the theatre where the coronation was staged both as a living tableau and as a puppet show.

Afterwards Gay waited with his friends to see what post he would be given when the Court was reorganized. There was reason to hope. The *Fables* for Prince William were a success and he got on well with George II's mistress Mrs Howard. But her influence with the King was dwindling. Pope, too, over estimated his influence with Walpole, speaking in August of making himself 'troublesome' at the Great Man's 'Sunday-tables, & disturbing his Sabbath-days of Rest'.[24] No doubt he had pleaded Gay's cause. He was all the more astounded and incensed therefore when his friend was offered an appointment as Gentleman Usher to the infant Princess Louisa, a post so negligible as to be virtually an insult. With the poet's approval, the disappointed and chastened Gay declined the appointment.

Shortly after this Pope wrote to Swift, telling him the poem on Dulness, sal-vaged from the flames, was finished and would show him 'what a distinguished age we lived in.'[25] At the same time Gay had finished the *Beggar's Opera*. This was another work written partly at Swift's suggestion. Years earlier he had mentioned to Gay that it would be a good idea to write 'a Newgate pastoral, among the whores and thieves.'[26] He had brought up the subject again during his last visit to England. Gay liked the notion and had been busily writing since the summer. Now, as he added the finishing touches to his opera, he told Swift that, since he was not to study the courtiers at close hand, he had time to do the next best thing – to go to Newgate and study the convicts.[27]

Notes

1. G.V. Bennett, *The Tory Crisis in Church and State 1688–1730* (Oxford: Clarendon, 1975), p. 276.
2. *Corr.* 2: 218.
3. *Corr.* 2: 325.
4. *Corr.* 2: 152.
5. Ibid.
6. *The Drapier's Letters to the People of Ireland*, ed Herbert Davis (Oxford: Clarendon, 1935), 2nd edn, 1965.
7. *Corr.* 2: 321–2.
8. *Corr.* 2: 372 and note.
9. *The Correspondence of Jonathan Swift*, ed Harold Williams, 5 vols (Oxford: Clarendon, 1963–65) 3: 130.
10. Robert Halsband, *Lord Hervey* (Oxford: Clarendon, 1973), p. 121. Hervey was describing dinners at Houghton but the standard of hospitality was much the same at Chelsea.
11. *Corr.* 1: 359.
12. *Corr.* 2: 380.
13. *Corr.* 2: 381.
14. *Corr.* 2: 412.
15. *Corr.* 2: 384.
16. *Corr.* 2: 413.
17. *Corr.* 2: 412.
18. *The Craftsman 1726–1736.* Nos 1 to 511 (London: R. Francklin, 1737), Dedication to Volume 1.
19. John 'Orator' Henley in *The Hyp-Doctor*, 2–9 November 1731. See also Simon Varey, '*The Craftsman*: A Historical and Critical Account,' unpub. diss. (Cambridge University, 1976).
20. *John, Lord Hervey, Some Materials Towards Memoirs of the Reign of George II*, ed Romney Sedgwick, 3 vols (London: Cresset, 1931), 1:24.
21. *The Prose Works of Jonathan Swift*, ed Herbert Davis and others, 14 vols (Oxford: Clarendon, 1939–68), 2: 219.
22. *Corr.* 3: 81.
23. *Corr.* 2: 442.
24. *Corr.* 2: 441.
25. *Corr.* 2: 456.
26. *Corr.* 1: 360.
27. *Corr.* 2: 455.

CHAPTER SEVENTEEN

Into the Arena

On 29 January 1728 Pope went to the Lincoln's Inn Fields Theatre for the first night of the *Beggar's Opera*. As he sat waiting for the performance to start he was apprehensive. Cibber had turned the work down for Drury Lane, not only because he had quarrelled with Gay, but because he did not think this low life piece could succeed. Reading the text over, Congreve said, 'It would either take greatly, or be damned confoundedly.'[1] It did not help Pope's state of mind that now, before the curtain went up, the audience was restive because there was no introductory music. The manager sent one of the actors out front to apologize. He was nervous too and stammered, 'Ladies and Gentlemen, we – we – beg you'll not call for first and second music, because – because you all know, that there is never any music at all in an opera.'[2] This put everyone back in a good humour. There was no sign of a cabal, such as the one that killed *Three Hours After Marriage* and, as soon as the show began, the audience was quiet, almost too quiet. But, during Act I, Pope glanced over to the next box where the Duke of Argyll was sitting and heard him mutter, 'It will do – it must do! I see it in the eyes of them.'[3] Argyll was right. The people in the audience were silent because they were listening to every word spoken and sung on stage. When it was all over, they brought the house down in a clamour of applause.

At a time when a play was a success if it ran for more than a fortnight, Gay and Pope were able to report to Swift that the *Beggar's Opera* had played for fifteen, then forty nights and looked set to last the whole season. Which it did, this first run having sixty-two performances. Gay made about £800. Lavinia Fenton, who starred as Polly, became the toast of the town and married the Duke of Bolton – after understudying that part for twelve years. On hearing her mezzotint was on sale in all the London bookshops, Swift asked Gay to send him a copy to show his curious Irish friends, before they saw and enjoyed the opera themselves, when it was put on in Dublin at the end of April.

Swift also wanted to know whether Walpole had received the Newgate pastoral as an 'affront to him' and prayed to God he had 'for he has held the longest hand at hazard that ever fell to any Sharper's Share.'[4] According to Lord Hervey, Walpole knew full well the opera was about him.[5] On the night the first minister went with his brother Horatio to see it, the audience turned and stared pointedly in his direction during the song, 'That was levell'd at Me.' He smiled back and, with his customary aplomb, called for an encore.[6] The theatre goers were disarmed, but no small part of their delight over Gay's exuberant piece

17.1   John Gay. Godfrey Kneller, *c.* 1713

came from their appreciation of the apt comparison between the way Walpole ran his Ministry and the way Peachum managed the pickpockets and highwaymen who passed in and out of Newgate. Even Sir Robert's colleagues, who knew what a very able chief minister he was, had no illusions about his morals. There was hardly any need to explain the political allegory in the *Beggar's Opera* to men and women who were used to seeing Walpole feature regularly in the *Craftsman*, thinly disguised as one reprobate after another, from assorted countries and times. But just in case the audience had missed any of the finer points, on 17 February no. 85 of that Opposition journal was devoted to an explication of the political parallels in Gay's work.

The *Dunciad*, the third Scriblerian attack on Walpole's England, was supposed to come next but instead, a few weeks after the *Beggar's Opera* opened in London, Pope published *Peri Bathous, Or, The Art of Sinking* on 8 March. Apparently the poem on Dulness was too long to go into the *Miscellany*, for which it had been intended and, in any case, Pope was still revising it. The prose piece and the poem were closely related, both of them being about bad writing, with Pope naming those contemporaries he considered guilty. In both works, therefore, Pope was acting as a literary gatekeeper, laying down the criteria by which poetry, including his own, should be judged.[7]

The Art of Sinking, like *An Essay on Criticism*, was a literary manifesto. When Pope was twenty-one, he gave Longinus pride of place among the critics he commended in the *Essay*. Now, at the age of forty he took the author of *On the Sublime* as his chief mentor, *The Art of Sinking* being an upside down version of the Greek treatise. When Longinus lists the things that are necessary for great writing he gives as sources of literary excellence: notable language, vigorous feeling, a unified structure and, most important of all, 'a firm grasp of ideas.'[8] Pope pursues this last point with hilarious vigour throughout *The Art of Sinking*, identifying writers who fail to measure up. He finds no shortage of fatuous utterances but gives the literal-minded Theobald a special commendation for his line, 'None but himself can be his own parallel.'[9]

As an overture to the *Dunciad*, Pope's treatise did two things. It prepared readers for one of the mock epic's main themes, which was that a cultural decline reflected a moral decline in the nation, a theme also upheld in the *Craftsman*. At the same time, because it was all about writing, it deflected the attention of the public away from politics and encouraged readers to expect that the *Dunciad* would be more of the same, in particular, the poet's revenge on his literary foes. In the event, the majority of people read both works in this way. However the poem also contained the political attack on the Whig administration, hoped for by Swift and Gay. Pope indulged in diversionary tactics before its publication because, even though he now had active Tory supporters again, he still felt vulnerable as a Papist and in need of camouflage.

Pope continued to be politic rather than political. Well before the *Dunciad* appeared, he instructed Richard Savage, to spread rumours about it in Grub

Street. This strategy succeeded, if the frenzied scene on 18 May is anything to go by. According to Savage:

> On the Day the book was first vended, a Crowd of Authors beseig'd the Shop. Entreaties, Advices, Threats of Law, and Battery, nay Cries of Treason were all employ'd to hinder the coming out of the *Dunciad*. On the other Side, the Booksellers and Hawkers made as great efforts to procure it.[10]

As well as concentrating the minds of readers on one aspect of the poem, how better could a writer have organized the advance publicity for his work?

Pope had three main targets in the *Dunciad*: his own enemies, Whig party hacks and bad writers in general. These groups overlap so that, as often as not, one victim is all three things at once. Nevertheless it is useful to view Pope's poem from different angles, seeing it, first of all, as an act of personal vengeance, next as a political poem and, finally, as a comment on the cultural scene in 1728.

There is no doubt Pope was determined to wreak his revenge on the nest of hornets that had plagued him, virtually since the beginning of his career. Year after year the attacks came, all of them hard hitting, some of them obscene. Since the law of libel, as we know it, did not exist in the eighteenth century, no legal redress was available to Pope against Gildon, Oldmixon, Burnet, Duckett and others, no matter what they said about him. Given that he was congenitally incapable of not retaliating, it was only to be expected that he would go on the offensive, sooner or later. The only surprising thing was the comprehensive and original form of his counter attack.

Some of the people Pope pilloried could take care of themselves. When Richard Bentley found his way into the *Dunciad*, he dismissed the matter with a growl, 'I talked against his Homer,' he explained, 'and the portentous cub never forgives'.[11] Nothing a portentous (or poetic cub) cub said was likely to change men's minds about Bentley, whose reputation was established, while less illustrious members of the *Dunciad* cast could be sure of the price of a meal if they penned counter attacks – which they did by the score.

Sawney (1728), one of the more adroit of these attacks, was the work of James Ralph, who then found himself impaled in the *Dunciad Variorum*. Ralph was also the author of a neo-gothic poem called *Night*. This has not conferred immortality on him, but Pope ensured we know about it with a couplet:

> Silence, ye Wolves! While Ralph to Cynthia howls,
> And makes Night hideous – Answer him ye Owls!
>
> (*Dunciad* 3: 165–6)

Ralph then complained 'that he had near been famished by this line. None of the Booksellers would employ him'.[12] Actually though, Ralph went on to have a successful career as a journalist, ending up with a Government pension of £300 a year.[13] So one could argue that Pope did him a good turn by discouraging his poetic ambitions.

Nevertheless, there were writers whose posthumous reputations have suffered because they featured in the mock epiç. This was particularly the case with women who were often marginalized in the literary world and, until recently, only remembered because of what Pope said about them. For instance, while Elizabeth Thomas lived there were those who knew her as Dryden's 'Corinna,' because Dryden suggested she adopt that pen-name and paid her a back handed compliment in telling her that her verses were 'too good to be a Woman's'.[14] Then, after she died in 1731, her lively satires were forgotten, until Roger Lonsdale included some of them in the *Oxford Anthology of Eighteenth-Century Women Poets* in 1989. Up to that point, she had been remembered, if at all, as Cromwell's Sappho, who let Curll have Pope's youthful letters to his friend for ten guineas and was punished in the *Dunciad*. There she makes an unforgettable entrance during the games. Curll has just overtaken Lintot in the race when suddenly:

> Full in the middle way there stood a lake,
> Which Curll's Corinna chanc'd that morn to make,
> (such was her wont, at early morn to drop
> Her evening cates before his neighbour's shop),
> Here fortun'd Curll to slide ... (*Dunciad* 2: 69–73)

When Cromwell protested about these lines, pointing out that Mrs Thomas had sold Curll the correspondence because she was almost penniless, Pope issued a half-hearted retraction, which appeared in the next few editions of his poem, only to be withdrawn in 1735.

Pope rarely humiliated anyone to the extent he humiliated Mrs Thomas, nor was he always so obdurate. According to one of his contemporaries, he relented even towards Lady Mary before the end.[15] However, Pope did not punish Mrs Thomas just because she had sold his letters. It looks as though the two of them had never got on very well. For one thing, she had been an ardent supporter of King William, which would not have predisposed Pope towards her when they first met. How their relationship developed thereafter is suggested by one of the counter-attacks on the *Dunciad* published by Curll in 1728. *Codrus ... To which is added, Farmer Pope and his Son. A Tale* was anonymous but Pope, who employed Savage to find out who had written what, did not doubt that Mrs Thomas was the author.

Codrus describes Pope as Mrs Thomas would have known him, when he first came to London and was taken up by Wycherley and Cromwell. It gives much the same view of him as the one held by Gildon who, seeing an awkward boy in homespun clothes, with his own cropped hair, mistook him for one of Wycherley's tenants. Whether Pope was right or not in supposing Mrs Thomas had written *Codrus*, he obviously associated her with those people on the literary fringe who had been snobbish and patronizing at the beginning of his career.

The author of *Codrus* made much of Pope's humble origins, saying he was only excused from labouring alongside his father in the fields because he was consumptive, adding he was poor and able to stay in London, only because Wycherley paid for his board and lodging. Mrs Thomas had touched a raw place in Pope who had made himself accepted as a gentleman. He minded being sneered at as a parvenu, just as he winced at the thought that the coffee house clientele laughed because they saw him as the tall and imposing Wycherley's stunted hanger-on.[16] In her poems such as 'True Effigies of a Certain Squire,' Mrs Thomas viewed men with a caustic eye. To Pope she was like 'Phillis' – perhaps she was 'Phillis'. Significantly, in 1710, when he sent Cromwell his rondeau on the lady who had ridiculed his physical shortcomings, he had said, 'I desire you to show Sappho'.[17]

In the days when Pope was a poet anxious to make his name, Sappho, alias Dryden's Corinna, had been a superior person, too genteel to write for 'sordid Gain' or 'popular Applause'.[18] In 1728 Pope derived unholy satisfaction in driving home how she had degraded herself, by selling her soul (as well as his letters) to London's most unsavoury publisher.

Pope was unconcerned when the public decided the mock epic was his response to individuals who had attacked him. If men believed he was waging a personal vendetta, this was less dangerous than being named as the author of an anti-Government poem. Yet this is one of the things the *Dunciad* was. So to be on the safe side, Pope protected himself from possible prosecution by publishing his work anonymously. While to save his printer, he pretended the poem was published in Dublin. His friends knew the poem had a political dimension. Some months before it appeared, Swift hoped to see 'Pope's Dulness knock down the *Beggar's Opera*,' though not until it had 'fully done its Jobb,' just as earlier the opera had 'knockt down Gulliver'.[19] He thought of all three works as blows struck for the Tory Opposition.

Pope struck his blow for the Opposition by attacking Walpole's rapidly expanding propaganda machine. The *Dunciad* is a palimpsest, its sub-text visible as soon as we ask which political side the dunces are on. Pope does not say but, almost without exception, the men and women he arraigns are Whigs. One third of the men and women he pilloried were writers for, and publishers of, political newspapers and journals. They made up the largest single group of victims. A token number: Mist, Molloy and Roper, opposed the Government. All the rest defended it

The rewards Whig propagandists received for their services ranged from a pittance to a pension while some joined the ranks of placemen. To give just a few examples; Pope's long term enemy George Duckett, who was one of the *Pasquin* authors, was made Commissioner of Excise, Thomas Gordon was bought by Walpole with the office of First Commissioner of Wine Licences and, at different times, Edward Roome and Philip Horneck were appointed Solicitor to the Treasury.[20] James Pitt (dubbed 'Mother Osborne' by the

Craftsman, to put him on a par with Mother Wiseborne, the Covent Garden 'Madam'), was given a post in the Customs House for his work on the *London Journal* and the *Daily Gazeteer*. While Matthew Concanen who wrote for the *Daily Courant*, afterwards becoming Editor of the *British Journal*, was made Attorney General of Jamaica in 1732.[21]

The strategies Pope had employed to protect himself, while launching an attack on the Whig journalists, succeeded in the short term. It was another three years before one of Walpole's paid informers, John Henley, wrote of the *Dunciad* 'abusing certain Gentlemen on a parallel Motive as the *Craftsman* traduces the Government.'[22]

As well as waging a personal vendetta and a political campaign in the *Dunciad*, Pope mounted a defence of culture against what he thought of as barbarism. A self-appointed guardian of critical standards, he saw himself as a warrior hero, though now he figures more as a literary Canute. Well before the end of the twentieth century the Western cultural tradition came under attack because it excluded so much. In the process Pope was seen first as an elitist, largely responsible for establishing 'the distinction between "classic" and "popular" writers and writing.'[23] While, more recently, he has come to be regarded as a reactionary, opposed to the literary market place and the emergence of the professional author.[24]

Pope was undoubtedly an elitist and proud of it. He had an exalted idea of poetry. Homer was his first mentor, followed by Longinus and the most acclaimed writers in the ancient and modern world. He believed that a poet must serve an apprenticeship, such as the one he had undergone himself, if he was to write well. This did not mean, however, that he was opposed to popular culture. He contributed to it – rather more often than other leading English poets have done. As well as rumbustious pamphlets, aimed at Curll and others, he wrote broadsheet ballads, set to familiar tunes – the kind of thing sold by street hawkers for twopence or threepence a copy. So, even as he was composing the *Dunciad* in 1727, he penned *The Discovery or, The Squire turn'd Ferret*. This 'Excellent New Ballad' sung to the '*Tune of High Boys! Up go we*,' told the story of Mary Toft of Godalming who had caused a sensation that year when she claimed to have given birth to rabbits![25] The part of Pope's many-sided nature that led him to express himself in such works helps to account for the cheerful atmosphere in the *Dunciad*, commented upon by several readers.[26] The dunces, presided over by the Smithfield Muses, are enjoying themselves as if they were at Bartholemew Fair. Pope's mock-epic describes a carnival.

It is true that in the *Dunciad* popular writers such as Tom D'Urfey and Ned Ward get short shrift but their unpretentious ephemera caused Pope no pain. He was however alarmed by a growing body of authors who wanted to be taken seriously, yet could not be bothered to learn their craft and/or lacked intellectual integrity.

17.2   An Author & Bookseller. Thomas Rowlandson, engraved by the artist

James Ralph, for instance failed on both these counts. When someone suggested he studied how plays were constructed before he wrote one, he smiled cheerfully and assured his adviser that 'Shakespeare writ without rules'.[27] Then when he found his niche as a political journalist, he turned his coat at regular intervals. He was employed as a hack for Walpole on the *Daily Courant* until 1735. He found himself out of a job in that year however, when various Government newspapers were amalgamated to form the *Daily Gazeteer*. Whereupon he lost no time offering his services to the Opposition. Later on in life he wrote anonymously for Lord Bute, even while he was receiving a pension from Bute's failing rival, the Duke of Newcastle.[28] Over the years he proved himself to be an effective and mischievous journalist, producing sensational copy, guaranteed to appeal to the mob. In one of his last assignments he wrote a series of articles attacking the 1753 Bill to grant Jews naturalization. In this campaign he produced arguments that were to become depressingly familiar in later centuries, conjuring up the idea of a conspiracy, claiming the Government was controlled by Jewish money – in particular, the money of Sampson Gideon. 'England' Ralph thundered, was becoming a 'Country where Gideon the Fleecer would take the place of all the Genius, Knowledge and Virtue it ever produc'd.'[29]

One of the things that has always pained readers of the *Dunciad* is Pope's lack of pity for writers who did not know where their next meal was coming from, as if as James Ralph said, 'Want of a dinner made a fool'.[30] Possessing supreme talent himself, Pope could not understand the compulsion which causes the less gifted to gamble on achieving fame and fortune through writing, when there are easier ways of making a living. Furthermore these hacks, obstinately pursuing a career for which they were unfitted, were letting the side down. Pope had striven to make himself respected and accepted in genteel society as a professional writer. One of his motives in writing his poem was to disassociate himself from Grub Street.

Taking the larger view, he also foresaw a time when the bad would overwhelm the good. As was suggested earlier the *Dunciad* describes a carnival. Carnivals, particularly the medieval ones analysed by Mikhail Bakhtin, provided a necessary outlet in strictly ordered societies just because, while they lasted, hierarchies were overturned, rules flouted and the participants delighted in all that was grotesque and indecent.[31] This was something that Pope with his anarchic streak was drawn to. Carnivals however are temporary. Should they become permanent, civilization cannot survive and as Pope concluded, 'universal Darkness covers all'.

In the *Dunciad* Pope was reacting to the new commercial world of literature. He was part of this world himself, keeping an eye on the market and driving hard bargains with publishers. It was no secret that he made money from poetry. But he did not sell his soul. Nor was he alone in objecting to those who produced trash for cash. As the century wore on there was widespread concern about the proliferation of these drudges of the pen, with both Dr Johnson and Oliver Goldsmith, professional writers themselves, calling them to book.[32]

The world Pope described is a familiar one to readers in the twenty-first century. It would not be difficult to find modern equivalents for his contentious academics, journalists who hitch their star to the nearest band wagon and publishers who market sensational trivia and, were he writing today, Pope would be able to add to his list of targets – including among them, female biographers of famous poets, perhaps. Furthermore, according to a recent survey, impoverished authors still predominate in a latter day Grub Street.[33] However, the fear that art and learning would be totally eclipsed has not been realized – as yet. Writers whose works bear rereading continue to co-exist with the purveyors of fashionable ephemera.

The eighteenth century dunces took their revenge but, despite the uproar it caused, no one took legal action over the mock epic. Everyone wanted to read it, including George II. So Walpole presented him with a copy of the *Dunciad Variorum*, whereupon the King declared the poet was 'a very honest man'.[34] A year later Arbuthnot, writing to Swift told him, 'Pope is now the great reigning poetical favourite'.[35]

The *Dunciad* was both a personal and public statement. In the first place Pope was defending himself when he launched his onslaught on his political and literary opponents. Similarly by setting himself up as the 'Lord Paramount-wou'd-be of Mount Parnassus,' as one of his victims put it, he was attempting to fix the principles by which he expected his work to be judged by readers.[36]

Pope's career was flourishing again even though he was troubled in his private life. His circle of old familiar friends was shrinking. First Congreve died suddenly on 19 January 1729. Then Gay was virtually adopted by the Duke and Duchess of Queensberry and went to live with them on their Wiltshire estate. Partially offsetting these losses, Patty Blount was now the poet's constant companion, though he was embarrassed by Teresa, who drew the attention of the Catholic community to this fact, when she herself began a much talked of affair with a married man. Worse still, Pope's mother fell ill and when she recovered he realized she was going senile. And if that was not enough, his health was also worse than it had been before. Piles were a new misery, in addition to headaches and recurrent digestive disorders. Early in 1728 he went to Bath for ten weeks, without feeling any better at the end of that time.

None of these things stopped Pope's creative flow. Having rediscovered himself as a poet, the writing of poetry became the central thing in his life again. When he was engaged in doing what he knew he could do so well, he was completely absorbed and the everyday world with its problems and pains was excluded from his consciousness.[37] The first possible reference to *An Essay on Man* came in November 1729, in a letter from Bolingbroke to Swift. In it he spoke 'with abundant partiality' of a poem his friend at Twickenham was writing. Pope enclosed the letter with one of his own, explaining the work mentioned was 'a system of Ethics in the Horatian way'.[38] He now spent much of his time with Bolingbroke, who over the next few years became the closest friend he had.

Notes

1. Spence, 244.
2. William Oxberry, *Dramatic Biography* (London, 1825), iv, 177.
3. Spence, 245.
4. *Corr.* 2: 475.
5. *Lord Hervey's Memoirs*, ed Romney Sedgwick, 3 vols (London, Cresset, 1931), 1: 98. For discussion of Gay's political stance see *John Gay and the Scriblerians*, eds Peter Lewis and Nigel Wood (London: Vision Press, 1989), especially J.A. Downie, 'Gay's Politics', pp. 44–61.
6. *Memoirs of Macklin* (London, 1804), pp. 53–7.
7. Mihaly Csikszentmihalyi, *Creativity: Flow and the Psychology of Discovery and Invention* (New York: HarperCollins, 1996), p. 262.
8. *'Longinus' On the Sublime*, ed D.A. Russell (Oxford: Clarendon, 1964), 8: 14.
9. *The Prose Works of Alexander Pope, Volume II 1725–1744*, ed Rosemary Cowler (Oxford: Blackwell, 1986), p. 199.
10. *A Collection of Pieces in Verse and Prose ... By Mr. Savage* (1732), p. vi.
11. James Henry Monk, *The Life of Richard Bentley, D.D.*, 2 vols (London, 1833), 2: 372.
12. *Notes and Queries*, cciii (1958), 348.
13. John Burke Shipley, 'James Ralph: Pretender to Genius.' Unpublished dissertation, Columbia University, 1963.
14. *Eighteenth-Century Women Poets*, ed Roger Lonsdale (Oxford University Press, 1989), p. 32.
15. William Ayre, *Memoirs of the Life and Writings of Alexander Pope* (1745), 2: 199. Nevertheless, it is thought widely that Pope was unduly harsh about women writers. See, for instance, Brean S. Hammond, *Professional Imaginative Writing in England 1670–1740* (Oxford: Clarendon, 1997), ch. 6 and Christa Knellwolf, *A Contradiction Still: Representations of Women in the Poetry of Alexander Pope* (Manchester University Press, 1998), ch. 4.
16. Edmund Curll and Elizabeth Thomas [?] *Codrus: Or, the Dunciad Dissected: Being the Finishing-Stroke. To Which is Added, Farmer Pope and his Son* (London, 1728), p. 7.
17. *Corr.* 1:90.
18. William Ayre, quoted Lonsdale, p. 33.
19. *Corr.* 2: 484.
20. J.A. Downie, 'Walpole "The Poet's Foe"', in *Britain in the Age of Walpole*, ed Jeremy Black (London, Macmillan, 1954), pp. 171–88.
21. *Dictionary of National Biography*.
22. *The Hyp-Doctor*, 29 June 1731.
23. Brean S. Hammond, *Pope* (Brighton: Harvester Press, 1986), p. 129.
24. Brean S. Hammond, *Professional Imaginative Writing in England 1670–1740, 'Hackney for Bread'* (Oxford: Clarendon, 1997). Contrast Hammond's view of Cibber, Ralph and Co. with that given by Pat Rogers two decades earlier in *Hacks and Dunces: Pope, Swift and Grub Street* (London: Methuen, 1975).

194   POPE RECREATES HIMSELF

25. TW. 6: 259–64.
26. See for instance, Howard Erskine-Hill, 'The "New World" of Pope's *Dunciad*', *Renaissance and Modern Studies*, 6 (1962), 47–67 and Emrys Jones, 'Pope and Dulness' in *Pope: Recent Essays*, eds M. Mack and J.A. Winn (Brighton: Harvester Press, 1980), pp. 612–51, especially p. 639. Also, James Noggle, 'Skepticism and the Sublime Advent of Modernity in the 1742 *Dunciad*', *The Eighteenth Century: Theory and Interpretation,* vol. 37, no.1 (Spring, 1996), 22–41.
27. Pope's note, TW. 5: 165.
28. Shipley, ch. 12 and 13. See also *Dunciad in Four Books*, ed Valerie Rumbold (London: Longman, 1999), editorial note pp. 238–9.
29. Shipley, p. 520.
30. *Sawney. An Heroic Poem* (1728), p.vii.
31. Mikhail Bakhtin, *Rabelais and his World*, trans. Helene Iswolsky (Cambridge, Massachusetts: MIT Press, 1965).
32. John Brewer, *The Pleasures of the Imagination: English Culture in the Eighteenth Century* (New York: Farrar Straus Giroux, 1997), pp. 146–9. In the eighteenth century, as now, pessimists and optimists were in opposing camps regarding the future of civilization. In 1733 Samuel Madden wrote his *Memoirs of the Twentieth Century*, with its futuristic vision of London as the cultural capital of the world. Then James Thomson in *Liberty* (1735–36) and Paul Whitehead in *Manners* (1739) came to optimistic conclusions. Nowadays, the pessimistic view of civilization and culture is maintained by John Lukacs, *A Thread of Years* (Yale University Press, 1998) and by many others.
33. Kate Poole, 'Love, not Money', *The Author* (Summer, 2000), cxi, 2, 58–66.
34. *Corr*. 3: 26n.
35. *Correspondence of Jonathan Swift*, ed Harold Williams, 5 vols (Oxford: Clarendon, 1963–65).
36. *The Gentleman's Miscellany: In Verse and Prose ... Dedicated to the Most Fallibly Fallible Pope Alexander or Alexander Pope. By Sir Butterfly Maggot, Kt.* (1730).
37. For a description of the main elements in the 'flow experience' see Csikszentmihalyi, pp. 110–13.
38. *Corr*. 3: 81.

CHAPTER EIGHTEEN

Bolingbroke:
The 'Master of the Song'?

If Pope's contemporaries had voted on who was the most gifted man of his generation, the clear leader in such a poll would have been Bolingbroke. Gay took it for granted he was 'the most accomplished of his species.'[1] Soon after they met, Swift said he was 'the greatest young man' he 'ever knew' and later told him, 'It is you were my hero.'[2] Chesterfield, who was not given to hero worship, described the effect he had on his political opponents in the days when, as a brilliant, young Secretary of War, he spoke in Parliament. 'Like Belial in Milton, "He made the worse appear the better course"'. All the internal and external advantages and talents of an orator are undoubtedly his: figure, voice, elocution, knowledge.'[3]

Chesterfield might have added energy and stamina. Bolingbroke was a hard drinker (mostly burgundy and champagne) and made no secret of his strenuous sex life. There was usually some story doing the rounds about his more flamboyant escapades, such as one recounted by a startled old gentleman who came upon the minister running with some of his companions, inebriated and naked, across St James's Park. He needed little sleep. Whether he was up till dawn with a bottle and whore, or reading through papers in his office, he could still appear, clear-headed and forceful, at Queen Anne's cabinet meeting a few hours later. He was only thirty-six when Anne died and he was dismissed, never to enter Parliament again.[4]

By the time Bolingbroke returned to live in England at the age of forty-seven, he had settled down somewhat. He now got up at the time he used to go to bed, but he had lost none of his charisma. He made as great an impact on his Whig enemies as he did on his Tory friends. Lady Mary Wortley Montagu recorded a single meeting with him, when she said, 'He appeared in the corner of the drawing-room, in the exact similitude of Satan.'[5] He evoked some of this supernatural horror even in Walpole who, in 1734, stood up in the House of Commons to denounce the man whose presence was never seen, but always felt there. In a blistering speech pointing out how his rival had betrayed every leader and every cause he espoused, Walpole did not name Bolingbroke, but referred to him throughout as the Anti-Minister, thereby conjuring up a vision of Anti-Christ.

In the five years before Walpole made that speech, Bolingbroke had pressed him hard, using William Pulteney and Sir William Wyndham as his spokesmen in the Commons. Each year after the newly formed Opposition got into its

18.1   Henry St John, Lord Bolingbroke. Godfrey Kneller, *c.* 1713

stride, the Commons was the scene of a major drama, directed by Bolingbroke.

In 1730 this was the Dunkirk issue. Bolingbroke spent £4000 of his own money on preliminary investigations. These being completed, Wyndham stood up in the Commons on 10 February and exploded a bombshell as he told members how, contrary to the agreement signed with England, the French had rebuilt the fortifications at Dunkirk. Wyndham had ships' captains waiting at the door to give facts and figures. The House was in an uproar. Walpole had not expected any of this, but he calmed everyone down by inviting the captains to come in and make their report. Then he played for time. After ten days of intensive negotiations with France, and much lobbying at home, he was ready to face the House again. By then he had received, and had read, an assurance from Fleury, his French counterpart, that the clandestine fortifications were already being dismantled.[6] This episode was characteristic of a political campaign in which Bolingbroke went on the offensive and the chief minister outmanoeuvred him, retreating if he had to, but never allowing himself to be routed.

Walpole was sceptical when the Opposition roused the people with cries of 'Patriotism' and 'Liberty.' He was the hedgehog who knew one thing, his concern being the peaceful prosperity of England. He was superb at coping with immediate problems, but rarely troubled himself about the long term implications of his policies. Bolingbroke was the fox who knew many things. He often changed his mind and course of action, but he was more imaginative than his rival. He could argue that the corruption Walpole fostered, in order to keep the Whigs in power, would ultimately undermine the constitution and said the chief minister's determined efforts to control the press paved the way to tyranny.

Actually the press was harder to control in this period than one might suppose. Newspapers were not allowed to report Parliamentary debates, but Bolingbroke made sure the issues involved reached the public with the articles he and his supporters wrote each week in the *Craftsman*, even though that journal was investigated eight times in the first four years of its existence by a Government committee, responsible for looking into cases of seditious libel.[7]

Once he was in England again, Bolingbroke cultivated Pope's acquaintance assiduously. By 1730 Mrs Pope was so vague and forgetful that her son hesitated to go far from Twickenham. He went on no rambles that year, telling Gay in October that he had not spent more than three days in London in the last four months. When he was not at home he was at Dawley, only four miles away. Few men were immune to Bolingbroke's personal magic and Pope was no exception. Nor was the spell ever broken. Spence, visiting Twickenham in the last few months of the poet's life, mentioned Bolingbroke saying, 'I really think there is something in that great man which looks as if he was placed here by mistake.' Pope assented eagerly. 'There is so', he replied, 'and when the comet appeared to us a month or two ago I had sometimes an imagination that it might possibly be come to our world to carry him home, as a coach comes to one's door for other visitors.'[8]

Bolingbroke said *An Essay on Man* was written at his instigation.[9] Pope also discussed the work in progress as he composed the poem, writing some of it in the library at Dawley. So the question of how far he was influenced by his forceful and persuasive friend inevitably arises. Bathurst had no doubt about the matter. He told a friend he had seen a prose draft of the *Essay* in Bolingbroke's handwriting 'and that Mr. Pope did no more than put it into verse.'[10] Unfortunately the manuscript he spoke of disappeared and since then the matter has been exhaustively debated.[11]

Without rehearsing all the arguments here, it is worth mentioning that Pope, unlike Bolingbroke, had a religious temperament. His aim in the *Essay* was to reconcile the theories of modern Christian theologians and the ancient pagan philosophers in a new synthesis. Because many of the beliefs Pope held intuitively would have been impossible to prove logically, it is unlikely he discussed them with his exclusively rationalist friend when they talked about the poem. Bolingbroke, in his turn, concealed the extent to which he was a religious sceptic. His more explicit thoughts on theological questions were not published until after his death. They found a common meeting ground in that neither of them was narrowly sectarian, believing that to be so produced the bigotry that divided men and prevented them working for the common good. Both were looking for a religious philosophy that would be acceptable to all reasonable men. However, even that basis for agreement was less solid than we might suppose because they had different definitions of reason.

Reason for Bolingbroke was the deductive faculty that makes four by adding two and two. Reason for Pope was more complex. There was 'simple Reason', corresponding to intuition and 'Wit oblique', corresponding to our analytical ability (III: 230–31). 'Simple reason' was a steady light which enabled our primitive ancestors to arrive at a knowledge of God. 'Wit oblique' illuminated fragments of the truth in dazzling flashes but distorted the total picture. Pope did not invent the distinction he made here. It had an ancient history and had been kept alive by (among many others) Benjamin Whichcote, a follower of Pope's favourite theologian Erasmus. Whichcote wrote of a 'highest purest reason' which makes us 'acquainted with the inwards of things', contrasting this with the inferior analytical, deductive faculty which 'makes no impression on the inward sense.'[12]

The opening lines of *An Essay on Man* make it clear the work is addressed to Bolingbroke, while the poem ends with twenty-five lines in his praise as 'master of the poet and song' (IV: 347). Pope's friend was the audience he kept in mind as he composed his *Essay* – the intelligent, modern reader he must convince – but the song had more than one master and there are more things in it than were dreamed of in Bolingbroke's philosophy.

The overall aim of the *Essay* was to edify mankind. 'Mr. Pope's present design is wholly upon human actions and to reform the mind,' wrote Spence in May 1730 and, a few months later, the poet spoke of contributing 'some honest and moral purposes in writing on human life and manners, not exclusive of religious regards.'[13] When Pope decided to instruct his readers in this way, he was both giving expression to his pedagogic side – one of the many disparate elements in his personality – and responding to the mood of the times, which was becoming increasingly moralistic as the century wore on. Pope's change of direction was also an example of his instinctive feel for the demands of the marketplace.

An Essay on Man was to be primarily a work of ethics therefore, its aim being to teach men how to live, the main message to men being to love one another – 'All Mankind's concern is Charity' (III: 308). Bolingbroke would have endorsed this edict. He thought all Christian precepts about brotherly love were a matter of common sense. For men to try and live in any other way was impractical because it was destructive. He wrote in *The True Use of Retirement and Study*, 'The Christian religion is extremely plain, and requires no great learning or deep meditation to develop it.'[14]

However Pope's ethical system is raised on a metaphysical belief which he embraces with an emotional fervour, far removed from his friend's cool deism. His poem gives a picture of the universe which has an underlying order and harmony. This was his abiding conviction.[15] Everything is interdependent. It is a harmony because, although 'ALL subsists by elemental strife' (I: 169), the opposing elements are reconciled and the Many are ultimately One. God is immanent as well as transcendent and his world is not dead and wooden but vital and magic. Pope's muse soars in the passage where he describes the universe as he feels it to be:

> All are but parts of one stupendous whole,
> Whose body Nature is, and God the soul;
> That, chang'd thro' all, and yet in all the same,
> Great in the earth, as in th'aethereal frame,
> Warms in the sun, refreshes in the breeze,
> Glows in the stars, and blossoms in the trees,
> Lives thro' all life, extends thro' all extent'
> Spreads undivided, operates unspent,
> Breathes in our soul, informs our mortal part,
> As full, as perfect, in vile Man that mourns,
> As the rapt Seraph that adores and burns;
> To him, no high, no low, no great, no small;
> He fills, he bounds, connects, and equals all. (I: 257–80)

Man is presumably in mourning for a fallen world. The golden age is no more, yet the emphasis in these lines is on earth as a wonderful and noble star.

In speaking of Man, Pope describes him as a microcosm of the universe he inhabits, so that in him too, opposites must be reconciled to produce a harmonious whole. In the golden age when there was 'Union the bond of all things' (III: 150), men lived in accord with themselves, with each other, and with the rest of creation. This happy state of affairs came to an end when men came to see themselves as separate from the rest of creation, instead of an integral part of it. They had walked with beasts, joint tenants of the shade but then they turned on animals and killed them. After that they turned on each other and waged wars. Their present task was to try and recreate, in themselves and in the societies they formed, the harmony they had lost.

In Man's own being passion and reason are opposites that can be reconciled. In Pope's philosophy neither passion nor the flesh are deplored. 'Each sex desires alike, 'till two are one. / Nor ends the pleasure with the fierce embrace; / They love themselves, a third time, in their race' (III: 122–4). Sexual love, therefore, can lead to a more comprehensive regard for one's partner, then to love of a family and thence to the love of the larger family of mankind. The whole process begins with self love, which implies man's acceptance of his human nature, not a puritanical denial of it.

The wish to describe a natural religion acceptable to all reasonable men meant that Pope did not include anything in his system of belief made known to men through Biblical revelation. So he did not use the Fall and the concept of Original Sin to explain why the world had declined from its first perfection. As a result the least successful part of the *Essay* is where he discusses the problem of evil. He does not explain evil so much as explain it away. For him, as for some of his Christian and pagan predecessors, evil was unreal.[16] So he can sound glib and complacent even if what he says is doctrinally sound. Those who believe the Creator is just and good have to believe 'Whatever is, is right' (I: 294). The earliest manuscript gives us a gloss for this line, 'Thy Will be done, on earth as it is in Heaven.'[17] But in formulating his aphorism Pope leaves no room for grief. He, if anyone, is entitled to say, 'See ... the cripple sing' (II: 267), but in saying so he chooses to ignore the many men and women who are dehumanized and destroyed by suffering, whether this is the result of natural disaster, or is inflicted on them by their fellows. A determination to look on the bright side was in the philosophical air during the Enlightenment, its most famous expression being the Leibnizian theory that all is for the best in the best of possible worlds.[18] Even in the eighteenth century Voltaire found this idea risible.[19] In the twenty-first century such an approach makes *An Essay on Man* seem facile.

It has to be remembered that one of Pope's aims in his poem was to give a view of the world that would be acceptable to Bolingbroke, who approving of the ethical system outlined, could smile at some of the metaphysical flights in the *Essay* as examples of poetic licence.[20] In due course Pope came to doubt Bolingbroke's capabilities as a theologian, saying of him, 'If he ever trifles it must be when he turns Divine.'[21]

It was a different matter when it came to political science. This was Bolingbroke's forte. He was praised for his writings on the subject by Disraeli, who credited him with laying 'the foundation for the future accession of the Tory party to power' because he 'threw to the winds' outmoded and suspect doctrines Tories had previously been saddled with, such as the divine right of kings and passive obedience to them.[22] When Pope touches on politics in *An Essay on Man* he shows he is in complete accord with the philosophy his friend formulated, which gave the Opposition campaign its ideological basis.

In Epistle III Pope describes how men were saved from anarchy at the end of the golden age. They followed nature, observing 'The Ant's republic, and the realm of Bees' (184), forming societies on the same lines. Bolingbroke believed that God instituted 'neither monarchy, nor aristocracy, nor democracy, nor mixed government.'[23] Pope says, 'Thus States were form'd; the name of King unknown, / Till common int'rest plac'd the sway in one' (209–10). Bolingbroke's preferred form of government was a hereditary monarchy, as long as this was divested of mystic significance. Pope too, makes it clear a king's power rests on a contract formed with the people, 'Nature knew no right divine in Men' (236). The people's choice of monarchical government follows nature because a king enacts the same role in the nation as a father does in the family.

Pope goes on to describe what happened in the distant past when kings abused their power and became tyrants. Then a 'Poet or Patriot' (early proto-types of himself and Bolingbroke) came forward to remind men of the lessons taught by nature, 'Relum'd her ancient light' (III. 285ff.). Under their benign influence conflicting interests were reconciled to produce the music of 'a well mix'd State' (294). The well mixed state is Pope's term for Bolingbroke's concept of a balanced government in which the King, the Lords and Commons all have their appointed roles and work for the common good. Pope reinforces his friend's argument at this point by showing how the well mixed state mirrors harmony in the universe, 'Such is the World's great harmony, that springs / From Order, Union, full Consent of things!' (295–6).

By 1730 Bolingbroke was arguing that the political parties had degenerated into factions, dominated by self interest and the wish for power for its own sake. He pointed out that Tories and Whigs now agreed about such fundamental principles as the exclusion of the Stuarts, the right to resist tyranny and the independence of Parliament. So there was no longer any need for parties at all, or rather there must be one party, 'authorized by the voice of the country. It must be formed on principles of common interest. It cannot be united and maintained on particular prejudices, any more than it can, or ought to be, directed to the particular interests of any set of men whatsoever.'[24] Pope showed the same indifference to party divisions when he concluded the political section of *An Essay on Man* by saying, 'For Forms of Government let fools contest; / What e'er is best administer'd, is best' (303–4). An efficiently run tyranny, in which the people are oppressed, is not included in this blanket approval. At the back of Pope's lines is Aristotle's comment in *Politics* that governments are judged by how effective they are in achieving the aim of every good state, the happiness of its inhabitants. Like Sir William Temple, Pope believes that 'those are generally the best Governments where the best Men govern; and let the Sort or Scheme be what it will, those are ill Governments where ill Men govern.'[25]

Because a nation's well being depended on the moral character of those in charge of it, Bolingbroke and Pope agreed that reform began with men, not with the system. Believing that Walpole's Government had gone astray because of egotism and greed, Pope spoke of the need for the poet and patriot to 'restore the Faith and Moral, Nature gave before' (III. 285–6). His work as a satirist and, willy-nilly as a party political writer, was founded on principles laid down in *An Essay on Man*.

Notes

1. *Corr.* 2: 413.
2. Swift's remark, made in 1711, is in *Journal To Stella*, ed Harold Williams, 3 vols (Oxford, 1963), 2: 401 and Gay's, made in 1729 is in *Corr.* 3: 63.
3. 'Lord Chesterfield's Character of Lord Bolingbroke' in David Mallet's edition of Bolingbroke's *Works* (1777), 1: lv.
4. Oliver Goldsmith, 'The Life of Henry St. John, Lord Viscount Bolingbroke', *Collected works of Oliver Goldsmith*, ed Arthur Friedman (Oxford, 1966), 3: 439.
5. Spence, 755n.
6. J.H. Plumb, *Sir Robert Walpole: The King's Minister* (London: Cresset, 1960), pp. 208ff.
7. Simon Varey, '*The Craftsman*: A historical and critical account.' Unpublished dissertation, University of Cambridge, 1976, ch. vii. As Varey points out, Bolingbroke had been responsible for prosecuting political libellists 1710–14, and so (as gamekeeper turned poacher) knew ways round the law. See also Varey's paper on *The Craftsman* in *Telling People What to Think: Early Eighteenth Century Periodicals*, ed J.A. Downie and Thomas Corns (London: Frank Cass, 1993).
8. Spence, 275.
9. *Corr.* 3: 213.
10. Bathurst to Hugh Blair, April 1763 in James Boswell, *Life of Johnson*, ed G.B. Hill, 6 vols (Oxford, 1971), 3: 402.
11. Brean S. Hammond, *Pope and Bolingbroke: A Study of Friendship* (University of Missouri Press, 1984) argues Pope was deeply influenced by his friend. Maynard Mack, *Alexander Pope: A Life* (Yale University Press, 1985), p. 921 suggests the influence was a 'two-way street.' For other contrasting discussions of the origin of Pope's ideas, see Douglas H. White, *Pope and the Context of Controversy: The Manipulation of Ideas in An Essay on Man* (University of Chicago Press, 1970), A.D. Nuttall, *Pope's Essay on Man* (London: Allen & Unwin, 1984) and Ernest Lee Tuveson, *The Avatars of Thrice Great Hermes* (University of Bucknell Press, 1982), pp. 125–35.
12. 'Eight Letters to Dr. Anthony Tuckney and Benjamin Whichcote', included in *Moral and Religious Aphorisms ... published in MDCCIII by Dr. Jeffrey. Now republished with very large additions, by Samuel Salter* (1753). For a fuller account

of Pope's concept of Reason than is given in this chapter, see N. Goldsmith, 'A Reconciliation of Opposites: Concepts of Mind in Pope and Coleridge', *Prose Studies* (May, 1984), pp. 3–23.

13. Spence, 295 and *Corr*. 3: 155.
14. *Works of Lord Bolingbroke*, 4 vols (Philadelphia, 1841), 4: 106.
15. It has sometimes been suggested that Pope's yearning for order and form was, in part a reaction to his disordered and misshapen body. For a recent elaboration of this theory, applied to Pope's polished couplets, see Helen Deutsch, *Resemblance and Disgrace: Alexander Pope and the Deformation of Culture* (Harvard University Press, 1996).
16. Augustine's contention that evil was an absence of good had been expressed by Plotinus, who said evil had no positive value. See *Enneades*, trans. Stephen Mackenna, 2 vols, 3rd edn, rev. B.S. Page (London, 1956), 1: viii. Also Whichcote, *Moral and Religious Aphorisms*, no. 253.
17. Maynard Mack, *Collected in Himself* (University of Delaware Press, 1982), p. 332.
18. *The Theodicy* (1710).
19. *Candide* (1759).
20. As well as the lines 257–80 from the first Epistle quoted here, another passage, lines 7–26 in the third Epistle sees Pope converting the old concept of a Chain of Being into a 'Chain of Love' and endorsing the neoplatonic theory of 'plastic nature', an early version of the life force.
21. The phrase quoted replaced 'he is grown a great Divine', written in a letter to Swift in 1725, *Corr*. 2: 350 and *Works of Alexander Pope*, ed W. Elwin and W.J. Courthope, 10 vols (London, 1871–89), 2: 43.
22. *A Vindication of the English Constitution* (1853).
23. *Works* (1841), 4: 234.
24. 'A Dissertation Upon the Parties', *Works* (1841), 2: 48. Originally published in *The Craftsman*, 1733–34.
25. *Works of Sir William Temple*, 2 vols (1720), 1: 259.

CHAPTER NINETEEN

A New Battlefield

Once Pope had begun to write *An Essay on Man* he stood back from the literary war he had provoked with the *Dunciad*. His foes continued to snipe away in poems and pamphlets but, if and when, Pope returned their fire, he did so indirectly via items he wrote, or got his friends to write, in the *Grub Street Journal*, a new Tory periodical which started up in January 1730. He also showed compassion to one or two of his victims, contributing to a pension for John Dennis and placating Aaron Hill who had objected to being included among the dunces.

By 1730 Pope was on good terms with Walpole, the Court and a cross section of the aristocracy. Pope enjoyed being wooed. 'I now fling off Lords by dozens', he said on one occasion.[1] As that remark suggests, Pope was able to choose his aristocratic friends and when we look at whom he did choose – men such as Harcourt, Burlington, Oxford, Cobham, Bathurst and Bolingbroke – we find they had two things in common. In the first place he found their view of the political and cultural scene broadly sympathetic. Secondly, and even more importantly, they were in a position to help him in any one of a number of ways. In this he had more in common than he would have cared to admit with Colley Cibber, of whom it was said, that he 'above all other Poets of his time, was the *Peculiar Delight* and *Chosen Companion* of the Nobility of England' and as he freely admitted, wrote 'certain of his Works at the *earnest Desire* of *Persons of Quality*.'[2]

Cibber was castigated by Pope and his friends as a shameless sycophant and moron. Their view of him was summed up in 1729, when the Duke of Grafton announced Cibber was to become Poet Laureate. 'Tell, if you can', one of them wrote, 'which did the worse,

> Caligula or Gr[afto]n's gr—ce?
> That made a Consul of a Horse,
> And this the Laureate of an Ass.'[3]

It suited the Opposition to call Cibber a fool which he was not, though he was a banal poet. He had been honoured, despite this shortcoming, because he was shrewd. His system of networking was not really very different from Pope's but, being a Whig and a Protestant, he was an insider, so career building was a simpler matter for him. He did not have to look over his shoulder when he wrote quasi political works. His highly successful *Non-Juror*, which cashed in on the anti-Stuart, anti-Papist hysteria that prevailed after the 1715 rebellion, expressed his own views as well as those of the Government. Later, he said that the fact he was the author of this popular play gave him the edge over several competitors for the Laureateship. Pope had not played an active part in the debate over who should be Laureate. However, his attempt to stay on the sidelines in current controversies came to an abrupt end, as soon as he published his *Epistle to Burlington* in December 1731. In this poem the peer, who was a notable architect and patron, exemplifies the principle laid down in *An Essay on Man*, in that he recreated in his buildings and gardens the harmony and order underlying the universe. By contrast, another magnate whom Pope called Timon, offended against this canon because vanity led him to erect a house and plan an estate merely to display his wealth and enhance his prestige. Timon's Villa flouted nature and was neither beautiful nor useful. Pope considered his poem innocuous. He was reprimanding folly, not vice.

An uproar greeted the *Epistle to Burlington*, which not only took Pope by surprise but was disturbing because he found himself on a new battlefield, no longer Grub Street but the Court and drawing rooms of St James's. The attacks focused on the description of Timon's Villa and were politically inspired. Bolingbroke realized what had happened before his friend did. Somewhat earlier he had prophesied 'The time will come, and who knows how near it may be, when other powers than those of Grub Street, may be drawn against you.'[4] That time had come. Pope was now considered as much an Opposition writer as any of the contributors to the *Craftsman*, one of whom he was suspected of being.

By 1731 the circulation figure of the *Craftsman* had risen to 9,000, with each copy having up to forty readers.[5] After several failed attempts to quell this persistent voice of the Opposition, the Government managed to bring a successful prosecution against its printer Richard Francklin, after the paper leaked details of confidential negotiations between Walpole and the Hapsburg Emperor in January 1731. Francklin was sentenced to one year's imprisonment and fined heavily. However, even this act of retribution failed in its main purpose, as the printer's friends raised the money demanded (over £2,000), and the *Craftsman* continued to pillory the chief minister as usual.

A more effective measure for dealing with Opposition propaganda was Walpole's decision to recruit his own writers to put the Government's point of view to the public. Of these the foremost was Lord Hervey who wrote pamphlets for Walpole from 1729. In 1730 he came to the Minister's aid with a paper which fudged the facts about the Dunkirk fortifications and, as a reward, he was appointed Vice-Chamberlain to the King's Household, as well as being made a Privy Councillor. In September of that year he wrote three more refutations of particular charges made in the *Craftsman*. Then, one dawn in January 1731, he went in the lightly falling snow to Green Park and fought a duel with William Pulteney, who had published a letter calling him a 'delicate hermaphrodite' that is, a homosexual.[6] Each was slightly wounded before the seconds parted them. The duel was the talk of the town. The fact that Hervey had come out of an awkward situation rather well did not inhibit his critics. Quite apart from the *Craftsman*, which naturally backed Pulteney, there was was a brisk sale in ballads, poems and prints commemorating the event, some of which contrived to bring in Walpole. One caricature showed him squinting through a window at the duellists saying, 'Let them cut one another's throats.' As the cartoonist knew, there was no love lost between the chief minister and his conscientious assistant.[7]

The *Epistle to Burlington* appeared therefore in an acrimonious political atmosphere which brought forth a new lampoon of Walpole almost every day. The battle lines were clearly drawn and it was impossible for Pope to keep in with both sides, even though he believed it was better for him as a poet not to be labelled party political. However, staying out of London and controversies did not save him from being associated with the Opposition campaign. Six months before the *Epistle* appeared John Henley made a connection between attacks on the Government in the *Craftsman* and the *Dunciad*.[8] Nor had it escaped notice that for much of the early part of 1731 Pope virtually lived at Dawley, where he went on the supposedly invigorating asses' milk diet. At other times Bolingbroke and his Tory colleagues gathered at the Twickenham villa, soon nicknamed the 'Little Whitehall.'[9]

It has been suggested that, when the Ministry looked at the *Epistle to Burlington*, someone decided Timon's Villa was meant to be Houghton which Walpole had luxuriously refurbished. Whereupon a Government journalist Leonard Welsted was told to write a pamplet, deflecting the public's attention from the chief minister's house, by suggesting that Pope was satirizing Cannons, the equally luxurious home of the Duke of Chandos.[10] Pope always insisted he had not described any specific house in Timon's Villa, though ever since possible models for it have been suggested.[11]

There were seven attacks on Pope in the first part of 1732, all accusing him of ingratitude to Chandos, even though the Duke himself had written to the poet saying he did not believe he was the object of his satire.[12] So Pope used his extensive list of contacts to find out who was behind this latest, disconcerting campaign against him. He discovered there was a cabal, consisting of a few prominent Whigs and courtiers, chief among whom was Hervey, with the journalists Welsted and Concanen as its instruments. Pope named most of his new foes in an ironic defence of his poem which he called *A Master Key to Popery*. Hervey made a first appearance in this pamphlet in the guise of 'Lord Fanny.' However Pope did not publish his counter attack, merely circulating it among his friends. He decided it was better to let the brouhaha die down.

Pope lay low for the rest of 1732. When he had to go to London to see his publisher he stayed incognito in Lord Oxford's house in Dover Street with only Lion the family dog for company.[13] There he spent his time collecting material for the *Epistle to Bathurst*.

The new poem was subtitled *Of the Use of Riches* and was about the responsibilities of wealth. Bathurst had the right attitude because he used his money for public splendour and private charity. The poem's hero, however, is the Man of Ross who, on a comparatively modest income of £500 a year, achieved charitable wonders. He ran his own welfare service, dispensing food and medicines to the needy as well as providing, at his own expense, a waterworks, almshouses and other desirable amenities for the town where he lived. The Man of Ross existed. He was John Kyrle. If Walpole's henchmen had decided to teach Pope a lesson when they raised a storm about Timon, the poet had learned one. From now on he would name a good many of his heroes and villains himself. He also decided to concentrate on castigating vice more than mere folly. Like many another writer he proved better at depicting vice than virtue. His portrait of the 'thrice happy' (l. 275) Kyrle is somewhat cloying, whereas those miserable wretches Vulture Hopkins and Old Cotta are as fascinating as they are appalling. Cotta the miser activates the gothic strain in Pope's imagination. He lives on gruel in the 'old Hall', alone, save for the 'gaunt mastiff growling at the gate.'

> Tenants with sighs the smoakless tow'rs survey,
> And turn th'unwilling steeds another way:
> Benighted wanderers, the forest o'er,
> Curse the sav'd candle, and unop'ning door. (189ff.)

There were plenty of villains, worse than Cotta, for Pope to choose from, Denis Bond of the Charitable Corporation for instance. The Charitable Corporation was founded by a number of gentlemen, some of them Members of Parliament, to lend money to the poor at low interest. When one of the directors suggested they actually do this, Bond turned on him with, 'Damn the Poor' and suggested they go, with the funds they had collected, into the City where they could 'get Money.'[14] When this scam was discovered, the three MPs involved were expelled from the House of Commons. Bond lived the scandal down though. Three years later he was appointed churchwarden of St George's, Hanover Square.

Bond's ringing cry found its way into the *Epistle to Bathurst*. It seemed to speak for a society in which greed had become a virtue. When Pope commented on a society which produced overweening entrepreneurs, crooked financiers and rapacious money lenders, he was reacting to the less attractive aspects of emergent capitalism. His was one of the first voices to make itself heard about the problems capitalism produced – and continues to produce. Furthermore, the solution he came up with has a familiar ring today. Put simply, he advocated tempering the excesses of money men in a competitive society with compassion for one's fellows and unselfish concern for the public good.

Pope did not contemplate overturning the economic system on which society was based. Indeed he was a participant, using entrepreneurial skill in marketing his poetry, speculating in South Sea Company shares and, later, buying stock in

Sun Fire, the first insurance company formed in England. His role as a social and economic moralist was a complex one because, as usual, he strove to reconcile opposites – in this case individual enterprise, necessary for success under capitalism, with love of one's neighbour which was part of the Christian tradition. In seven of his poems he waged war on the attorney Peter Walter, who was also a land agent and a money lender, not only because he thought Walter was dishonest but because, as he noted in *To Bathurst*, his 'wealth was unseen and his bounty unheard of' (125n). Throughout his career Walter was guided by the maxim that 'business is business' or, as he himself put it, 'our affections should never run away with our money.'[15] He was miserly as well as grasping, hoarding most of his gains. He had begun his career as a scrivener. When he died he left behind him £282,401.

Not that Pope had any objection to men becoming rich nor, being a merchant's son with a merchant's instincts himself, did he believe that wealth should be based on land. Without having any strong feelings about how money was made, as long as it was made honestly, he did, however, have strong feelings about how money was used. A man of modest means, such as Kyrle, could help those who had little or no money. A rich man ought to be a benefactor, as was Burlington who inherited a fortune, as was Ralph Allen who made one. Pope, along with his contemporaries, had only a rudimentary concept of social engineering – the welfare state was a long way off. He placed most of the burden of caring for others on the shoulders of the individual. In this respect (if not in every other) he practised what he preached, giving away a sizeable proportion of his income each year for charitable purposes.[16] Pope finished his *Epistle to Bathurst* well before the end of 1732 but, unsure how it would be received, decided to delay publishing it until the following January.

The year 1733 was Excise year, in which Walpole was very nearly brought down. Bolingbroke and his friends found their most popular cause when they decided to spearhead resistance to the chief minister's plan for reorganizing the import duty system.[17] Nothing Walpole had thought up before provoked such a furore. The protests, both in and outside Parliament, were not just about a new method of taxing wine and tobacco. Few wanted to read the carefully reasoned account of the scheme Hervey wrote for his master. Some of those who laid their hands on his pamphlet, ostentatiously burned it. Gut reaction as well as papers 'dispersed by thousands all over the City and country' convinced ordinary Englishmen that excisemen were about to demand entry 'into all houses, private or public, at any time, by day, or by night.'[18]

Walpole, believing his scheme to be both reasonable and efficient, was prepared to ignore mammoth petitions, Opposition arguments and all the broadsheets, ballads and savage cartoons representing public opinion. However, some of his ministers took fright. He saw his support in both Houses melting away. On 10 April he told a few allies over dinner, 'This dance it will no farther go, and tomorrow I intend to sound the retreat.'[19] Accordingly, he stood up in the Commons the next day and withdrew the Bill. When he came to leave after the announcement, it took forty constables and a personal bodyguard of supporters (one of whom was Hervey) to save him being lynched by the mob. Drunken crowds thronged the streets all that night. They let off fireworks, lit bonfires and burned Walpole in effigy.

The Opposition was much encouraged. The Great Man may have eluded them yet again but it was obvious he was the object of widespread hatred. Chesterfield, who had voted against Excise, now joined Bolingbroke and Pulteney. So did other Whigs, including Cobham, whom Walpole punished by depriving him of his regiment. All of them looked forward to the next year's General Election.

The impassioned but narrow debate over Excise was not one that called for Pope's special talents. While it was going on he continued to ponder over what he saw as a fundamental malaise afflicting the England of his day and, even at the beginning of this phase in his career, when the Opposition regarded him as their own, preferred to take the longer view. He remained aware of the vanity of all human endeavour. Also he was reminded again that we live in the shadow of death when he lost two more friends, Atterbury and Gay, in 1732, the one dying in exile, the other 'hurrried out of this life in three days.'[20] It is no accident therefore that some of most celebrated lines Pope wrote are the ones in *To Bathurst* on the perennial theme of *sic transit Gloria mundi* (so passes earthly glory). In this passage his dramatic sense and ability to select the right visual detail come to the fore, as he recreates the legend (from the previous century) of how the brilliant Duke of Buckingham died:

> In the worst inn's worst room, with mat half-hung,
> The floors of plaister, and the walls of dung,
> On once a flock-bed, but repair'd with straw,
> With tape-ty'd curtains, never meant to draw,
> The George and Garter dangling from that bed
> Where tawdry yellow strove with dirty red,
> Great Villars lies – alas! How chang'd from him,
> That life of pleasure, and the soul of whim!
> Gallant and gay, in Cliveden's proud alcove,
> The bow'r of wanton Shrewsbury and love,
> Or just as gay, at Council, in a ring
> Of mimick'd Statesmen, and their merry King.
> No Wit to flatter, left of all his store!
> No Fool to laugh at, which he valu'd more. (299ff.)

Pope's decision to wait before publishing his *Epistle to Bathurst* had the desired effect in that there was no concerted outcry against him this time, despite Hervey's hope that someone would 'teach him the proper use of cudgels.'[21] At the end of January Pope was able to tell Caryll that the 'preacher' was 'less railed at than usually those are who will be declaiming against popular or national vices.' Then the energetic, combative side of his nature surfaced again as he promised, 'I shall redouble my blow very speedily.'[22] He was probably referring to his first *Imitation of Horace* (*Sat*. II.i.) which was published on 15 February.

This poem was written during a flu epidemic that swept through England that winter. It killed many but Pope got off lightly with a fever. While he was recuperating, Bolingbroke came to see him and happened to pick up a volume of Horace which was on the bedside table. The politically wary Pope was worrying about the risks of being a satirist, at a time when the Ministry was all too sensitive to the written word. Bolingbroke suggested how well it would put the poet's case if he were to translate the verses Horace had written when he was in a similar predicament. Pope lost no time. The result was in the bookshops in just over a fortnight.

The *Satire*, cast in the form of a dialogue between Pope and Fortescue who was a member of Walpole's staff, is an indirect address to the chief minister. Fortescue begins by advising the poet not to write at all or if, as he claims writing is a compulsion with him, like Darteneuf's longing to eat ham pie, then he should follow Cibber's example and write only praises of the royal family. For his part, Pope seeks to reassure his rulers that he stands outside political faction. Towards the end of the poem, having listened to the satirist's plea that he is 'To VIRTUE ONLY and her FRIENDS, A FRIEND', Fortescue warns him that there have been times in England when 'A Man was hang'd for very honest Rhymes' (121 & 146). He tells him to study the law of seditious libel. Whereupon Pope says he has no intention of writing libel, 'But grave *Epistles*, bringing Vice to Light ... Such as Sir Robert would approve' (151ff.).

Whether Sir Robert approved or not, he was worried by more immediate dangers than those presented by the poet. A furious Lady Mary did not get very far when she complained to him about the fate Pope said befell her associates, 'P-x'-d by her Love, or libell'd by her hate' (84). However, she found an ally in Hervey, mentioned in the *Satire* as 'Lord Fanny' who spins a thousand lines of weak verse a day (6). Together they produced *Verses Address'd to the Imitator of the First Satire of the Second Book of Horace* which appeared in print on 9 March.

Verses Address'd, mainly Lady Mary's work, were written with ferocious skill. Having taunted the poet with his 'birth obscure' and lack of sexual attractiveness, the lines mount to an eldritch curse:

> Like the first bold Assassin's be thy Lot,
> Ne'er be thy Guilt forgiv'n, or forgot;
> But as thou hate'st, be hated by Mankind,
> And with the Emblem of thy crooked Mind,
> Mark'd on thy Back, like *Cain*, by God's own Hand,
> Wander like him, accursed through the Land. (p. 8)

The disparate sides of Pope's nature appeared in sharp juxtaposition in 1733. As well as exchanging unchristian diatribes with Lady Mary, he published the first

19.1   Robert Walpole, 1st Earl of Orford. Arthur Pond

three books of *An Essay on Man*. No doubt he enjoyed the irony of the situation when, in the same week he read *Verses Address'd*, he looked at the signature on a letter forwarded to the anonymous author of the *Essay* saying, it was 'above all commendation, and ought to have been published in an age and country more worthy of it.'[23] The signature was Leonard Welsted's.

Very few people knew Pope was writing the *Essay*. He had kept it a secret even from Swift and Caryll because he wanted to see what an unbiased reaction to the work would be. The initial result was gratifying. Welsted's unqualified admiration was shared generally by English readers. Writing to Richardson, the poet was able to say, 'I see a glut of praise succeeds to a glut of reproach. I am as much overpaid this way now, as I was injured that way before.'[24] Richardson knew who had written the *Essay* because Pope had asked his help in getting the poem transcribed.

Later in the year Pope called on Richardson again. On 7 June Mrs Pope died at the age of ninety-one. Her son wanted the artist to paint her portrait before she was laid in her coffin. Watching his cheerful, sociable mother lose her mental faculties in her last years had been painful. He loved her – not even his enemies denied that. In her memory, he erected the obelisk which stood at the end of an avenue of cypresses, becoming the focal point in his garden.

Notes

1.   Spence, 379.
2.   TW. 5: 269n.
3.   *Grub Street Journal*, 24 December 1729.
4.   *Works of Lord Bolingbroke*, 4 vols (Philadelphia: Carey and Hart, 1841), 3: 42.
5.   The details given here of the history of this journal are taken from Simon Varey, '*The Craftsman*: A Historical and Critical Account', University of Cambridge doctoral dissertation, 1976.
6.   *The Craftsman*, 20 January 1731.
7.   Robert Halsband, *Lord Hervey* (Oxford: Clarendon, 1973), p. 117. Halsband lists and discusses Hervey's political writings from 1729.
8.   *The Hyp-Doctor*, 29 June 1731.
9.   *Corr.* 3: 406.
10. Kathleen Mahaffey, 'Timon's Villa: Walpole's Houghton', *Texas Studies in Literature and Language*, 9 (1967), 193–222.
11. Suggested parallels range from Versailles to Dawley. Pat Rogers has argued for Chatsworth in *Essays on Pope* (Cambridge University Press, 1993), pp. 88–92.
12. *Corr.* 3: 263.
13. *Corr.* 3: 280.
14. *Epistle to Bathurst*, l. 100 and note.
15. Staffordshire Record Office, D. 603, quoted by Howard Erskine-Hill, *The Social Milieu of Alexander Pope* (Yale University Press, 1975), p. 125. My information about Peter Walter comes from relevant chapters in this book.
16. Spence, 356 and note. As well of disapproving of the selfish greed which led men to ignore their responsibilities to charity, Pope was taken aback by the mad folly of

some speculators intent on getting rich quick, for example Joseph Gage and Lady Herbert. For an accurate account of the saga of this pair see Martin Murphy, 'Pope's "Congenial Souls": Joseph Gage and Lady Herbert', *Notes and Queries.* 237 (1992), 470–73.

17. Paul Langford, *The Excise Crisis: Society and Politics in the Age of Walpole* (Oxford: Clarendon, 1975) gives a detailed analysis of this episode.

18. 'A Letter from a Member of Parliaament from a Borough in the West', quoted by J.H. Plumb, *Sir Robert Walpole: The King's Minister* (London: Cresset Press, 1960), p. 262.

19. Halsband, *op. cit.*, p. 146.

20. *Corr.* 3: 334.

21. *Lord Hervey and his Friends, 1726–38*, ed Earl of Ilchester (London: John Murray, 1950), pp. 124–5.

22. *Corr.* 3: 345.

23. *Corr.* 3: 255–6.

24. *Corr.* 3: 352.

CHAPTER TWENTY

The Credentials of a Moralist

After Editha Pope's funeral her son needed to get away from the house at Twickenham, where he had been pent up in recent years. So he set off on a series of rambles. Over four months he went to spend time with friends, including Burlington and Cobham, whom he had not seen much of lately. He had a crowded schedule and no visit was longer than the three-week ones he made at Ladyholt to see Caryll and at Bevis Mount, the country home of Lord Peterborough. He finally got back to London and Twickenham in October.

At the end of November he read a new attack on him. Hervey had not intended to publish *An Epistle from a Nobleman to a Doctor of Divinity* but when it was printed, without his authorization, he was not displeased, particularly when he heard Pope was disturbed by it. 'Pope is in a most violent fury', he wrote to his lover Stephen Fox, 'and j'en suis ravi' (I am delighted about it).[1]

There was nothing in the text of the *Epistle from a Nobleman* to arouse his fury. It was mild as attacks on Pope went, its main point being that he was a second rate poet. Pope was disturbed not by what was written but by whom it was written. The *Epistle* aroused those fears for his personal safety and career as a poet that never lay far below the surface. This was because, if Hervey chose to use his influence, he could make life difficult for a Papist writer. If anything, he was more firmly established at Court than when he had made mischief over Timon's Villa. Then he had been a commoner, his title being a courtesy one. Now he had been rewarded for his support of Walpole with a barony and spoke in the Upper House.

Pope wrote a reply to Hervey's *Epistle*. His *Letter to a Noble Lord* was a temperate, even timid, response to the accusations and abuse heaped on him, both by Lady Mary and her ally, in recent months. Its wording shows just how vulnerable he felt as a member of a suspect religious minority, faced with the enmity of a man so highly placed in the Protestant establishment. 'I beseech your Lordship to consider' he began 'the Injury a Man of your *high Rank* and *Credit* may do to a *Private Person*, under *Penal Laws* and other disadvantages.' He also reminded Hervey that he had never written 'a Line in which the *Religion*, or *Government* of this *Country*, the *Royal Family*, or their *Ministry* were disrespectfully mentioned.'[2] As he had done with *A Master Key to Popery*, he showed this self defence to a few people but decided not to publish it. Some of his friends however took up the cudgels for him. Their anonymous pamphlets with titles such as *A Tryal of Skill Between a Court Lord and A*

Twickenham Squire and *An Epistle from a Gentleman at Twickenham to a Nobleman at St. James's*, in drawing attention to the social inequality of the two opponents, made a plea for sympathy for Pope as the underdog. This, together with the fact that Hervey was not wildly popular, meant that the middle class Catholic poet's fears that he was in serious danger were not realized. He took courage again and, as on previous occasions, bided his time before launching a public counter attack.

Meanwhile he continued to bring forth new poems. In January 1734 he published *An Epistle to Cobham* and the fourth book of *An Essay on Man*, the latter provocatively dedicated to Bolingbroke. Later in the year two more *Imitations of Horace* appeared.

Throughout most of the 1730s Pope was intent on recreating himself and with presenting the public with his new self. If he was to be listened to when he moralized his song, it was important that he established his credentials as a moralist and seemed to practise what he preached. For instance, having decided to reprove some of his contemporaries for their excesses and self indulgence, he published a sermon on moderation in July 1734. This was the *Second Satire of the Second Book of Horace*, dedicated to his naturally temperate friend Hugh Bethel. In the poem Bethel is made to hold forth on the golden mean as the way to good health and a contented mind. After which Pope elaborates on his own modest and simple way of life at Twickenham. 'No Turbots dignify my boards' he tells his readers, 'But gudgeons, flounders, what my Thames affords. / To Hounslow-heath I point, and Banstead-down, / Thence comes your mutton, and these chicks my own' (141ff.). The trouble with this exercise in image making was that even Pope's friends knew it was not entirely accurate. Admittedly abstemiousness was sometimes forced upon him by ill health, and plain living by an ever present wish to cut down on his household expenses but, given the chance, he was a sybarite. Bathurst, who had a keen eye for Pope's foibles, wrote to Lady Suffolk (formerly Mrs Howard) about the poet's conduct during his visit to Cirencester in 1734, 'You do well to reprove him about his intemperance', he wrote, 'for he makes himself sick every meal ... Yesterday I had a little piece of salmon just caught out of the Severn, and a fresh pike that was brought from the other side of your house out of the Thames. He ate as much as he could of both, and insisted upon his moderation, because he made his dinner upon one dish.'[3]

Pope might have been forgiven if all he had ever done, in constructing his new identity, was deceive others (and himself) about his gourmandism. Unfortunately it did not stop there. As time went on and he continued to castigate his fellow men and women for their vices, he felt impelled to recreate himself as a latter day Savonarola. This not only astonished his enemies at the time, who accused the bawdy little man they thought they knew of hypocrisy, but has had an unfortunate effect on his modern critics. Some of these, in the earlier part of the twentieth century, have tended to take Pope at his own value, creating a uniformly high minded image of him that is far too solemn. More recently, other commentators have found Pope's last representation of himself over-weening and self satisfied.[4] The pendulum has swung back so far that a few modern critics, like his eighteenth-century enemies, appear to believe he was deluding himself about almost everything.

Perhaps the way out of the impasse is not to expect Pope to have a fixed identity. He was a poet who, like Keats, had no 'unchangeable attributes.'[5] When he adopted roles, he brought to the fore one side of his nature. One part of him was the stern moralist, another was the tolerant humanist, yet another was the would-be rake. Sometimes he was the heroic protagonist, at others he was the insecure Papist. These contradictory aspects of himself refused to be suppressed and, as we shall see, surfaced, whether he willed them to or not.

In an effort to establish himself as a worthy critic of the social mores, intent on telling the truth without fear or favour, Pope put together *An Epistle to Dr. Arbuthnot* in the summer of 1734. It was written for his friend, with whom he had discussed the ethics of satire, as a public compliment. There was need for haste because the Doctor was ill, with enough knowledge of his condition to realize he would not recover.

By the time the *Epistle* was published, a month before Arbuthnot's death, it had taken the form of an apologia, outlining the way Pope now wished to be considered by his readers. It was also, as the Advertisement makes clear, a considered response to Lady Mary and Lord Hervey. Having explained that the poem was written at different periods, some lines in it years earlier, Pope goes on, 'I had no thoughts of publishing it till it pleas'd some Persons of Rank and Fortune [the Authors of *Verses to the Imitator of Horace* an of an *Epistle to a Doctor of Divinity from a Nobleman at Hampton Court*] to attack in a very extraordinary manner, not only my Writings (of which being publick the Publick judge) but my Person, Morals and Family.'[6]

In the event Lady Mary is barely mentioned in *An Epistle to Dr. Arbuthnot* but Hervey is central to it. In the process of making a unified whole out of the many parts that contributed to his poem, Pope builds up to a climax with the portrait of his latest and worst enemy as his antithesis, both as a man and as a writer.

Pope's literary biography is given as a flashback. Before he embarks on it he gives the first description in English of the disadvantages of being a celebrity. With comic gusto he conjures up a picture of himself in a state of siege, beset with hangers-on, flatterers and a host of would-be authors who demand his help.

After this energetic prologue which establishes, in a self-mocking context, Pope's current position as England's leading poet, he goes back to the beginning to tell us how it all started when as an infant he 'lisp'd in Numbers, for the Numbers came' (l. 128). Then follows a roll call of his literary relationships, from the days he was encouraged by Walsh and damned by Dennis, on

20.1   John, Lord Hervey. John Fayram (?)

to the period of his quarrels with the Buttonians. He gives the impression he maintained a dignified silence throughout the war waged on him by his enemies. 'I never answered' he says, speaking of Dennis (l. 154), air-brushing out of this literary biography those rowdy pamphlets in which he sent the old man up.

All the while he is moving nearer to the present again, and to Hervey. Just before he gets there, it becomes clear that the main theme in the poem is integrity. He devotes twenty lines or so to saying that the greatest crime in the literary world is when a writer or patron denies his commitment to truth. With Addison and Bufo this happened because their vanity got in the way. But the lines are especially relevant to the portrait of Sporus, which comes immediately after them, because Pope believed that Hervey was responsible for spreading lies about Timon being Lord Chandos.

Pope's denunciation takes the form of a malediction and so deliberately echoes the conclusion of *Verses Address'd*. 'Curst be the Verse,' he begins, 'how well so e'er it flow, / That tends to make one worthy Man my foe' (ll. 283–4). As he goes on it becomes clear he has Hervey in mind as he speaks of 'That Fop whose pride affects a Patron's name, / Yet, absent wounds an Author's honest fame' (ll. 291–2).

The portrait of Sporus is, among other things, a reply to a man who had injured the poet and a piece of political journalism. Not least it is a brilliant caricature, the equivalent in words of Hogarth's depiction of the bloated and slothful judges in *The Bench*, or the lecherous clergyman canting from the pulpit to *The Sleeping Congregation*. With the poet, as with the painter, the art of caricature lies in 'disproportionately increasing and emphasizing the defects of the features, so that the portrait as a whole appears to be the sitter himself while its elements are all transformed.'[7] Selectivity is all.

Though we do not doubt that Pope detests the man to whom he is making this meditated reply, there is no hint in the lines of a personal grievance. He presents Sporus as a public enemy, an individual representative of a type we always have with us. He is universally recognizable as the trivial, two-faced, back-biting sycophant. He is an individual because his exaggerated, girlish good looks and bisexuality are made to reflect his moral corruption. Pope's lines would command attention even if the reader of them had never heard of Lord Hervey.

However, as soon as the Sporus portrait appeared, everyone knew who it was meant to be, not least because of the emphasis on Hervey's notorious sexual ambiguity, beginning with the name he is dubbed with. Sporus was Nero's creature, a boy he fell in love with, castrated and took as a wife. The homophobic elements which offend modern readers would have passed without question in the 1730s. Hervey was not persecuted for his sexual tastes but he was mocked. Pope's contemptuous innuendos were just another, more vitriolic, contribution to satirical squibs about 'Vicey' or the 'Lady of the Lords' that had appeared in the Opposition press.

By 1734 Hervey had revealed a talent for making enemies that matched Pope's own. He was a prime political target for good reasons. For one thing his intimacy with the Queen was regarded as dangerous because, while he influenced her, it was commonly believed that this clever woman influenced her obstinate husband regarding Ministerial policy. The intimacy between Caroline and her favourite had recently been ratified when she presented him with a gold snuff box and persuaded the King to add another thousand pounds to his salary. Furthermore, Hervey was the Government's spin doctor. Ten thousand copies of his sixty-page pamphlet *The Conduct of the Opposition* were distributed throughout the country, helping Walpole to win yet another term in office.

The portrait of Hervey is a hatchet job, one as yet unsurpassed in the language. It is effective because Pope the caricaturist highlights features which his target possessed. This is not to say the picture Pope paints is fair, but everything he says can be backed by evidence, some of it provided by the victim himself. The description of Sporus, who 'at the Ear of *Eve*, familiar Toad, / Half Froth, half Venom, spits himself abroad, / In Puns, or Politicks, or Tales, or Lyes' (ll. 319–21) is hardly contradicted by an entry in Hervey's *Memoirs*. There he tells how, in the summer of 1734, Caroline gave him a hunter, so that 'on Hunting-days he never stirred from her chaise. She called him always her "child, her pupil, and her charge;" used to tell him perpetually that his being so impertinent and daring to contradict her so continually, was owing to his knowing she could not live without him; and often said, "It is well I am so old, or I should be talked of for this creature".'[8] Hervey had a face as lovely as a woman's. Then, because his wretched health gave him a deathly pallor, he used paint. So when Pope speaks of 'Beauty that shocks you' (l. 332), he is giving what must have been a common reaction to a garishly feminine appearance.

As an artistic creation Sporus is complete, though the picture of the Roman catamite is not a complete account of Lord Hervey. Caricatures work by what they leave out as much as by what they put in. A few of the things missing from the picture are Hervey's capacity for hard work, stoicism and the physical courage he showed from his boyhood days when, as a fearless gentleman jockey, he won the Queen's Plate at Newmarket, much to his father's delight. He respected and loved his father incidentally, even though the Earl of Bristol listened to his son's speeches in Parliament and then, voted for the other side.

Hervey was neither a knave or a hero. He was an insider, completely at home in the world he lived in. That world was the Court. Country life 'sacred to sweat and spaniels', as he put it, bored him.[9] He was not a reformer. He once said, 'I cannot imagine what people mean, when they sigh over the degeneracy of the age and badness of the world. In my opinion and to my taste, they are both delightful. I had rather live in these times than in any times or country I ever read of.'[10]

Pope had worked on *An Epistle to Dr. Arbuthnot* while staying at Bevis

Mount, Lord Peterborough's hilltop house, overlooking the sea and the Isle of
Wight. Charles Mordaunt, the third Earl of Peterborough had long been one of
Pope's heroes. After dropping out of Christ Church, Oxford at the age of sixteen
to go to sea, he had had a career as an Admiral, General and Ambassador, acting
in all those posts with considerable panache. Pope once said he would have
made an ideal leader of a Jacobite invasion.[11] Now at the age of seventy-six his
energy and gaiety were undiminished. He swept all before him. He even swept
the poet into his yacht and took him sailing round the coast. Pope loved him and
envied him a little, not least because he had always been successful with
women, paying court to Mrs Howard as well as keeping the celebrated diva
Anastasia Robinson as his mistress, until it eventually occurred to him to
propose marriage to her. That had been in 1722 and the wedding had been kept
secret.

Peterborough was not a heartless rake but he had learned his sexual morals
growing up during Charles II's easy reign. With such a friend at his side Pope
worked on *Sober Advice from Horace*, at the same time he was putting together
the poem for Dr Arbuthnot. The two poems are so different that *Sober Advice*,
which is all about sexual behaviour, has proved somewhat embarrassing for
those readers who have a picture in their minds of the mature Pope as a
consistently lofty moralist. Indeed, the poem embarrassed the poet himself, to
the extent that he tried afterwards to pretend he had not written it. Perhaps some
of the responsibility for it should be borne by Peterborough, not because he told
the poet what to write, but because his gallant presence reactivated a side of
Pope's personality that was dormant, though not dead.

In *Sober Advice* Pope exchanges his more exalted image of Virtue's
champion for the less portentous one of a man of the world who knows just
how much, or how little, can be expected of his peers when it comes to sex.
According to Bolingbroke, Pope toned down some of the images when he
revised the poem, so as not to 'hurt chaste ears overmuch.'[12] Addressing the
average sensual man, he advises him to leave his friends' wives alone, if only to
avoid the furious husbands and barking dogs concomitant upon an adulterous
intrigue. For he says, even putting married women to one side, 'Hath not
indulgent Nature spread a Feast?' (l. 96). Continuing in this vein, he adds that
the amorous adventures of Bolingbroke, 'who trades in Frigates of the second
Rate' (l. 62) and Bathurst, who confines himself to willing nymphs, harm no
one.[13]

When Pope sent *Sober Advice* to Caryll he warned him not to think it was one
of his own works because 'In truth I should think it a very indecent Sermon after
An Essay on Man.'[14] Nevertheless, it expresses a view of sex he had held ever
since his youth, when he exchanged mildly bawdy letters with Cromwell and
tried to play the rake himself. In *Eloisa to Abelard*, written when he was in love
with Lady Mary, he had recognized that sexual passion can be a transfiguring
obsession, but he also realized such an experience is rare and believed, as did

many of his friends, that to pursue casual amours adds excitement to life. It was a peripheral activity but none the worse for that. Sex was 'God's good thing' (l. 103).[15]

In the world Pope had left behind, while he was visiting Bevis Mount and other country estates, things had not gone well with his friends in Westminster. Indications of a split in the Opposition ranks had come in March 1734, when Pulteney and his Whig followers failed to back the Tories as energetically as they might have done in Bolingbroke's campaign to get the Septennial Act repealed. Walpole, on the other hand, was quite single minded about winning back the support he had lost because of the Excise scheme. In the months leading up to the Election he poured money into bribing the electorate, and into the printing and distribution of Government newspapers.[16] The 1735 Election was rougher than usual – some of the Whig candidates were stoned by their constituents. Nevertheless Walpole won it.

Bolingbroke was in eclipse. It had also been in the year 1734 that the chief minister had gone on the offensive against the unofficial leader of the Opposition. After denouncing him dramatically in the Commons as the Anti-Minister, Walpole wrote a pamphlet called, *The Grand Accuser; the Greatest of All Criminals*. It was a well documented account of his rival's intrigues (including Jacobite ones) over a twenty-year period. It confirmed the feeling, already growing in Opposition circles, that Bolingbroke was a liability. He, in his turn, was never a man to fight when his back was to the wall. If he had been, his career might have been different. He decided to return to France and did so the following spring, telling Wyndham, 'My part is over, and he who remains on the stage after his part is over deserves to be hissed off.'[17]

During the election year Dr Arbuthnot died at his house in Cork Street on 27 February. Shortly afterwards Pope learned of the incurable illness of Lord Peterborough. Both men departed from this world in the manner they had lived in it. Just before the end, when Pope asked him about his health, the realistic Doctor had replied that as his case was hopeless, the kindest wish his friends could have for him was euthanasia.[18]

Peterborough, the man of action (suffering agonies after futile surgery without an anaesthetic) put his affairs in order, including making his marriage to Anastasia public. Then he invited Pope and other close friends to Bevis Mount for a last reunion, after which he said he would take his 'leap towards the clouds ... to mix among the stars.'[19] In the event, more dead than alive, he took his yacht and sailed into the Mediterranean. It was like those final voyages of the old Norse chieftains, from which there was no return. He died on 25 October 1735.

After saying goodbye to Peterborough at Bevis Mount, Pope had made his way via Oxford to Stowe. There he met Patty, who had come with the Countess of Suffolk (the former Mrs Howard) to stay with Lord Cobham. Quite often when Pope visited friends these days Patty would be one of the guests. The previous autumn she had been in Bath, again with Lady Suffolk, when Pope visited the spa in the company of Burlington and Bolingbroke. In February 1735 he had published the *Epistle to a Lady* which was dedicated to her.

Notes

1. *Lord Hervey and his Friends*, ed the Earl of Ilchester (London: John Murray, 1950), p. 183.
2. *The Prose Works of Alexander Pope, Volume II 1725–44*, ed Rosemary Cowler (Oxford: Blackwell, 1986), pp. 454–5.
3. *Suffolk Correspondence*, 2: 81, quoted *Corr.* 3: 414n.
4. See John Richardson, 'Defending the Self: Pope and his Horatian Poems', *Modern Language Review*, vol. 95, pt. 3 (July 2000), 623–33. In this essay Richardson warns critics against commending Pope 'on the grounds of whether or not he can be co-opted as a contemporary political ally', p. 623. He goes on to argue that Pope's experience was not that of a citizen living in a liberal democracy. It was more like that of a dissident living in a single-party state. His stridency arises out of fear and insecurity, not self-satisfaction.
5. Letter to Richard Woodhouse, 27 October 1818. *Letters of John Keats*, ed M.B. Forman (Oxford University Press, 1948), p. 228.
6. TW. 4: 95. For details of the parts that made up the *Epistle* see Maynard Mack, *The Last and Greatest Art* (University of Delaware Press, 1984), pp. 419–54.
7. Filippo Baldinucci (1681), quoted *Oxford Companion to Art*, ed Harold Osborne (Oxford: Clarendon, 1970), 204. See also, J.H. Hagstrum, 'Verbal and Visual Caricature in the Age of Dryden, Swift and Pope' in *England in the Restoration and Early Eighteenth Century: Essays on Culture and Society*, ed H.T. Swedenberg (University of California Press, 1972).
8. *Lord Hervey's Memoirs*, ed Romney Sedgwick, 3 vols (London: Cresset, 1931), 2: 348–9.
9. Ibid. p. 86.
10. Ibid. p. 66.
11. Spence, 257.
12. *Corr.* 3: 414.
13. When Bolingbroke was appointed Minister one of the ladies of the town is supposed to have cried, 'Seven thousand guineas a year, my girls, and all for us.' Bathurst, as well as fathering seventeen legitimate children, pursued 'willing nymphs' throughout most of his life. He lived to be ninety-one.
14. *Corr.* 3: 447.
15. As late as 1742 Pope produced the following *bon mot*, 'The marriage state seems to be directly opposite to that of Paradise. In Paradise man was to forbear one tree and enjoy all the rest, in matrimony men are obliged to eat of one tree and forbear all the rest.' Spence, 577.
16. By 1735 there were four of these: *The London Journal, Daily Courant, Free Briton* and a new one *The Corn Cutter's Journal*.
17. Quoted, Walter Sichel, *Bolingbroke and his Times*, 2 vols (London, 1901–2), 2: 310.
18. *Corr.* 3: 417.
19. *Suffolk Correspondence*, 2: 129–30.

CHAPTER TWENTY-ONE

Pope and the Women

Pope is supposed to have nailed his sexist colours to the mast when he published his *Epistle to a Lady* on 8 February 1735. In the 1980s there were those that were sure Pope believed all women were contemptible.[1] Since then, however, the idea that he was ambivalent about them has been gaining ground.[2] In which case he was not all that different from a large number of men, both before and since his day.

One thing that is apparent from the *Epistle to a Lady* is that Pope was fascinated by women, without understanding them. Of a poet who finds it incongruous that Rufa goes from studying Locke to surveying the talent in the park, one can only ask whatever makes him think that scholarly ladies do not flirt? Pope is wonderfully observant of the way women appear and behave, without comprehending how they think or feel. He showed the same lack of understanding in his personal relationships as well. When he first met Lady Mary Wortley Montagu he was mistaken about her eminently practical nature and he may well have been wrong about Patty Blount. The closest he came to entering into the female pysche was when he recognized, in the opposite sex, traits that he possessed himself, such as Belinda's wish to be admired, or the role playing of the women in the *Epistle to a Lady*.

The framework for his poem is a stroll through a gallery with its author talking to Patty Blount about the portraits of the beautiful and often charming ladies that adorn the walls. These women have chosen to be painted as figures from myth and story. The Countess of Pembroke appears in one picture as a shepherdess, in another as modest Fannia, gazing fondly at her husband, and in yet another as 'naked Leda with a Swan' (l. 10). This type of portraiture was a convention of the age, but at the same time Pope implies that, in life as in art, the Countess and her peers play a series of roles for a male audience. These roles may be thrust upon them. Caroline can only appear as the Queen. In all her portraits and public appearances, 'That Robe of Quality so struts and swells, / None see what Parts of Nature it conceals' (ll. 189–90). It is this recognition that women are acting a part in public which produces the opening statement – the one that has got Pope into so much trouble – 'Most women have no Characters at all' (l. 2).

Yet as far as Pope was concerned it was not just the female sex that lacked a stable identity. As has long been known, La Bruyère made a similar observation about men, declaring that they 'have no certain Characters; or if they have any, 'tis that they have none which they always pursue, which never change, and by which they may be known.'[3] The lack of fixed identity in the male sex had been Pope's starting point in the *Epistle to Cobham*, published the year before his poem on women. While, as long ago as 1709, he had told Henry Cromwell that man was like an actor, 'much better known for having the same Face, than by his keeping the same Character. For we change our minds as often as they can their Parts, & he who was yesterday Cesar is to day Sir J. Daw.'[4]

As was mentioned earlier in this book, the question of whether or not man had a permanent identity became a popular talking point when Pope was a young man. It was a debate, stimulated by Locke, taken up by the Scriblerians and discussed in the *Spectator*.[5] Most people wanted to believe that the individual had a stable self, but Pope veered towards scepticism. In 1730 he told Spence that Montaigne's essay, 'Of the Inconstancy of our Actions' was 'the best of his whole book.'[6] Pope's ideas about human nature were reinforced by reading and discussion, but originated in self-analysis – in his awareness that like the women who appeared in portraits as Magdalen one day and as Saint Cecilia the next, he played the part his company expected of him. As a young man not only was he 'Grave and Godly' in his father's house, after acting the rake in town, he even went to the length of learning 'without book a Song of Mr. Tho. Durfey's' in an attempt to appear a jolly good fellow for the benefit of Binfield's hunting fraternity.[7]

In *To a Lady* Pope depicts contradictory female nature in all its variety. As it happens no woman he describes is as volatile and inconsistent as Wharton in the *Epistle to Cobham* but, unlike the men in the earlier poem, none of the women in the picture gallery are of any consequence. Nothing they do matters in the public world. Rufa who reads Locke, and Narcisssa who immerses herself in theology are dilettantes, their studies one more distraction without purpose. The female sex therefore is a prey to whim and emotional excess. One moment Flavia is an avid devotee of *carpe diem* (making the most of the day) then, out of sheer boredom, she is 'all for Death ... Lucretia's dagger, Rosamonda's bowl' (ll. 91–2). Pope sees this clearly but does not ask himself what impels a woman to study philosophy or theology or, like Lady Mary shut herself up in a library to learn Latin and Greek. Nor does he envisage how in a different social system they might be different.

Yet because Pope's portraits of women are not forced into the ruling passion straitjacket, as the accounts of men in *To Cobham* were, they have more vitality than their counterparts in that poem. In *To Cobham* Pope had developed a theory that we could resolve the contradictions in the male character once we had detected the dominant motive in a man which determined his every action. In painting women, despite saying they are ruled by 'Love of Pleasure, and the Love of Sway' (l. 210), Pope allows for complexity and mystery. So although society has changed since he wrote his poem, we recognize the modern counterparts of Calypso, 'Less Wit than Mimic, more a Wit than wise' (l. 48) and Atossa who 'Finds all her life one warfare upon earth' (l. 118).

Furthermore Pope dislikes very few of the women he describes. He is condescending but not misogynistic. Even his picture of Sappho (Lady Mary) in a grubby petticoat 'at her toilet's greasy task' (l. 25) is unlikely to have the effect Swift's account of Corinna dismantling herself at bedtime had on one contemporary reader, who threw up when she read it.[8] Swift, in contrast to his friend, felt the need to keep women at a distance.[9] Pope's greater sympathy with women stemmed, in part, from his recognition that their vagaries were his. Sometimes the resemblance is startling. The poet who describes Narcissa, 'Now deep in Taylor and the Book of Martyrs, / Now drinking citron with his Grace and Chartres' (ll. 63–4), is the same man who went within the hour from contemplating infinity with Whiston to cracking jokes with the irreligious old rebrobate General Tidcombe.[10] Having a volatile nature himself Pope did not dislike women for theirs, '''Tis to their Changes that their charms they owe' (l. 42).

Yet, as he points out, women are vulnerable who pursue pleasure and employ their sexual attractions to captivate men. They can only do so as long as their youth and looks last, though any ballroom has its quota of aging belles who have refused to give up:

> As Hags hold Sabbaths, less for joy than spight,
> So these their merry, miserable Night;
> Still round and round the Ghosts of Beauty glide,
> And haunt the places where their honour dy'd (ll. 239–42).

In these lines Pope is writing tragedy. The hags in the ballroom suffer the fate of women who have allowed men to typecast them. Early in life they were urged to play their roles as male sex objects. Now they are no longer desirable, they cannot hold their audience. But, if they quit the boards, the only thing that awaits them is 'an old Age of Cards' (l. 244). Pope understood that women face greater problems in achieving a rounded identity in society than men do, if only because they are slaves and men are their masters. His solution for this problem was not to redress the balance. He paid no attention to early feminists, such as Mary Astell, who wished to change society. Instead he advised women to retreat from it. 'Bred to disguise, in Public 'tis you hide' (l. 203), Pope tells the female sex, 'A Woman's seen in Private life alone' (l. 200). Only by avoiding an unending round of futile dissipation that destroys them, can they find some calm refuge where they can create themselves.

Nor was it women only who needed a refuge. For even though 'in Public Men are sometimes shown' (l. 199), they too can become shadows if they spend too long in society. Pope knew this to his cost. After one of his hectic visits to London, he wrote to Broome, 'A man who lives so much in the world does but translate other men; he is nothing of his own.'[11] Many different people recognize this feeling but poets, with their heightened power of empathy, are especially aware of it perhaps. Keats in 1818 said something like Pope when he observed, 'If I am ever free from speculating on the creations of my own brain, then not myself goes home to myself; but the identity of everyone in the room begins so to press upon me that I am in a very little while annihilated.'[12] Pope's solution, when he felt the world annihilating him, was the same one he recommended to women; he retired into private life. Pope went to his villa by the Thames to find himself. Given his recognition that he had no permanent, unchanging identity, this meant creating his own character in the poems he wrote.

The portrait of the woman with which Pope ends his *Epistle to a Lady* has been given a chance to create a character for herself. It was inspired by Patty Blount who, in real life, no longer had to spend all her time living up to (or down to) male expectations of her. Pope tells us she was denied the money that would have bought a husband to become her 'Tyrant' (l. 288). We know that after leaving Mapledurham she inhabited an all-female household. When, for reasons of economy, she had to retreat out of the full glare of society for a while, she made the best of it. For several years from 1727 she and her mother spent their summers quietly at Petersham. Later on Fortescue let Patty have the occasional use of the Shepherd's Hut, the cottage he owned near Richmond. During these summer months she passed hours with people she could be at ease with including Pope, his mother and their friends; or she read and walked, wearing her old gowns to save money, to pay for the winter in town. So she did not have to live in disguise as much as many women of her class did. Her personality was given space in which to evolve.

Nevertheless, the portrait of Patty Blount in *To a Lady* disappoints both male and female readers. Nothing disturbs her or fires her imagination. She is unfailingly cheerful and sensible and a bit dull.[13] A few questions arise as we read the portrait. First of all, is Pope really telling us why he likes her and, if not, what is he doing? Second, is the account of Patty true to life and did Pope ever know her truly? All these questions are closely interrelated.

Pope's picture of his friend is without foibles, let alone warts and is, for him, unusually abstract. We do not hear Patty say anything as we hear Papillia say, so revealingly, 'Oh, odious, odious Trees'! (l. 40). Nor do we see her as we see Chloe who, 'while her Lover pants upon her breast, / Can mark the figures on an Indian chest' (ll. 167–8). Instead we are given a catalogue of her virtues and the description that emerges is muted and nebulous. It would seem that Pope is giving an edited version of why he likes Patty, missing out her high spirits and free manners, qualities which led that barometer of conventional opinion, Magdalen Rackett, to call her a 'great romp and by no means a prude.'[14]

It would be surprising if Pope had chosen as his constant companion a woman as lacking in vivacity as the one he holds up for our admiration in his poem. All his life he was attracted by lively, spirited women who spoke their minds. During one of his early visits to Bath he wrote to Patty of his delight in meeting Lady Sandwich, 'who has all the Spirit of the last Age, & all the gay

Experience of a pleasurable Life', adding, 'She is, in a word, the best thing this Country has to boast of, & as she has been all that a Woman of Spirit and delight could be, so she still continues that easie, lively & independent Creature that a sensible woman always will be.'[15] He formed enduring friendships with women who were vocal and forceful including, as mentioned previously, the Countess of Burlington and the Duchess of Marlborough. Dorothy Boyle, as well as drawing witty caricatures, was a passionate opera-goer. Eyebrows were raised when, in 1727, she engaged in a slanging match with Lady Pembroke across the auditorium of the theatre, while Cuzzoni and Faustina, the different *prima donnas* they favoured, set about each other on the stage.[16]

All the women Pope admired were, or had been good looking and he was unkind about the ugly ones. It was the intimidating size of Lady Darlington (the half sister of George I), together with her masculine stride and loud theatrical voice, which put him off, more than the fact she read 'Malbranche, Boyle and Locke.'[17] Indeed, there is no clear evidence that Pope shared the distaste some of his male contemporaries' had for intelligent, witty women. Unlike those men, he never doubted he could hold his own. When he fell in love with Lady Mary, he was understandably indirect in expressing his physical feelings for her, but unstinting in his praise of her mental attributes. In his ballad *Sandy's Ghost* he complimented her on her 'brains.'[18] He was also in the vanguard in championing her campaign for inoculation against smallpox.[19] He did not object to her wit until, in some unspecified way, she turned that wit against him. When his feelings for her were beginning to cool, he turned to the less acerbic Judith Cowper, in the hope perhaps that she could become the new object of his devotion. However, the fond and gentle Miss Cowper proved not to be to his taste and before long she was lamenting that he had forgotten her.[20]

During his brief correspondence with Judith Cowper Pope told her that the attraction of the 'brightest Wit in the world' declines like the glaring sun 'without better qualities of the heart',[21] and it is true that Pope disliked women, when he did, if he decided they lacked those 'better qualities of the heart.' He once told Patty, 'There are but two things in the World which can make you indifferent to me which I believe you are not capable of, I mean Ill nature & Malice.'[22] He turned against her sister Teresa when she proved to be spiteful and increasingly bad tempered. Not surprisingly, he was appalled to learn that she was given to 'striking, pinching and pulling her mother about the house.'[23] Patty was more amiable, but it is doubtful that she was as subdued as Judith Cowper.[24] She would have bored Pope if she had been. So why did he present his readers with a toned down portrait of her in *To a Lady*?

The answer to that question might be that Pope was writing a defence of Patty Blount of whom a number of people disapproved. In presenting an idealized portrait of her as the kind of self effacing, sensible and, above all, modest woman extolled in the *Spectator*, he was answering her critics who thought her loud and disreputable. Some of these critics were in the Catholic community, including her godfather John Caryll. We do not know if Caryll believed Pope in 1725 when he denied Patty was his mistress.[25] But, whether he did or not, the gossip continued. Nor did it help when, in 1729, Teresa embarked on her much talked about love affair with the married Captain Bagnell.[26] The two sisters lived together and were tarred with the same brush. By the time Pope wrote *To a Lady* Patty no longer heard anything from Mrs Caryll.[27]

Patty had her admirers, notably Swift and George Lyttelton but neither of them knew her for very long and, for an amiable woman, she aroused a fair amount of hostility, not all of which was to do with her moral reputation. Warburton and Bolingbroke, if they agreed on nothing else, agreed in disliking Patty. Warburton refused to allow that Pope's portrait in the *Epistle* was about her, declaring instead that the lady was 'imaginary',[28] while Bolingbroke ignored her arrival on one occasion when they were together at Twickenham.[29] Furthermore, some of her closest friendships with women came to an unexplained end – the one with Lady Suffolk, for instance. Equally inexplicable was the Duchess of Queensberry's decision, by 1740, not to invite Patty to her assemblies any more.[30]

Which bring us to our last question. How well did Pope know Patty Blount? He could make mistakes about the women he loved, as he did about Lady Mary. Evidence about Patty's character is hard to come by and there has been a tendency to accept Pope's evaluation of her and disregard the views of anyone who was hostile to her, such as Warburton and Magdalen Rackett, because they had reason to be biased. Pope once said that his friend was 'one of the most considerate and mindful people in the world.'[31] Yet, a story told by the Bishop of Bristol, who had no reason to invent it, makes us wonder about her tact. He said that Ralph Allen had explained how an awkward situation had arisen when Patty was his guest because she had demanded his coach to take her to the Mass-house in Bath. The request had been all the more embarrassing because he had been Mayor at the time.[32]

Pope also said his friend had one of the 'sincerest and gentle of hearts.'[33] Magdalen Rackett doubted her sincerity, noting how her manner changed as soon as Pope came into the room.[34] Nor did her gentle heart stop her from telling him things that were likely to hurt his feelings, as when she reported that few of his friends in town remembered to ask about him.[35]

Pope was a very useful friend to have. He had always tried to please women by offering them assistance and he helped Patty in numerous ways, from getting her lottery tickets, seats in the theatre and persuading his illustrious acquaintances to invite her to their houses, to advising her on investments and trying to ensure her brother Michael paid her allowance on time. There is no indication she loved him but she was willing to please. We do not know if they were sexual partners, though their contemporaries obviously believed they were. Nor do we know if Pope ever asked her to marry him. Given his views on marriage, he probably did not. He did not need a wife. He needed an object of devotion. In the process of choosing Patty to fill this role, he reinvented her – twice. Once, as his own ideal woman in his everyday life and again, in the portrait he drew of her in his *Epistle to a Lady*. Theirs was not a conventional relationship, but it worked.

Of the poems Pope published in 1735 an *Epistle to a Lady* aroused less controversy than many of his writings. Bolingbroke, who read it earlier in manuscript, regarded it as the poet's masterpiece.[36] For the time being Hervey was bereft of words after the *Epistle to Dr. Arbuthnot*. Pope was no longer welcome at the Court of George II and Caroline, but was favoured by George's son Frederick, who disagreed with his parents about most things. He resented Hervey's hold over his mother and was convinced she had given the gold snuff box to her favourite to spite himself. In October the Prince of Wales paid a surprise visit to the villa at Twickenham, staying four or five hours. Unfortunately Pope fell asleep over dinner. The Prince was encouraged to visit Pope by some of the younger men in the Opposition who had come to the fore since the last election. He came as an unwitting harbinger of a political initiative they were to launch – one in which he was eccentrically cast as Arthur and the poet as Merlin.

However, after Bolingbroke left England in 1735, Pope retired from the political scene for a while, and he did not bring out any new satires for twenty-two months after the Tory leader departed for France. Instead he was engaged in a new project – yet another way of establishing the image he wanted the public to have of him. To this end he spent most of 1736 preparing an edition of his letters, which he published the following spring.

Notes

1. Laura Brown, *Alexander Pope* (Oxford: Blackwell, 1985), pp. 102, 107 and Ellen Pollak, *The Poetics of Sexual Myth: Gender and Ideology in the Verse of Swift and Pope* (University of Chicago Press, 1985), p. 127.
2. Felicity Nussbaum, *The Brink of All we Hate: English Satires on Women 1660–1750* (Lexington: University of Kentucky Press, 1984), p. 140. Valerie Rumbold, *Women's Place in Pope's World* (Cambridge University Press, 1989), pp. 262–3, 274–5, 277–9. Christa Knellwolf, *A Contradiction Still: Representations of Women in the Poetry of Alexander Pope* (Manchester University Press, 1998).
3. *The Characters, or the Manners of the Age* (1700), p. 248.
4. *Corr.* 1: 71.
5. Christopher Fox, 'Locke and the Scriblerians: the Discussion of Identity in Early Eighteenth-Century England', *Eighteenth-Century Studies,* 16 (1982), 1–25.
6. Spence, 318a.
7. *Corr.* 1: 81.
8. This was the reaction of Laetitia Pilkington's mother on reading 'The Lady's Dressing Room', *Memoirs of Laetitia Pilkington*, ed A.C. Elias, Jr, 2 vols (Athens and London: University of Georgia Press, 1997), 1: 314.

9.   Felicity Rosslyn, 'Deliberate Disenchantment: Swift and Pope on the Subject of Women', *Cambridge Quarterly*, xxiii, 4 (1994), 293–302.
10. *Corr.* 1: 185.
11. *Corr.* 2: 302.
12. *Letters of John Keats*, ed M.B. Forman (Oxford University Press, 1931), p. 228.
13. Andrew Varney, 'The Motion of the Things it Represents: The Verbal and the Visual in Early Eighteenth-Century Culture', *European Journal of English Studies*, 4, 1 (April, 2000), 10–24. Varney also points out how, in the portrait of Miss Blount, Pope abandons the metaphor of the poet as painter, which he uses elsewhere in the poem and often adopts when he is most inspired.
14. George Sherburn, 'New Anecdotes about Alexander Pope', *Notes and Queries* (1958), p. 349.
15. *Corr.* 1: 261.
16. James Lees-Milne, *Earls of Creation*, revised edn (London: Century Hutchinson, 1980), p. 131.
17. Artemesia (TW. 6: 48–51) has been identified as Charlotte von Kielmansegg, who became Countesss of Darlington, by Lois Kathleen Mahaffey, 'Pope's "Artemesia" and "Phryne" as Personal Satire', *Review of English Studies*, 21 (1970), 466–71.
18. TW. 6: 170–76.
19. *Corr.* 2: 77.
20. *Corr.* 2: 209n.
21. *Corr.* 2: 139.
22. *Corr.* 1: 261.
23. *Corr.* 3: 41.
24. Miss Blount urged Pope so forcibly to clear up the reasons why Ralph Allen was angry with them both, that Nathaniel Hooke got the impression 'she would have Mr. Pope fight him.' Spence 361 and note.
25. *Corr.* 2: 353.
26. Valerie Rumbold, *op. cit.*, p. 53. It is not absolutely certain that Captain Bagnell was Teresa's lover but it looks as if he was.
27. *Corr.* 3: 451.
28. TW. 3.ii: 46.
29. Samuel Johnson, *Lives of the Poets*, ed G.B. Hill, 3 vols (Oxford: Clarendon, 1905), 3: 190.
30. *Corr.* 4: 212.
31. *Corr.* 4: 177.
32. Spence, 361n.
33. *Corr.* 3: 414.
34. 'New Anecdotes', p. 349.
35. *Corr.* 4: 212.
36. *Corr.* 3: 349.

CHAPTER TWENTY-TWO

What the Letters Tell Us

Pope had always regarded his letters as part of his literary output. Many of them were carefully revised and some were set pieces, such as his entertaining account of a ride with the enterprising Mr Lintot to Oxford.[1] In 1730 Swift told his friend, 'I find you have been a writer of Letters almost from your infancy, and by your own confession had Schemes even then of Epistolary fame.'[2] Pope denied this but Swift, who knew him better than many men did, was probably right. Added to which, in the 1730s, Pope saw how an edition of his correspondence might provide a companion portrait to the one he was giving of himself in the Horatian satires. This prose portrait could go into more detail than was possible in the economy of verse and show him, not only as the loyal subject of King George and the friend of Virtue's but also as the valued friend of peers, country gentlemen and other illustrious writers. Pope's decision to publish his letters therefore was part of his persistent endeavour to answer his enemies and direct the way his readers felt about him. If this latest project was to succeed, Pope knew the letters would need rigorous editing – and this he gave them.

As early as 1712 Pope asked Caryll to return his correspondence. Caryll was reluctant to do so and the subject was dropped until 1726. In that year the matter became urgent when Curll managed to buy, and publish, the poet's letters to Cromwell. Lord Hardwicke's landmark decision, stating that letters were the writer's personal property, not to be disposed of at will by the recipient, was still fifteen years off.[3] Pope was alarmed when Curll printed the Cromwell letters not only because he resented others cashing in on anything he had written, but because he was worried by the thought of what the predatory publisher might get hold of next. There were some things he had no wish to see in print, such as indiscreet comments he was supposed to have committed to paper during the Atterbury trial.[4] Soon he wrote to Caryll asking again for his letters, though it was more than two years before he got them because Caryll's daughter Catherine was secretly transcribing them for her father.

In the meantime Pope wrote to other men asking them to return his correspondence, giving as his excuse the need to keep it out of the hands of Curll. In the beginning he was particularly anxious to get back anything he had written to his fellow Catholics, many of whom had Jacobite sympathies. So, at the same time he wrote to Caryll in 1726, he asked Edward Blount's widow to return the letters he had sent her husband. When he got this correspondence he played about with it extensively, reassigning some of it to other people.[5]

In the end he allowed very few Papist missives to get into print. There are none from his 'particular friend', the Catholic lawyer Nathaniel Hooke, or from the Jacobite fund raiser Father Southcote, or the Chevalier Ramsay, a tutor to Bonny Prince Charley, though we know letters were written.[6] In addition there are gaps in the correspondence, one of the longest being in the weeks before the 1715 rebellion. Whatever Pope's feelings about the Jacobites, he was, as ever, looking over his shoulder at those ready to accuse him of being one of them. Also missing are certain letters from members of the Opposition. There are none from Lord Cornbury, while the ones from Bolingbroke have been carefully culled. Finally it is probable that Pope omitted anything that might give his enemies ammunition when charging him with being two-faced. Laetitia Pilkington was shocked by a letter, which has since disappeared, but shown her by Swift, containing a 'great many satirical' remarks on the success of the *Beggar's Opera*.[7]

Pope admitted he burned three-quarters of the material he gathered together. Yet even after he had finished the weeding out process he was able to tell Lord Oxford in 1729, the collection was 'of some bulk.'[8] It was going to be stored in the Earl's library at Wimpole and, as Pope got ready to send it there, he added 'I think more and more of it; as finding what a number of Facts they [the letters] will settle the truth of, both relating to History, and Criticisme, & parts of private Life & Character of the eminent men of my time.'[9]

For the modern reader, the letters, both Pope's own selection and the twentieth-century edition in five weighty volumes, are of interest mainly in giving us a picture of the poet which is incomplete but not totally false. On the whole he appears amiable and charitable, which he was some of the time. We also note that he was clear-headed and had an excellent sense of humour. We do not see much of his ambitious and aggressive nature, still less of his deviousness and penchant for stratagems. But perhaps, in view of his enduring image as the wasp of Twickenham, the most striking thing about Pope, which is clear from his letters, is that his capacity for making friends fully equalled his capacity for making enemies. We also see something of his swiftly changing moods and attitudes as he adapts himself to his various correspondents, frivolous one day, philosophic the next, climbing onto a pedestal, only to jump off when it gets boring up there.

When Pope sent the letters to be stored at Wimpole he did not tell Lord Oxford that he wanted to see them in print. There was a tradition that one did not publish private correspondence and, although Pope thought this was 'prudery', he wanted to avoid the criticism he would face if he ignored a well-established convention without some good excuse.[10] One good excuse would be if there was a danger of the letters being published by anyone else. So Pope decided the solution to his problem was to lure Curll into piracy. The manoeuvres he engaged in to achieve this end tell us as much about him as the letters do themselves, bringing to the fore qualities he did not care to make too obvious when constructing his public image. These included his delight in intrigue, which he enjoyed, both because he liked pitting his wits in a complicated game of skill and because intrigue, along with the undercover activities often accompanying it, offered dramatic possibilities – of the sort that accompanied that mysterious delivery of the *Gulliver's Travels* manuscript to a publisher at the dead of night.

In 1733 Curll advertised for facts about the poet's life for one of his infamous biographies and Pope seized his chance. He decided to answer this advertisement himself. Signing his letter 'P.T.', he fed Curll with a lively blend of fact and fiction, including laying claim to aristocratic ancestors for himself.[11] Then, a month later, using the same pseudonym, he offered the publisher a collection of letters he happened to have by him, on condition that Curll took full responsibility for possession of them.[12] Curll could see himself being prosecuted for theft if he was not careful, so he did nothing for sixteen months. Then he wrote to Pope, enclosing the notes from P.T., offering to be his partner in a publishing venture. The poet took up the offer – in his own way.

The next thing that happened was that a short, squat gentleman arrived at the publisher's shop. This was James Worsdale, one of the shadier characters who were as much part of Pope's extensive network of useful contacts as peers such as Lord Oxford. A former pupil and reputed natural son of Godfrey Kneller, Worsdale sometimes made copies of his master's paintings for Pope. He was also a professional actor.[13] Dressed as a clergyman with lawyers' bands, he introduced himself to Curll, somewhat unimaginatively, as 'Smith.' Then he produced a bundle of the poet's letters, saying there were more where they came from.[14]

When Curll looked through the loose sheets, which were printed, he realized that only Pope could have sent them. They included some correspondence with Wycherley and came from the *Posthumous Works* of the dramatist, edited by the poet in 1729. After the book was suppressed because of a copyright dispute, Curll knew Pope had collected sheets from the printer. However, he thought he could still make money if he went along with 'Smith.' Accordingly Curll's edition of his sparring partner's correspondence came out in May 1735.

Predictably Pope raised a storm about the publisher's 'shameless industry.'[15] The illicit volume was, of course, as much the work of Pope as the legitimate one it paved the way for. Nevertheless, Curll showed he could still give the poet a few uncomfortable moments. When Pope announced he would have to produce his own authentic edition, Curll said that if he did, he would reprint from it, as he now had the copyright. He accused the poet of trickery in *Fog's Journal* but Pope forced the paper to issue a retraction.[16] Curll also promised to include letters from the indiscreet Duchess of Buckingham and from Atterbury in a further volume of the correspondence. This had Pope arriving on Fortescue's doorstep in an effort to get the volume banned.[17] An injunction was taken out but failed. This did not matter, however, because Curll did not have any letters from Jacobites. In fact he soon ran out of genuine ones of any kind and, by the time he published a third volume, he was forced to fabricate some from the poet to Patty Blount.

All these literary skirmishes took place in a blaze of publicity which helped to sell the book. So Curll made money, while Pope found the letters he had selected for his unacknowledged business partner impressed the wider public as favourably as he had intended they should do. The reaction of the Reverend Mather Byles of Boston, Massachussetts was not unrepresentative. Byles, who had never met Pope, wrote to him in 1736 to say he had read the letters in Curll's volume 'with particular pleasure' because they led him 'into the First Thoughts, and Domestick Character of so great a Man.'[18] By that time Pope was working on his own edition which another admirer offered to subsidize.

The admirer was Ralph Allen who visited Twickenham to make his offer in January 1736. Pope took a liking to his visitor but he did not want a patron. So a compromise was reached, with Allen getting his way about a de luxe format for the edition, which was then sold by subscription, with several of the poet's friends, including Fortescue, Bethel and Spence helping to recruit subscribers. Not everyone was taken in by Pope's machinations but that did not prevent the authorized and expanded version of his correspondence getting as many readers, and as much acclaim, as the unauthorized one had done.[19]

Meanwhile Pope added his would-be benefactor Allen to his list of friends.

Notes

1. *Corr.* 1: 371–5.
2. *Corr.* 3: 92.
3. Pat Rogers, 'The Case of Pope v. Curl', *Essays on Pope* (Cambridge University Press, 1993).
4. *Corr.* 2: 206.
5. *Selected Prose of Alexander Pope*, ed Paul Hammmond (Cambridge University Press, 1987), pp. 232–89. Hammond shows how Pope's own version of his correspondence, in which letters are grouped according to the people written to, gives a different impression from the strictly chronological sequence in George Sherburn's 1956 edition. See also, Maynard Mack, 'These Shadows of Me,' in *Collected in Himself* (University of Delaware Press, 1982), pp. 348–71 and Wendy Jones, *Talking on Paper: Alexander Pope's Letters* (Victoria BC: University of Victoria Press, 1990).
6. *Corr.* 3: 185 and Spence, 306.
7. *Memoirs of Laetitia Pilkington*, ed A.C. Elias, Jr, 2 vols (Athens and London: University of Georgia Press, 1997), 1: 34.
8. *Corr.* 3: 54.
9. Ibid.
10. Spence, 349.
11. *Corr.* 3: 387–8.
12. *Corr.* 3: 395–6.

13. *Dictionary of Irish Artists*, ed W.G. Strickland, 2 vols (Dublin and London, 1913).
14. *Corr.* 3: 461.
15. *Corr.* 3: 455.
16. Having entered thoroughly into his role, Pope offered a reward of £20 for information about 'Smith.' *Corr.* 3: 461.
17. *Corr.* 3: 472.
18. *Corr.* 4: 17.
19. For further details of this complicated story see, *The Correspondence of Alexander Pope*, ed George Sherburn, 5 vols (Oxford: Clarendon Press, 1956), 1: xii–xv and 3: 458–67 for a reprint of Pope's anonymous *The Narrative of the method by which the Private Letters of Mr. Pope have been Procur'd and Publish'd by Edmund Curll, Bookseller.*

CHAPTER TWENTY-THREE

The Patriots:
A Game of Hide and Seek

Ralph Allen, after starting off in life with few advantages except a good deal of native ability, made a fortune out of reorganizing the postal system. By the time Pope met him he was a philanthropist of a very practical kind. Not only did he regularly look after his workmen when they and their dependants were sick or old, he also opened a new quarry ahead of time, one hard winter, so as to provide jobs for men in his neighbourhood. Then, as he grew wealthier, he began filling in the gaps in his education. This is where Pope came in. He found a way of returning his new friend's generosity after Allen built a splendid house for himself near Bath. The poet not only helped plan the garden, as he did for many of his friends, but also suggested books for the library and found pictures for the gallery at Prior Park.

If Allen had not existed, Pope would have had to invent him. He was a living example of the honest entrepreneur with a social conscience and a respect for the Arts, whom the poet had in mind as an ideal when he savaged the crooked land agents and hard hearted money men, who were Allen's opposite.

The admirable Allen stood out in a world that had not improved since Pope had written his last moral satire. But he was not the only virtuous man to court the poet at this time. Writing to Swift in March 1736, Pope told him 'Here are a race sprung up of young Patriots that would animate you.'[1] He was referring to George Lyttelton, George Grenville and a hard-up young wonder William Pitt. They, and one or two others, were closely associated with Lyttelton's uncle Lord Cobham, and so were sometimes referred to as 'Cobham's cubs.' Fresh, energetic and full of optimism, they had picked up the torch thrown down by Bolingbroke. Although they had not been sorry to see their erstwhile leader go, they did not abandon his ideas. They endorsed his theory of kingship and carried on the task, he had already begun, of winning over the Prince of Wales, who they hoped would lead them into battle against the aging Walpole, and out of the moral squalor into which, as they saw it, the Minister had plunged England. Pope was attracted by their idealism, whereas he suspected the older anti-Ministry leaders, Carteret and Pulteney, of being no more than careerist politicians.

The enthusiasm of the young patriots was infectious. Nevertheless Pope was hesitant when they made it increasingly clear they wanted him to write for them. On the one hand, he was glad to have a support group. It gave him protection, in that, when he criticized the Government as one of a recognized party that included Protestant Whigs, he felt less vulnerable than he did as a solitary Papist and suspect Jacobite. On the other hand, he had no wish to become the Opposition's captive. In everyday life Pope was a double dealer, unscrupulous when it came to protecting and furthering his career but he never compromised his integrity as a poet. When he wrote verse, he wrote the truth as he saw it.

However the 'golden boys of Britain's future' pressed him hard.[2] George Lyttelton was the most insistent. He was an earnest, worthy man, a minor author as well as a politician who, in both these capacities, was more remarkable for his 'great flow of words' than for clarity of thought.[3] Pope esteemed him up to a point as 'one of those whom his own merit' had led him 'to contract an intimacy with.'[4] However he kept this particular patriot at arm's length when he tried to dictate, not only the subject matter of his poems, but the style in which they were to be written. In *An Epistle to Mr. Pope, from a Young Gentleman at Rome* (1730) Lyttelton had told Pope that satire was demeaning, urging him instead to 'raise / A lasting Column to thy Country's Praise' (ll. 5–6).[5] The kind of work he had in mind was provided by Richard Glover whose *Leonidas*, in nine books, recruited the Spartan opponent of the mighty Xerxes as a prototype Opposition hero. This tedious, almost forgotten epic was hugely successful at the time it was written, because it captured the public mood.

Lyttelton, who was to become the Prince of Wales's Secretary, would also have liked Pope to be Frederick's mentor and 'Animate him to Virtue.'[6] The Patriots had taken over the Prince's education but Pope was sceptical from the beginning about the abilities of 'Poor Fred'.[7] It seemed unlikely that this cordial mediocrity could be turned into Bolingbroke's wise monarch, capable of overriding factional party politics and uniting the country under his enlightened rule. Pope declined to teach him. Instead, as a goodwill gesture, he gave him one of Bounce's puppies with a quizzical inscription on the collar.

Resisting all efforts to take him over as a poet, Pope was nevertheless willing to contribute to the Patriots' campaign in his own way, doing what he did best which was writing satire. The result was that, for a year and a half from 1737, he was drawn into becoming more of a party writer than at any other time in his life.

Apparently he even agreed to write for a new Opposition newspaper, *Common Sense*. Though, as always happened when he was asked to contribute to party political journals, it is not known what, if anything, he wrote for this new one, which Charles Malloy started up in February 1737.[8] However, the poems Pope wrote at this time became increasingly bold in their attacks on prominent public figures, from George II on down.

Pope returned to the political arena in an eventful year. Throughout 1737 Walpole found himself faced with one crisis after another and although he kept cool and survived them all, it seemed his luck was running out at last.

At the opening session of Parliament the Opposition introduced a motion to

23.1   Alexander Pope, later in life. Arthur Pond

increase the Prince of Wales's allowance to £100,000 a year. It was a popular measure but abhorrent to Frederick's parents who loathed their son with a virulence, astonishing even for Hanoverians. So Walpole had to ensure the motion was defeated. It was – after Hervey wrote an eloquent pamphlet and after the chief minister spoke about the evils of dividing a father and his son. Later, Walpole boasted that the whole operation had only cost £900. Yet the margin of thirty votes by which he won was a narrow one, considering that half the Members of Parliament now depended on him for places or pensions. Such a small majority was an ominous sign for the future.

The debate over the Prince's allowance was no sooner out of the way than it was followed by an embarrassing dilemma over the Porteous Riots. A lynch mob in Edinburgh had hanged Captain Porteous of the Town Guard. As the Scots refused to name the culprits, Walpole would have liked to impose harsh penalties on the entire city. The Opposition hoped he would, as any Draconian action was sure to cause trouble with the forty-five Scots in Parliament. Pulteney and his followers fanned the flames but, to their disappointment, Walpole backed down.

While the Opposition launched their sorties on the Walpole citadel – with less success than they looked for, Pope published his first satire of the year on 28 April. In it he rehearsed the reservations he had about his capacity as a poet to reform society. The *Second Epistle of the Second Book of Horace* is addressed to one of the Dormer brothers, old friends whose home was Rousham in Oxfordshire, a house where Pope stayed most years during his summer rambles. General James Dormer and his brother Robert, a colonel, were former supporters of the Ministry who had become disenchanted.

In the last 300 lines of this satire Pope discusses whether or not he should stop being a poet. The main reason he gives for calling a halt to his career is that he does not see how he can do any good. Indirectly he is trying to explain to the Patriots why he has been slow to answer their call. He assumes the friend he is addressing in the poem will agree with him, maybe because he too is pessimistic about the possibility of changing society. Pope counsels retreat:

> Learn to live well, or fairly make your will;
> You've play'd, and lov'd and eat, and drank your fill:
> Walk sober off; before a sprightlier Age
> Comes Titt'ring on, and shoves you from the stage (ll. 322–5).

That last theatrical image is reminiscent of the one used by Bolingbroke, when he left England and wrote, 'My part is over, and he who remains on the stage after his part is over deserves to be hissed off.'[9] The similarity suggests Pope was thinking of Bolingbroke in this, the first poem he had published since his friend returned to France. Unlike the young Patriots who were new to the game, both men had seen too many political ventures fail to be confident of success now.

The departure of Bolingbroke and the comparatively recent deaths of such close allies as Gay and Arbuthnot helped to bring to the fore, in this new poem, that perennial theme of Pope's – loss. 'Years foll'wing Years, steal something every day,' pleasures, mistresses, friends. But this thought produces its own argument against retirement. For as Pope ruminates on Time, 'this subtle Thief of Life' he asks, 'What will it leave me, if it snatch my Rhime?' (ll. 72ff.). He cannot stop writing poetry because writing gives his life meaning.

Less than a month after telling his readers that he had no other choice than to be a poet, Pope published the *First Epistle of the Second Book of Horace*. It appeared in print soon after Richard Glover, whose *Leonidas* was taking London by storm, had spent a few days as Pope's guest at Twickenham. During the visit they were 'one evening honoured with the company of the Prince of Wales', escorted by Lyttelton.[10] We do not know what Pope thought of Glover or his epic but he had no intention of being upstaged. His new satire was his most daring so far, for its target was Frederick's father.

George II was an unpopular monarch. When his subjects thought he was lost at sea in December 1736, they viewed the matter with equanimity. 'How go the winds?' was the question asked in the London taverns, the answer being, 'Like the nation – against the King.'[11] The general populace was scathing about George's habit of spending so much time in Hanover, which he did all the more after 1735 when he found a new mistress there, Madame Walmoden.[12] The courtiers thought him a bore. The writers knew he was not interested in ideas or literature. His wife's fondness for philosophy and poetry exasperated him, though he knew what he liked in Art. Caroline and Hervey once spirited away a 'gigantic, fat Venus' from the wall of the great drawing room in Kensington Palace but he made them put it back.[13]

Such was the man Pope addressed as Augustus in the poem he published on 25 May 1737. In Pope's first Horatian satire, written four years earlier, Fortescue is supposed to have advised the poet to be like Cibber and write in praise of the royal family. Pope, who prided himself on being able to take advice, showed a friend's suggestion had not gone unheeded. The new poem was indeed a eulogy – one permeated with irony.

The tone of *To Augustus* is set by the compliment to George with which the epistle begins:

> While You, great Patron of Mankind, sustain
> The balanc'd World, and open all the Main;
> Your Country, chief, in Arms abroad defend
> ...

'Arms'? 'Walmoden's'? readers must have asked, but Pope does not hesitate to out-Cibber Cibber in phrases which parody the homage paid by the Poet Laureate in his royal birthday odes. 'Wonder of Kings'! Pope exclaims, 'like whom, to mortal eyes, / None e'er has risen, and none e'er shall rise' (ll. 29–30).[14] Another wonder is how Pope dared to commit such *lese majesty* except that, as he no doubt realized, it was virtually impossible to take him to task without admitting he had to be joking.

In the rest of the poem Pope steals an hour of his monarch's time to describe for him the state of the arts in England. The picture is one of decline with the deterioration in culture linked to moral decadence. Although George is not to be blamed if he is bored by poets who tire his patience by reciting nine hours out of ten, quarrel among themselves and write him epistles in the hope of a place or a pension, yet he owes it to his country to encourage the best in art.

Pope makes it plain what he believes is the best in poetry when he distinguishes between a mere man of rhymes and the true poet, imbued with fire and passion, yet in control of his material. He also argues that the poet is the guardian of moral values, singling out Swift for praise because, in campaigning against Wood's Halfpence, he fought for the oppressed and 'wrought a Nation's cure' (l. 222).

Pope wrote *To Augustus* when he was nearly fifty and showed that, since he had published *An Essay on Criticism* at the age of twenty-two, his standards had not wavered, nor had his ideas changed about the function of the true poet.

As had already been pointed out, it would have been difficult to charge Pope with mocking the King in his satire, but an uneasy Privy Council wondered if he could be prosecuted because of his compliment to Swift. The members of the Council discussed whether to take action but then thought better of it, though the fact they met at all meant they now had Pope in their sights.

Walpole, knowing how unpopular the King was, had been anxious to avoid a complete rift between him and his son, who was the people's darling. However a momentous row broke out in the royal family in August which culminated in George banishing Frederick from the Court. The Prince went to live in Norfolk House, St James's Square and, just as Walpole had feared, Frederick's new home became a centre, not only for members of the Opposition, but for disaffected courtiers as well. As the King refused to countenance anyone who visited his son, the establishment was now split in two. Worse was to come.

On 23 November Pope was in town, 'as sure to be there in a bustle' as Bathurst put it, 'as a porpoise in a storm.'[15] The Queen's death, three days earlier, had deprived Walpole of his best ally. For years, whenever he had a difficult proposition to put to the King, he approached Caroline first. To those who knew the Court, it was inconceivable that he could continue without such a mediator. During Caroline's painful, last days Chesterfield wrote to Lyttelton, 'In case the Queen die, I think Walpole should be looked on as gone too.' Then he counselled attacking him 'vigorously and personally as [one] who has lost his chief support.'[16] Actually Walpole was not finished yet but he showed signs of wearying in the face of an Opposition that went on, the following year, to do exactly as Chesterfield advised.

In 1738 the Opposition decided to concentrate on Walpole's foreign policy, in particular the complacency with which he regarded Spanish raids on English shipping in the Caribbean. The situation had been getting worse lately, with the guarda costas who claimed the right to search, behaving like pirates when they did so. On this issue, Pulteney and his followers had public opinion more solidly behind them than at any time since the Excise campaign.

Pope published a new satire on 7 March, a week after the beginning of the debate on Spain. The *First Epistle of the First Book of Horace* was addressed to Bolingbroke, a dedication that, quite apart from anything the poem said, was a provocation at the start of a political drama which reached a climax on 15 March, when Walpole's opponents produced a mutilated Captain Jenkins to give his testimony in the House of Commons. Jenkins told a plain, if not unvarnished, tale of his voyage to Jamaica seven years earlier. The guarda costas had boarded his ship, tied him to the mast, sliced off his ear and stripped the boat down to the bare timbers before turning it adrift.

Jenkins was followed by the up-and-coming William Murray, a friend of Pope, who was supposed to have coached him in the art of oratory. Murray's speech was one to fire the hearts of patriots, and was followed by Pulteney's call for measures against Spain that could easily lead to war. By now Walpole had only a dwindling band of supporters in the Ministry and as usual, when he was at bay, he played for time, with the result that he avoided coming to a clear decision until the following year.

The *First Epistle of the First Book of Horace* which Pope had published in March contributed to the Opposition campaign in arousing the patriotic feelings of the people. He deplored the mercenary values that stifled love of liberty and the national spirit, the cry of 'Get Mony, Mony still ... preach'd to all / from low St. James's up to high St. Paul' (ll. 79ff.) and, like the patriots, he called men back to their heroic selves asking:

> ... to which shall our applause belong,
> This new Court jargon, or the good old song?
> The modern language of corrupted Peers,
> Or what was spoke at CRESSY and POITIERS? (ll. 97–100)

Yet despite that clarion call to arms, the satire shows Pope was still not comfortable as a party writer. He was not an idealogue and it did not come as easily to him as it did to the politicians to think of issues in black and white terms. At the end of the poem he addresses Bolingbroke directly, telling him 'no Prelate's Lawn with Hair-shirt lin'd, / Is half so incoherent as my Mind' (ll. 165–6). He looks for guidance from his friend who is 'that reas'ning, high, immortal Thing, / Just less than Jove, and much above a King.' But Bolingbroke is no longer there and, having been moved to pay him the tremendous compliment just quoted, Pope shows just how divided his feelings are, about everything and everyone. In the last line of the poem he accuses his revered mentor, who has deserted him, of petulance, 'A Fit of Vapours clouds this Demi-god.'

Pope found it difficult to write simplistic verse himself but he was willing to help other more single minded writers. On 6 April 1738 James Thomson's *Agamemnon* opened. The play was party propaganda. Agamemnon represented George II, blamed for leaving his country for Hanover. Egisthus was Walpole who, in the King's absence, exerted a pernicious influence over Clytemnestra, alias Caroline. The work was dedicated to the Princess of Wales and Frederick went to see it twice. According to Cibber, Pope had written to two theatre managers when Thomson was trying to get his play put on. Then, when the premiere did not go as well as had been hoped, he met with other wits at the theatre the next day to slash the text, so as to make the drama better paced.[17]

Pope had been greeted with a round of applause by the audience when he entered his box on the first night of *Agamemnon*. No doubt some of the people sitting in the theatre had read the *Daily Gazeteer* which that same day had carried an attack on Pope, specifically aimed at his political stance. The journalist, who was probably John Henley, pointed out that in all the poet's current works 'the Friends to the present *Government* are continually the subject of his *Satire* as they who are the avowed Enemies to their Country are thought worthy of his Panegyricks.'

The *Daily Gazeteer* was now the main organ of ministerial opinion because, in 1735, Walpole had stopped subsidizing the myriad of journals there used to be, asking Nicholas Paxton to set up this one paper instead. It was well funded, ten thousand copies of it being regularly distributed, free of charge, by the Post Office.[18] The article on 6 April signalled that, whether he liked it or not, Pope was now regarded as a writer of political propaganda. It was one of some two dozen newspaper attacks on him that followed in the rest of 1738. These often blamed him for his praise of Bolingbroke who returned to England in July, but also revived the old charges of Papist disloyalty and Jacobitism. As always, Pope read what was being written about him but decided that, for the time being at any rate, it was still safe for him to carry on penning politically slanted verses.

Notes

1. *Corr.* 4: 6.
2. Christine Gerrard, *The Patriot Opposition to Walpole: Politics Poetry and the National Myth 1725–1742* (Oxford: Clarendon, 1994), p. 70.
3. *Lord Hervey's Memoirs*, ed Romney Sedgwick, 3 vols (London: Cresset, 1931), 2: 388.
4. *Corr.* 4: 134, Fielding's 'Epistle to Mr. Lyttelton' shows Pope and Lyttelton were friends by 1733. See Isobel M. Grundy, 'New Verse by Henry Fielding', *Publications of the Modern Language Association* (March, 1972), 213–45.
5. Gerrard, p. 77.

6.   *Corr.* 4: 138.
7.   The phrase 'poor Fred' is from an ironic epitaph quoted by Horace Walpole, *Memoirs of George II*, ed Lord Holland, 2nd edn, 3 vols (1847), 1: 436.
8.   Malloy, a Jacobite, informed the Stuart agent in Paris that Pope had offered to contribute to the new journal, as long as his participation was kept secret. *Stuart Papers*, 194, no. 10 and G.E. Jones, 'The Jacobite Charles Malloy and *Common-Sense*', *Review of English Studies*, 4 (1953), 144–7.
9.   'Letter to Sir William Windham,' November 1735, *The Works of Lord Bolingbroke*, 4 vols (Philadelphia, 1841), 1: 115.
10.   Joseph Warton, *An Essay on the Genius and Writings of Pope*, 2 vols 4th edn (1782), 2: 400.
11.   *Herveys's Memoirs*, 3: 913.
12.   Ibid., 2: 489.
13.   Ibid., 2: 202.
14.   Compare with Cibber's first New Year's Ode to George II in 1730: 'Hail, royal Caesar, hail. / Like this may every annual sun / Add brighter glories to thy crown, / Till suns themselves shall fail.
15.   *Corr.* 4: 88n.
16.   *Philip Dormer Stanhope, 4th Earl of Chesterfield, Letters*, ed Bonamy Dobrée (London, 1932), no. 608.
17.   Malcolm Goldstein, *Pope and the Augustan Stage* (Stanford University Press, 1958), ch. 3.
18.   Michael Harris, 'Print and Politics in the Age of Walpole', *Britain in the Age of Walpole*, ed Jeremy Black (London: Macmillan, 1984), p. 201.

Exit a Political Activist

When Pope read the attack on him in the *Daily Gazeteer* of 6 April, one particular insult struck home. The journalist had called him 'the calm Hero of a Couplet', writing verses in 'Twick'nam Bowers' that were, for all their misguided political bias, 'harmless Songs' that 'tinkle' in the ear. For Pope, who believed that great poetry stirred the heart, this sneer was of more immediate importance than the criticism of him as a supporter of the Opposition. He sensed that his days as a propagandist were numbered, but he had no intention of allowing his literary reputation to sink as one particular phase in his writing career came to an end.

He took the journalist's criticism so seriously that he devoted the next poem he wrote to answering it. Within weeks of the article in the *Daily Gazeteer* Pope's *Epilogue to the Satires: Dialogue I* was published on 16 May 1738. The poem begins with a 'Friend' playing the part of devil's advocate, expressing the view that Pope has grown 'correct that once with Rapture writ.' The courtiers gloat as they whisper, 'Decay of Parts, alas! We all must feel (ll. 3ff). The 'Friend' goes on to suggest that this is because the poet has taken Horace as his model. The Roman poet 'was delicate, was nice' (l. 11). He could afford to be. He was an accepted member of the establishment, whose 'sly, polite, insinuating stile / Could please at Court, and make Augustus smile' (ll. 19–20). Pope's situation is different. Despite his liking for Walpole as a man, he has taken up his stand against him as a Minister. Even his own side expects his attacks to be more hard hitting. '*Patriots* there are' the Friend says, 'who wish you'd jest no more' (l. 24). So be it. At the end of *Dialogue I* Pope shows his enemies and his friends what he can do with the couplet when he chooses.

In his description of Vice triumphant, sounding her black trumpet through England, Pope answers his critics with his most impassioned indictment so far of a society that not only protects the wicked if they have money and status, but worships them, a society in which 'Not to be corrupted is the Shame' (l. 160). The dramatic framework for the scene he creates combines a Roman Triumph with the presentation of the Whore of Babylon in the Book of Revelation.[1] The urbane voice of Horace is replaced by the thunderous tones of the Biblical patriarch. 'Let *Greatness* own her', Pope says of Vice, 'and she's mean no more':

> Her Birth, her Beauty, Crowds and Courts confess,
> Chaste Matrons praise her, and grave Bishops bless:
> In golden Chains the willing World she draws,
> And hers the Gospel is, and hers the Laws:

> Mounts the Tribunal, lifts her scarlet head,
> And sees pale Virtue carted in her stead!
> Lo! At the Wheels of her Triumphal Car,
> Old *England*'s Genius, rough with many a Scar,
> Dragg'd in the Dust! His Arms hang idly round,
> His Flag inverted trails along the ground!
> Our Youth, all liv'ry'd o'er with foreign Gold,
> Before her dance; behind her crawl the Old! (ll. 145–56)

The phrases about 'Old *England*'s Genius' being 'Dragg'd in the Dust' while 'His Flag inverted trails along the ground!' could not have been more timely. The day before the poem appeared Pulteney's Bill, to force Walpole into a war redeeming the national honour, was given a third reading – and was thrown out. No doubt the sceptical Pope had anticipated this blow to Opposition hopes.

The lines were also timely in another way. The picture of Vice is no abstract personification. She is doubly allegorical. According to Warburton, she is Theodora, the prostitute whom Justinian married.[2] Justinian, dubbed the Great, codified Roman law and was therefore an apt counterpart for Walpole who legislated for Britain. Moreover, for Pope's contemporaries, Theodora would have brought to mind Maria Skerret, Walpole's mistress, recently raised to the dignity of becoming the Great Man's wife.[3] In the spring of 1738 she was received at Court, with the Duchesses of Newcastle and Richmond vying for the honour of presenting her to the King. So the woman whom moralists called a whore became the symbol of a society which had accepted her as one of its own.

Fresh restrictions were in force on the right to speak out on public affairs, even as Pope wrote *Dialogue I*. A new Licensing Act was passed in June 1737. This law was supposed to apply only to the theatre but, while it was still being debated in Parliament, Chesterfield warned the Lords, 'It is an Arrow that does but glance upon the Stage: but it will give its fatal wound to the liberty of the Press.'[4] He was not far wrong. There was an immediate clamp down on Opposition journals. Nicholas Paxton, who directed Walpole's press, was given the task of studying all Opposition writing for evidence that it slandered the King or his Government.[5] He wasted no time. Within a month of the Act receiving Royal assent the *Craftsman* was prosecuted for its paper of 2 July 1737 and, again, for an issue that appeared on 10 December.[6]

Dialogue II was published on 18 July 1738, two months after the first poem in the *Epilogue to the Satires*. Pope begins his new work with a reference to Paxton. So far he has not been reported to the Secretaries of State but the situation might not last, 'And', he says, 'for that very cause I print today' (l. 3). He knows he is vulnerable because of his habit of naming names. However, by doing so, he states he has succeeded in discomforting those who are otherwise fawned on by society. *Dialogue II* is his final vindication of himself as a satirist. 'I must be proud to see' he admits, 'Men not afraid of God, afraid of me' (ll. 208–9). Pope also insists, as he has always done since he started writing satire, that he is a moralist, an independent critic of society as a whole, not a party political partisan:

> Ask you what Provocation I have had?
> The strong Antipathy of Good to Bad.

Pope's assertive self righteousness can strike modern readers as insufferable posturing. Who, after all was this fallible human being to set himself up as a judge of his fellow human beings? Yet if Pope failed to live up to his own virtuous principles, on occasion, this does not mean the principles were any less sincerely held. Furthermore, as one of his recent defenders points out, before we condemn Pope's strident tone, we should remember that, unlike us, he did not live in a comparatively liberal democracy.[7] In fact, his situation was more like that of a dissident living in a one-party state. Stung by the *Daily Gazeteer*'s contempt, Pope did not want to be labelled 'harmless' – or, worse still, pusillanimous. He was shrill because he felt insecure. It took courage for a Papist outsider to take on a powerful Government machine as he had done, especially as he could not know how real, or not, the danger of doing so was.

Actually by the time Pope wrote *Dialogue II* he had already been the target of one bit of unpleasantness. In the poem he refers to an evening when Paxton's men, bribed with 'double Pots and Pay' broke his windows at Twickenham while he was entertaining his friends to dinner (l. 141). The attacks on him in the press also gathered momentum. The following year another Paxton hireling would list him with Pulteney, Carteret, Chesterfield, Wyndham and Bolingbroke as one of the 'Six Incendiary Chiefs' of the Opposition.[8] *Dialogue II* ends as it began with Pope thinking about censorship as he reiterates, 'Yes, the last Pen for Freedom let me draw, / When Truth stands trembling on the edge of Law' (ll. 248–9).

There was talk of Pope planning a third dialogue and at least three different reasons are on offer as to why it did not appear. Two of the explanations come from William Warburton and the third from the poet himself. In 1740 Warburton said, 'Mr. Pope is tired of imitating Horace ... the great scheme he has in view is the continuation of the Essay [on Man].'[9] Writing seven years after the poet's death however, Pope's chosen editor said the poet had been silenced, like Paul Whitehead who was summoned to appear before the House of Lords in 1739, to answer for his satire, *Manners*. Warburton went on to refer to a third dialogue, 'more severe and sublime than the first or second' which was 'unfinished and suppressed' after 'Pope's enemies agreed to drop the prosecution.'[10] Meanwhile in 1740, when both dialogues were reprinted as the *Epilogue to the Satires*, Pope had added a final note which read,

> This was the last poem of the kind printed by our author, with a resolution to
> publish no more; but to enter thus, in the most plain and solemn manner

he could, a sort of PROTEST against that insuperable corruption and depravity of manners, which he had been so unhappy to live to see. Could he have hoped to have amended any, he had continued those attacks; but bad men were grown so shameless and so powerful, that Ridicule was become as unsafe as it was ineffectual.'[11]

All this is confusing but it may be possible to reconcile the opposite explanations as follows. It looks as if Pope was warned off but felt it would be humiliating to advertise the fact. Certainly, such an admission would not have accorded very well with his reinvention of himself as a secular Savonarola. At the same time, he was probably not sorry to have an excuse to stop writing party political verses. He had never been at ease with the politicians' urge to damn their opponents just because they were opponents. Even when he was writing for the Patriots he stood aside from the violence of opinion. In *To Bolingbroke* he had said of himself, 'Sworn to no Master, of no Sect am: / As drives the storm, at any door I knock' (ll. 24–5). For two years Pope had been a captive of the Opposition – he wanted to be free again.

We cannot be sure what happened in 1738 but the above explanation fits in with Pope's instinctive recognition that he needed a measure of independence if he was to be a true poet. His escape from writing propaganda is an instance of inner conviction he shared with other creative people, that he had to remain an outsider.

Writing to Swift in May 1739, Pope told him that he had 'written but ten lines' since his 'Protest' in the *Epilogue to the Satires*.[12] Yet if he had not written any more verses for the Patriots, he was still willing to help them in other ways. Bolingbroke had returned to England in July 1738 and stayed with Pope in Twickenham, while trying to sell his farm at Dawley. There, the two men were visited by the new, younger members of the Opposition. This group included 'a Lord Cornbury, a Lord Polwarth, Mr. Murray & one or two more' all of whom Pope greeted with initial enthusiasm, saying that with them 'he would never fear to hold out against the Corruption of the World.'[13] During this period he was also courted by another fierce opponent of Walpole, the old Duchess of Marlborough.

In addition to presiding over a little Whitehall at his villa again, Pope continued to advise on plays that were politically slanted. On 13 February 1739, resplendent in a red cloak, he went to see James Quin on the first night of David Mallet's *Mustapha*, a work on which he had offered helpful comments. The author dedicated it to the Prince of Wales. However, the Government was now determined to use the 1737 Licensing Act to prevent the Opposition using the theatre as a forum for its ideas. Two plays, with a political subtext, that Pope read in manuscript were banned in 1739, Henry Brooke's *Gustavus Vasa*, featuring Walpole as the villain, and Thomson's *Edward and Eleanora*. So a useful avenue for reaching the public was now closed.

Meanwhile Bolingbroke started writing his *Idea of a Patriot King* while he was at Twickenham. This treatise was designed to instruct a prince on his role once he succeeded to the throne. It brought into sharper focus ideas on the monarchy described earlier in the *Craftsman* and elsewhere, its basic thesis being that a King's role was to mediate between the demands of the aristocracy in the Lords and democracy in the Commons. Bolingbroke had jettisoned the belief in divine right but still thought there was a powerful magic which adhered to a hereditary monarch, enhancing his authority. Above all, a king must be the embodiment and the symbol of the best spirit of the nation.

Such a theory presupposed that, at the very least, the king was able to keep the respect of his subjects. Bolingbroke's favourite monarch was Elizabeth I. However, both he and Pope had their reservations about the capacity of Frederick to be a moral influence, still less an inspiration to the country.[14] Bolingbroke, having sold Dawley, returned to France in 1739. Before he went he gave the manuscript of the *Patriot King* to the poet, having asked him to get half a dozen or so copies printed for distribution among their friends.

The year 1739 was also when the first minister's attempts to negotiate a settlement with the Spaniards failed finally. War was declared on 19 October and the bells rang throughout the land, whereupon Walpole famously said, 'They now *ring* the bells, but they will soon *wring* their hands.'[15] The Prince of Wales, on the other hand went with the patriotic tide, toasting the mob from a City tavern. The following year he went to Clivedon for the first performance of the masque *Alfred*. This had in it a song by Thomas Arne voicing the current belligerency – *Rule Britannia*.

Pope, one of Nature's non-conformists, shared less of this general euphoria than might have been supposed. He sketched out another satire which he never completed. *1740: A Poem* expressed some of the doubts he had felt the year before as he listened to his friends discussing political strategies over dinners at Twickenham. It shows that he had become disillusioned, not just with the King and his Ministry but with the Opposition, whose ranks were thinning. In June 1740 Wyndham was killed in a riding accident. Then Pope's favourite among the newer men, Lord Polwarth was removed from Parliament on inheriting the title of Earl of Marchmont. He would not sit in the Lords as a Scottish peer until 1750. If that was not enough, Bolingbroke, away in Paris, was making fresh overtures to the Jacobites.[16] Out of those who were left to oppose Walpole, Pulteney was showing himself to be no less self-seeking than the men he fought against. Others lacked strength of purpose, including old friends of Pope.

It is unlikely that Pope criticised the guests who sat round his dinner table openly. Instead, as was his wont, he reserved the truth as he saw it for *1740*. Although the poem is only a skeleton, with some lines half written in and most of the proper names left blank (replaced by initials or cryptic symbols), the gaps have since been plausibly filled in so that the general drift is clear.[17] Pope begins by castigating the 'Patriot Race' (l. 4), including men he had

once admired. Cobham and Bathurst express concern for wretched Britain's
welfare, 'Unless the ladies bid them mind their cards' (l. 24), while Chesterfield
finds his country 'at best, the butt to crack his joke upon' (l. 28). When Pope
discusses the Government, he knows it consists of nonentities, except for
Walpole. His estimate of that pragmatic leader is close to the view taken by
posterity as he writes, 'Rise, rise great W[alpole] fated to appear / Spite of
thyself a glorious minister' (ll. 43–4). Certainly there was nothing to be hoped
for from George II, 'the people curse, the carman swears, / the drivers quarrel,
and the master stares' (ll. 73–4).

Pope concludes by saying:

> Alas! On one alone our all relies,
> Let him be honest, and he must be wise,
> Let him no trifler from his [father's] school'
> Nor like his [father's father] still a [fool]
> Be, but a man! unminister'd, alone,
> And free at once the Senate and the Throne;
> Esteem the public love his best supply,
> A [king's] true glory his integrity (ll. 85–92).

The subject of these lines appears to be Frederick, Prince of Wales but could
just as easily be Charles Edward, who since his birth had been the Jacobites'
hope for Britain. If Pope was thinking of Bonnie Prince Charley as he wrote,
then the deliberate ambiguity would have been characteristic of him.

It is doubtful whether we shall ever know for sure what Pope's connection
with the Jacobites was. There is no evidence he was ever involved in their plots,
though he certainly knew more about these than he cared to admit. After 1727,
when he became a reformer, he did not contemplate overturning the system. He
worked within it, having resigned himself to the Hanoverian *status quo*. The
rise to power of Walpole was one reason for this. Pope's attitude to the Whig
minister was always ambivalent. He knew that, though Walpole misused
power, he deserved the title 'Great Man', even if half the people who called him
that did so in mockery. Pope, who was patriotic but not a war monger, approved
of his long term aims of peace and prosperity for the country. Furthermore he
liked him as a man. Even at the height of the Opposition campaign, he paid
tribute to Walpole's warm and engaging personality:

> Seen him I have, but in his happier hour
> Of Social Pleasure, ill exchang'd for Pow'r;
> Seen him, uncumber'd with the Venal tribe,
> Smile without Art, and win without a bribe
>
> (*Dialogue I*, ll. 39–42).

Earlier Pope had thought to find in Walpole someone to whom he could turn
for protection and favours. He was encouraged when the first minister, for
reasons of his own helped to secure the Abbey at Avignon for Southcote. It is
possible too that he secured some kind of a deal with him after Charles Rackett

was arrested. However, any illusions he may have had about the extent of his influence were shattered when Walpole failed to provide for Gay. Eventually Pope had joined the Patriots in their campaign to expose a corrupt regime and oust the man who presided over it. Yet as he did so, he blamed the minions more than their leader saying, 'Sure, if I spare the Minister, no rules / Of Honour bind me, not to maul his Tools' (*Dialogue II*, ll. 146–7).

1740: A Poem shows Pope remained as mixed as ever in his feelings about Walpole. It also shows him deeply pessimistic about political solutions. When he wrote it he probably had no more faith in the Jacobites than in the Opposition. A wise, strong king would be the best thing for the country but Pope was not optimistic when he contemplated the rival claimants for the throne. The unimpressive Prince of Wales in England was at best, a 'little Short sighted.'[18] His charismatic counterpart was over the water. Any attempt to bring him back was likely to fail again. When Pope mused on the future of the monarchy, he could only say 'Alas!'

Notes

1. Compare: 'and I saw a woman sit upon a scarlet coloured beast, full of the names of blasphemy. And the woman was arrayed in purple and scarlet colour, and decked with precious stones and pearls, having a golden cup in her hand ... And I saw the woman drunken with the blood of the saints and with the blood of the martyrs.' *Book of Revelation*, ch. 17, verses 3ff.
2. *Works of Alexander Pope*, ed William Warburton, 9 vols (1951), vol. 4.
3. James M. Osborn, 'Pope, the Byzantine Empress, and Walpole's Whore', *Review of English Studies*, 6 (1955), 372–82. Maria Skerrett had been Sir Robert's mistress since about 1724. By 1735 she was drawing £1000 a year from the public funds. Walpole married her as soon as his wife died but Maria herself died soon afterwards in 1738.
4. Quoted by James Ralph in *A Critical History of the Administration of Sir Robert Walpole, Now Earl of Orford* (London, 1743), p. 322.
5. *Calendar of Treasury Books and Papers (1735–38)*, p. 422.
6. Laurence Hanson, *Government and the Press 1695–1763* (London, 1936), p. 67.
7. John Richardson, 'Defending the Self: Pope and his Horatian Poems', *Modern Language Review*, vol. 95, pt 3 (July, 2000), 623–33.
8. *A Hue and Cry After a Pack of Hounds, which Broke out of their Kennel in Westminster* (1739), p. 21.
9. Spoken to Charles Yorke. Quoted, George Harris, *The Life of Lord Chancellor Hardwicke*, 3 vols (1847), 1: 475.
10. *Works*, ed Warburton (1751), 4: xl.
11. *Dialogue II*, 254n.
12. *Corr.* 4: 178.
13. Ibid.
14. See also *Lord Hervey's Memoirs*, ed. Romney Sedgwick, 3 vols (London: Cresset, 1931), 1: 97 where Hervey said of Frederick that 'he had a much weaker understanding, and if possible, a more obstinate temper than his father.'

15. William Coxe, *Memoirs of Sir Robert Walpole* (1798), 1: 618.
16. Stuart Papers at Windsor, letter dated 18 April 1740 from Semphill, one of James's agents.
17. This work was done by Edmond Malone. See Comments TW. 4: 330–31.
18. *Corr.* 4: 142.

PART VI

Looking to Posterity

CHAPTER TWENTY-FIVE

A Closet Editor

At the beginning of 1740 Pope was staying at Allen's house in Bath. The very cold weather made travelling back to Twickenham difficult, especially as he was more than usually unwell – kidney trouble being an additional problem. So he remained at Prior Park for over three months. During the visit Allen did everything possible to ensure his guest was comfortable, including limiting the number of visitors who besieged the house while the poet was there. Pope settled down (he enjoyed being cosseted), not too sorry to have an excuse for staying out of the way of his Opposition friends for a while.

As yet Pope had not embarked on his next poetical project but he was not idle that winter. Having devoted a lifetime to directing what the public thought about him and his work, he turned his attention to promoting the reputation of two of his oldest friends, Bolingbroke and Swift. He wanted to give each of them his rightful place in history and had decided just how to go about this. In Bolingbroke's case, it meant revising the *Patriot King* and, in Swift's case, making sure his correspondence was published. Pope was never a man to leave things to chance. Nowadays we would be tempted to call him a control freak. The contrasting reactions of the objects of Pope's attention, when they discovered what he had been doing, were characteristic of them. Bolingbroke, the grand seigneur, was astonished and outraged at his protégé's presumption. Swift, a social equal and fellow writer, who knew very well what Pope was capable of, said nothing but, at the last minute, took charge, turning his friend's stratagems to his own advantage.

Pope had the manuscript of the *Patriot King* with him at Prior Park because, as has already been mentioned, Bolingbroke had asked him to have about ten copies of it printed, for distribution to their friends. When Pope read it through, he made changes. As no copy of the original manuscript has survived, we do not know what these changes were but it is unlikely Pope was tinkering with the style of such an accomplished writer. Bolingbroke had, however, written the *Patriot King* when he was contemplating the Jacobite option again. So it is feasible that Pope removed anything that suggested the work was written with Bonny Prince Charley in mind.[1] When he had finished he showed the revised version to his host. Allen, who was a staunch Hanoverian, liked what he read and it was agreed to have as many as 1,500 copies run off, probably with Allen's financial help. The edition was then left with the printer John Wright. It is hard to know what Pope planned to do next. Perhaps he hoped to persuade Bolingbroke to publish the revised work at an appropriate time later on.

Alternatively, he might have intended to publish the *Patriot King* himself, if his friend died before he did, so ensuring his posthumous fame.

However, Pope died first, whereupon Bolingbroke found out about the 1,500 copies stored in Mr Wright's shop. He made the discovery shortly before the Forty Five Rebellion when England was on full alert, expecting an invasion. He panicked. Not realizing that Pope had changed a possibly subversive text which could have led to the author's execution for treason, he ordered Marchmont to collect the books and made a bonfire of them on the terrace of his house in Battersea, but one or two copies escaped the flames.

Eventually in 1749, well after the failure of the Jacobite rebellion, Bolingbroke arranged for his own authorized version of the *Patriot King* to be published, along with an advertisement denouncing Pope for having dared to revise what he had written. Yet the text Bolingbroke published did not differ in essentials from the one Pope had had printed.

Without Bolingbroke's original manuscript, any explanation of what happened has to be hypothetical, including the one suggested here. However, it is a fact that the final published version of the *Patriot King*, which was similar to the one edited by Pope, enhanced its author's reputation. Its lack of party bias helped to make it popular. One contemporary reader praised it for giving a 'perfect system of practical politics.'[2] It was reprinted four times in the last half of the eighteenth century and appeared in German and two French translations. In 1780 it was quoted by those who preferred conciliation of America to war. Later it proved so adaptable that it could be used to bolster the arguments of American radicals as well as English constitutional monarchists.[3]

While Pope was staying at Prior Park during the winter of 1740, he also began putting together another collection of letters, this time of his correspondence with Swift. Getting the volume into print was going to prove as difficult as any task he had undertaken but, as ever, having made up his mind to do something, he persevered.

One major problem was Swift himself, who would have preferred Pope to write an epistle in his praise.[4] On 3 September 1735 he had tried to force his friend's hand by telling him that he had given instructions in his will for his executors to burn every letter he left behind him.[5] Pope, however, had set his heart on revealing to the world the evolving relationship between the two leading writers of the age. He intended to show how even if they had often exasperated each other, with Swift leaving the villa at Twickenham because he found his host sickly and complaisant and Pope berating the Dean for sending him unwelcome visitors and for being tactless on occasion, yet the two of them had an understanding of each other which enabled their friendship to survive. He decided the letters they had written to each other over the years demonstrated this and he promised Swift that, when they were published, they would show him to be one of 'the greatest men of the time.'[6] In due course Swift, tacitly if reluctantly, came round to the poet's way of thinking and

25.1 Jonathan Swift. Engraved by B. Holl after Charles Jervas

the two of them worked, in their different ways to publish their letters to each other.

However, Swift's recalcitrance was only part of the problem. When Pope had first published a volume of his letters, he had pitted himself against Curll, a wily but familiar opponent whose measure he took from the outset. Now, apart from the two men who had actually written the letters, the cast included an obtuse peer Lord Orrery, a possessive lady Mrs Whiteway, a hanger-on Deane Swift and an honest Dublin publisher George Faulkner.

In 1735 Orrery, who had estates in Ireland, began writing regularly to Pope to tell him how Swift was. At that time Orrery was a young man of twenty-eight who had succeeded to the earldom four years earlier. His father, not having a high opinion of his intellectual capacity, had bequeathed his library to Christ Church, Oxford.[7] Nevertheless his son nurtured literary ambitions and sought the company of celebrated writers.

The accounts Orrery sent of the Dean were alarming. Throughout the negotiations over the letters Swift was sane, though, as he constantly lamented, his memory was going. As he approached seventy his attacks of giddiness and deafness came with increasing frequency, plunging him into deep depression but, when the symptoms of Ménière's Disease receded, he was well and could be cheerful. Even though Orrery realized there were times when Swift appeared to be in 'perfect health', he tended to exaggerate the importance of the bad days, telling Pope that the Dean was getting 'worse and worse.'[8]

Pope was inclined to take the pessimistic view when he got Orrery's letters. He was equally worried when he realized that Swift was in the habit of showing his Dublin acquaintances letters written to him by famous men. Sometimes he let them borrow them. As not all the people he entertained were over-scrupulous, there was a danger the papers would be stolen. Pope began to bombard Dublin with requests for his correspondence. Whereupon he encountered another obstacle. This was Mrs Whiteway who, for reasons of her own, obstructed his wishes and then those of Swift, regarding the letters.

Mrs Whiteway was one of Swift's cousins, a competent woman in her forties who from about Christmas 1730 used to come and play cards with him. In 1735 she took over the management of his household, vetting his visitors and writing letters for him when he was unwell. Eventually she became his nurse and looked after him faithfully right up to the appalling end. She was indispensable but not popular in Swift's social circle. Over the years, several of the Dean's close associates disappeared from the scene for various reasons, which included his increasing awkwardness. It was Mrs Whiteway, however, who in 1738 told Tom Sheridan, one of Swift's oldest friends in Ireland, that he was no longer welcome at the Deanery.[9] Nor did she get on with Orrery who, in his turn, was suspicious of her.

By April 1736 Swift no longer spoke of burning his letters. Instead he told Pope he would instruct his executors to forward them to Twickenham after he died. Throughout the first three months of 1737, however, Orrery was writing to Pope, hinting darkly of people with 'Selfish views' and 'mean designs' who were trying to get Swift to change his mind.[10] Nevertheless, he persuaded Swift to let him have some letters to take to Twickenham in July. There were supposed to be sixty of these but when Pope opened the package, there were only twenty-five. Whereupon he and Orrery supposed Mrs Whiteway had held the other thirty-five back. At first she denied this but eventually said she had acquired some more letters after all.

A year went by before Orrery returned to Ireland. By the time he did so in 1738 he found he was rarely admitted to the deanery. A number of changes were under way there. In May Swift made a new will. There was no mention in this of his letters being forwarded to Twickenham. Instead he bequeathed all his manuscripts to Mrs Whiteway. She had also acquired an ally, a penniless Oxford graduate Deane Swift, who would marry her daughter in 1739. As this young man hoped to edit the works of his relative and namesake and also write his biography, he had every reason to help his mother-in-law safeguard Swift's papers. However, Orrery gave Pope a useful piece of information when he wrote, telling him that although 'the Lady's power [Mrs Whiteway's] ... encreases daily: at night her influence ends, that is She retires to her Lodging, and the Dean to his Bed.'[11]

Pope had been wondering how he could get in touch with his old friend without going through Mrs Whiteway. Now he knew. Before he left Allen's house in 1740, he had sent to a discreet printer the volume of Swift's correspondence, which he had been compiling that winter. Back in London, he contacted Sam Gerrard, an old acquaintance of Swift's. In May Gerrard went to Dublin, carrying with him a package which had been left at his lodgings. This he took to the deanery – after dark. It contained the printed copy of the letters, together with a note supposedly from Irish well wishers which began, 'The true Honour which all the honest and grateful Part of this Nation must bear you, as the most publick spirited of Patriots, the best of private Men, and the greatest polite Genius of this Age, made it impossible to resist the Temptation, which has fallen our Way, of preserving from all Accidents a Copy of the *inclosed Papers*.'[12] The letter went on to assure Swift there was no other copy of the book in any hands but his own.

Pope had composed this letter and sent the packet which, as he planned, reached his friend safely, unbeknown to Mrs Whiteway. So far so good, but what happened next came as a surprise. He had thought Swift would tell him about the arrival of the letters. They would then agree it was unlikely that only one copy of the printed volume existed, and this would provide an excuse to bring out an official edition which Pope was getting ready to launch. However, Swift was in good health and spirits when the book arrived. He read it through, added a few footnotes and an additional letter or two. Then he sent it round to Dublin's leading publisher George Faulkner, with instructions to go ahead and reprint it.

Swift's prompt action gave Pope a few sleepless nights as he could not be sure how much his friend had added to the volume. He was particularly worried about correspondence with Bolingbroke which might be included, especially letters written after Anne's death when Bolingbroke had gone over to James. Orrery was given the task of getting proofs of the Faulkner volume and bringing them to Twickenham so that Pope could vet them. Meanwhile Mrs Whiteway proved zealous in trying to stop Faulkner publishing the letters at all saying, as she did so, that she was on the poet's side, who had to go along with the fiction he created, pretending not to know where the volume he had sent Swift came from, and officially expressing disapproval of it.

Actually, by this stage, Pope might just as well have stopped plotting. Not for the first time, he had been found out. Apparently both Mrs Whiteway and Faulkner knew that the volume they were arguing about came from Pope.[13] Orrrery was the only person who remained in the dark. He told the poet he thought Deane Swift was the culprit, having had the letters printed in England in the hope of making money.

Then Orrery began to cause problems of his own. After reading the proofs through before he gave them to Pope, he told him the letters 'were never meant for print' because 'in the dean's are some sharp sayings of a very high nature.'[14] Pope disposed of this inept objection with masterly despatch, pointing out that Swift took 'a pleasure in these freedoms' adding, 'I believe the printing of them will give him more Satisfaction than the consequences can give him any pain.'[15]

So the volume sent to Faulkner was reprinted, uncensored. This enabled Pope to go ahead with the plan he had had in mind from the beginning of this saga, of launching his own edition of Swift's correspondence. His excuse was that he had been provoked into doing so by the 'dubious' Dublin one. Pope's collection appeared in April 1741 and included a few more letters which he had obtained from Mrs Whiteway – after some protracted negotiations.

Pope had stood to gain nothing personally when he arranged for a surreptitious edition of the *Patriot King* but the situation was a different (and more familiar) one when he engaged in his complicated manoeuvres to get Swift's letters into print. Pope's own publication of them formed part of his *Works in Prose: Volume II*. As that title makes clear, he took a proprietary interest in the correspondence. He was concerned with his own reputation as well as Swift's, hoping the publication of their letters to each other would show his readers, including his enemies, not only that Swift was one of the 'greatest men of his time, but that this same man had admired and loved him'.

As usual Pope did not admit he had been scheming to achieve his ends. Nevertheless he did sound a little embarrassed when he wrote to Swift in March 1741. By that time it is reasonable to assume Swift knew his friend had sent him the correspondence in Gerrard's parcel and that the poet knew he knew. There is a note of guilty self justification in Pope's assurances as he writes, 'Think it not possible my Affection can cease but with my last breath: If I could think yours was alienated, I should grieve but not reproach you ... whatever unpleasant circumstances the printing of our Letters might be attended with, there was *One* that pleas'd me, that the strict Friendship we have borne each other so long, is thus made known to all mankind.'[16] We do not know what Swift thought as he read Pope's attempt at conciliation in this the last letter he received from him.

Posterity however has reason to be grateful. It is doubtful that Swift would have collected his correspondence and published it of his own accord. Without Pope's machinations and his vision, the letters might have been edited by someone with the emasculating tendencies of Lord Orrery or, worse still, dispersed throughout Dublin.[17]

Notes

1. For various discussions of what happened see: F.E. Ratchford, 'Pope and the *Patriot King*', *Texas Studies in English*, 6 (1926), 157–77; Giles Barber, 'Bolingbroke, Pope and the *Patriot King*', *The Library*, 19 (1964), 64–89; F.T. Smallwood, 'Bolingbroke vs. Alexander Pope: The Publication of the *Patriot King*', *Papers of the Bibliographical Society of America*, 65 (1971), 225–41 and Simon Varey, 'Hanover, Stuart and the *Patriot King*', *British Journal for Eighteenth-Century Studies* (Autumn, 1983), 163–72.

2. David Armitage, 'A Patriot for Whom? The Afterlives of Bolingbroke's *Patriot King*', *Journal of British Studies*, 36 (October, 1997), 397–418, p. 404.

3. Armitage, *op.cit.*

4. *Corr.* 3: 492.

5. Ibid.

6. *Corr.* 4: 28.

7. *Dictionary of National Biography.*

8. *Corr.* 4: 73 and 226.

9. Irvin Ehrenpreis, *Swift, the Man, his Works and his Age*, 3 vols (London: Methuen, 1962–83), 3: 882.

10. *Corr.* 4: 54, 62 and 72.

11. *Corr.* 4: 226.

12. *Corr.* 4: 242.

13. *Corr.* 4: 279 and British Library, Add. 4244. f. 38r.

14. *Corr.* 4: 294.

15. *Corr.* 4: 301.

16. *Corr.* 4: 337.

17. In the opinion of Ehrenpreis, 'The most considerable and enduring monument to Swift, apart from his own works, was conceived and accomplished by Pope', *op. cit.*, 3: 882.

CHAPTER TWENTY-SIX

Pope's 'Bulldog'

In April 1740 the Reverend William Warburton came to dinner at Twickenham. It was his first visit there and Pope, the gourmet, arranged a feast for the occasion, though these preparations were lost on his guest.

'What do you never eat any'? asked his host as the theologian refused the lobster.

'I never did.'

'You hate it then?'

'I can't tell.'

Pope pressed on. 'You had as good try, how you like it.' 'No', came the reply, 'as I have never tasted it, I don't know why I should try now.' The abstemious visitor also turned down the poet's Cyprus wine with 'We have desires enough; why should we add to them?'[1] Pope was more amused than disconcerted. During the course of what was to prove a close association, he refused to be ruffled by the clergyman's censorious streak, except on one occasion when it manifested itself against Patty.

At first sight, Warburton was a somewhat surprising companion for Pope. One of Nature's Victorians, he had none of the unselfconscious goodness of Ralph Allen, nor did he have any of the panache that appealed to the poet in some of his aristocratic friends. Pope saw to it that his new acquaintance was introduced to a varied circle that included political figures such as Chesterfield, Murray and Lyttelton, the philanthropist Allen, the artist Jonathan Richardson and the historian Nathaniel Hooke, but Warburton did not become universally popular. One anonymous contemporary exploded at the thought of him with, 'He's an absolute fo-ol! I saw it the first time I was in his company, in the horrid massiveness of his look, and that *impenetrable taciturnity.*'[2] Actually Warburton was far from taciturn once he had found his feet in society. Then it was said of him that he was 'disposed to take to himself a somewhat larger share of the conversation than exact breeding is thought to allow', though the same speaker added that in 'mixed companies ... he was extremely entertaining.'[3] His manners in print were somewhat worse because he was so dogmatic. 'In his polemic writings', said Edward Gibbon, 'he lashed his antagonists without mercy or moderation.'[4] It was this quality that first brought him into Pope's orbit.

When Pope invited Warburton to dinner at Twickenham he had been anxious to entertain him for some time. Looking ahead, he already saw a possible editor for a complete edition of his works in the scholarly, pugnacious clergyman. While in the short term he owed him a debt of gratitude and wanted to find out

26.1   William Warburton. Engraved by Thomas Burford after Charles Philips

the best way of repaying it. This was all to do with *An Essay on Man*. The *Essay* was generally acclaimed in England and abroad for three years or more after it was published. Whereupon it ran into trouble on the Continent. In 1737 J.P. de Crousaz, in Lausanne, launched an attack on Pope's poem in his *Examen*, saying that the attempt in it to describe a religion acceptable to all men amounted to little more than pantheism. The following year de Crousaz repeated this charge and made other damaging ones, when he wrote his *Commentaire*. Both attacks were quickly translated into English. Pope was taken aback. Then, to his relief, he discovered he had an unexpected champion when William Warburton published the first of a series of five letters defending the *Essay* in December 1738. These were finally collected together and published, with a sixth letter, as *A Vindication of Mr. Pope's Essay on Man* in November 1739. Like Charles Darwin when he teamed up with T.H. Huxley, the poet had found his bulldog.

After their first dinner together Pope and Warburton saw each other whenever the clergyman came south from his parish in Newark. In the spring of 1740 they met in London, while Pope was paying one of his hectic visits to town and lamenting, 'I am everywhere.'[5] Warburton also stayed at Twickenham, a little surprised to note how much the company consisted of 'Anti-Ministerial Men.'[6] Even so, Warburton spoke of his host 'in strains of rapturous commendation' saying, 'his vivacity and wit is not more conspicuous than his humanity and affability.'[7] Pope, who first got the idea of choosing Warburton as an editor from the latter's interpretation of *An Essay on Man*, was on his best behaviour as he courted his new ally. The following summer he made a determined effort to secure an honorary Oxford degree for his friend, refusing the doctorate offered to himself when it proved impossible to obtain the same distinction for the theologian.

As Warburton's comment about the company at Twickenham shows, Pope was still seeing his Opposition friends regularly, but kept his promise to write no more political verses, even though Lyttelton was still urging him to fan 'Sparks of Publick Virtue' in the hearts of the patriots.[8]

The Opposition, having lost Marchmont and Wyndham, was faltering. So was the Government. Walpole was a discouraged and exhausted man. As his son wrote at this time, 'He who at dinner always forgot he was a Minister, and was more gay and thoughtless than all his company, now sits without speaking, and his eyes fixed, for an hour together.'[9] The war he had never wanted was going badly. England was ill-prepared after a quarter of a century of peace. An expedition to Cartagena failed and the one to Cuba was abandoned, after thousands of soldiers and sailors died of tropical fever.

At the end of 1741 Pope escaped to Bath again for another lengthy stay at Prior Park. As the urinary problems he had been suffering from for over a year were, if anything worse, he consulted the celebrated Dr Cheseldon who diagnosed a prostatic obstruction and offered to treat this by inserting a catheter.

The process offered temporary relief but, without an anaesthetic, was so excruciatingly painful that Pope decided he would rather endure chronic discomfort than go on with Cheseldon's treatment.

Even so, Pope did not let ill health stop him working. He still had plenty of nervous energy. This year in Allen's house he settled down to plan a fourth book for the *Dunciad*. Although he was now convinced that transferring power from one political group to another would do little more than bring about a superficial change in society, he had lost none of his reforming zeal. One problem was how to gratify this impulse without attracting the attention of Nicholas Paxton. At the end of 1741 Pope was still preoccupied with the effects of the 1737 Licensing Act. The *New Dunciad* was to contain three references to censorship in the first forty lines or so.[10]

Pope had turned away from party politics, not only because taking sides in the current debate going on had proved dangerous, but because he now took a larger, philosophic view of his world. A fundamentally religious man, he decided to write about what he saw as the modern slide into godlessness and the decline in moral fibre in his country's young male elite, who seemed to him to have become ever more self centred and trivial. As a way of doing this, his thoughts turned again to education, a subject on which he had once considered writing a treatise.[11] In adopting this line he was subscribing to a long standing tradition that was still very much alive. It had found expression in diverse writings well known to Pope and his readers. Rosicrucian manifestos, such as the *Fama* (1614), contained a vision of a new society achieved by educational reform.[12] Then there were various works that were about the training of a prince. Bolingbroke's *Patriot King* had as a predecessor Fénelon's *Les aventures de Télémarque* (1699), in which the son of Odysseus is taught the skills of an enlightened monarch. Pope had possessed an English translation of *Télémarque* since he was fourteen years old.[13] More recently he would have been encouraged to take education as his subject from the immense success enjoyed by his acquaintance the Chevalier Ramsay, whose *Travels of Cyrus* (1727) was destined to go into thirty editions in French and English before the end of the century.[14] In Ramsay's pedagogic novel Cyrus learns how to be 'a good legislator, rather than a conqueror', by travelling through the ancient world, conversing with all the sages.[15] He finds they mingle truth about the existence of the one, true God with errors. Ramsay then went on to show how these errors had modern equivalents, including materialism and the pantheism of Spinoza. Not only would Pope have agreed with Ramsay, he too wanted to have his say on false philosophy.

Pope was not short of ideas – his own and those of other writers. If all went well the *New Dunciad* would be a more profound work than the earlier one. Dulness would no longer be a local deity presiding in Grub Street. She had taken shape in Pope's imagination as the antithesis of Sapience in *Hymne of Heavenly Beautie*, 'The souveraine dearling of the *Deity*' (1. 84), whom 'Both heaven and earth obey' (l. 197). By now deeply pessimistic, Pope was haunted by the fear that civilization, as he knew it, was coming to an end.

Yet although Pope had a theme for the *New Dunciad*, he still had difficulty getting started. It looks as if he had not found a suitable framework, or central metaphor, for his poem. Fénelon and Ramsay could not help him here because their picaresque works were too diffuse to serve as models.

In November he wrote to Warburton asking him to join him at Prior Park, ostensibly so that they could work together on the final edition of the poet's works. From Pope's letter of invitation it is also clear that his chosen editor had urged him to go on writing, and that he had begun the new poem but was having problems with it. If Warburton wants him to be a 'Scribbler again' he should come to Prior Park, for Pope says, 'What I have done, I don't like.'[16] Eventually Warburton helped write the notes for the fourth book of the *Dunciad* but before that stage was reached, he also became Pope's last mentor, in that one particular theory he had outlined in the *Divine Legation of Moses*, helped Pope to find a suitable framework for the ideas on education that he wanted to express in his new work.

The *Divine Legation of Moses* (1738–41) is, in part, a study in comparative religion. Warburton was one of a number of men, who from the Renaissance onwards, had an abiding interest in seeing if Christian beliefs were anticipated in ancient theology.[17] He differed from some of his predecessors, however, who believed the 'one true God was generally known and worshipped in the Pagan world', maintaining instead, 'That the Doctrine of the *one, true God* was indeed taught in all places, but as a profound secret, to the Few, in the celebration of their mysterious Rites.'[18]

Warburton illustrated his argument with a detailed analysis of Book VI of Virgil's *Aeniad*. He said that, when Virgil described his hero's visit to the infernal regions, he was giving an account of the Eleusinian Mysteries, with Aeneas going through various trials before his soul is restored to a pristine state, so that he is fit to learn the most profound and secret truth. This initiation completes the education of Aeneas.

Throughout Warburton's discussion of the *Aeniad*, he emphasises its didactic purpose. Virgil wrote 'for the use of men and citizens, to instruct them in the duties of humanity and society' (*Divine Legation*, 1: 282). He also argues that Virgil designed his epic as 'a system of politics', with its hero being trained as 'the perfect lawgiver', whose education is religious, as well as practical, because his destiny is to found 'a great and virtuous empire' (*Divine Legation*, 1: 212, 213, 218).

Such comments by Pope's theological friend harmonized very well with an ambition to reform a nation by education, in a mock epic which, from the beginning had made ironic use of Virgil's *Aeniad*. Pope read Volume I of the *Divine Legation* with 'Veneration and Wonder' in June 1740, and Volume II 'with delight' the following year.[19]

In Pope's letter, in the spring of 1741, he wrote of the 'Instruction and Pleasure' he had received in reading a dissertation on hieroglyphics which appeared in the third volume of the *Divine Legation*. One can see why he singled out this section. It would have been of particular interest to a poet worried about censorship. According to Warburton, the ancient Egyptians used hieroglyphics to conceal knowledge from the uninitiated, and had expressed their most profound thoughts in 'allegorical enigmas' (*Divine Legation*, 1: 122). The Hebrews, influenced by the Egyptians, had followed this practice when they wrote about sensitive or dangerous topics. To prove his point, Warburton then went on to provide an exegesis of the Book of Job which he claimed was the work of a poet, writing an allegory about the captivity of the Jews.

Pope wanted to know more. Fascinated by Warburton's description of the pagan world, he told him, 'I travel thro' your book as thro' an Amazing Scene of ancient Egypt or Greece ... at every step wanting an Instructor to tell me all I wish to know.'[20] No doubt Warburton obliged – who could resist an invitation to discuss his work with such a receptive reader? The *New Dunciad* took shape as a result of Pope's interest in the *Divine Legation*. It suggested to him how he might present his criticism of the contemporary scene. He found his central metaphor when he decided to use the account of the Eleusinian Mysteries, that Warburton said were contained in Book VI of the *Aeniad*. All he had to do was to turn the initiation rites round, showing the youth of England undergoing various ordeals until they were deemed fit to learn, not the truth, but a lie. Such a scheme would enable him to make education the main subject of his Virgilian mock-epic. As well as a metaphor, Pope now had a plot for the moral tale about the world he and his readers lived in.

In Book IV of the *Dunciad* the reign of Dulness has begun, so fulfilling the prophecies uttered in 1728 at the end of Book III. Now, thirteen years later, the poet addresses the power of chaos and night, 'whose Mysteries restor'd' he will sing if they grant him 'one dim Ray ... As half to shew, half veil the deep Intent' (ll. 1–5). These lines and the accompanying note which says that in the work there are 'Mysteries' which the author 'durst not fully reveal', invite the reader to look below the surface of the text.

What meets our eyes at first is an eighteenth-century scene, set in a palace where a monarch is holding an audience. There are Pope's contemporaries: academics, courtiers, connoisseurs, politicians and fops. We can observe them clearly; the insufferable Bentley in the hat that 'never vail'd to human pride' (l. 204), and the young man of fashion, exhausted by idleness, 'stretch'd on the rack of a too easy chair' (l. 342). But even as we watch, the familiar scene shifts and dissolves and we realize we are in a much stranger place than the Court of St James. It has become a phantasmagoric world, where spectres and magicians emerge from darkness to engage in occult rituals.

Pope's palace corresponds to the Temple of Ceres in which the Eleusinian rites took place. The growing feeling of strangeness and wonder which Pope evokes in his readers, as they embark on Book IV, is similar to that experienced by the aspirant when he enters the temple where, as Warburton had explained, 'he sees many mystic sights and hears in the same manner a multitude of voices; ... and a thousand other uncommon things present themselves before him' (*Divine Legation*, 1: 239).

In the *Divine Legation* Warburton had described the Lesser Mysteries which prepared the aspirant for the Greater Mysteries which came later. The Lesser Mysteries involved labours, ordeals (some of them terrifying) and much journeying. Pope adapted Warburton's account of these preliminary trials in depicting the formal education of his hero at school and university, and has him make the Grand Tour, instead of travelling to the different regions of the underworld, as does Virgil's Aeneas.

In Pope's poem Dulness, instead of Ceres, mounts her throne and her ghostly subjects flow towards her. Among the first to pay homage is the apparition of Dr Busby, the erstwhile Headmaster of Westminster School. Instead of the Eleusinian myrtle, he wears a 'birchen garland' (l. 141). He also carries a 'dreadful wand' (l. 140) which is both a caduceus and the rod for which Busby was famous. At the sight of this 'o'er ev'ry vein' of every schoolboy 'a shudd'ring horror runs' (l. 143), so mirroring the terror felt by a candidate entering the Mysteries.

At the beginning of his address to the Goddess, Busby refers to the Samian letter 'Y', used in the ancient world by Pythagoras as a symbol for the different paths of Virtue and Vice. The Headmaster, however, chooses the opposite path to that taken by Pythagoras, the teacher of Plato. Busby boasts that in his school, 'Words we teach alone' (l. 150). Any youthful curiosity about what the words say is stifled as he and his ushers 'ply the Memory' and 'load the brain' with rote learning (l. 157). He teaches boys to remember, but not how to live.

The work of keeping youth 'within the pale of words till Death' (l. 160) is carried on by the Master of Trinity College, Cambridge. A necromantic Bentley, 'stern as Ajax's spectre' (l. 274), exorcises the other shades that flutter round his Goddess, with a ringing cry of 'Avaunt' (l. 210). After which he assures her that his sole concern, as a classical scholar, is with grammatical niceties, 'Disputes of *Me* or *Te*, of *aut* or *at*' (l. 220), adding that, should any student ask for 'Ancient Sense ... Be sure I give them Fragments, not a Meal' (ll. 229–30). Bentley's exclusively analytic approach to his subject in no way prepares youth to see 'How parts relate to parts, or they to whole, / The body's harmony, the beaming soul' (ll. 235–6). The teaching Virgil's hero receives leads him ever closer to the light. Instructed by Bentley and Busby the candidate for initiation is led into the dark.

Pope's description of the Grand Tour, which completes the education of a young Englishman, corresponds to Warburton's account of the journeys of

Virgil's hero through the different regions of the underworld. In Purgatory Aeneas sees the fate of those 'who had indulged the violence of their passions, which made them miserable rather than wicked' (*Divine Legation*, 1: 254). The wicked inhabit Tartarus and include atheists, those lacking in natural affection, and men who have betrayed their country.

During his travels Aeneas learns the perils of giving in to sensual temptation and evil notions. In contrast Pope's heedless hero, as he crosses the Continent, seizes every opportunity to gratify his most trivial passions, and pursues an egotistical course of action, unlikely to benefit his fellow men or his country. 'Safe and unseen the young Aeneas past' (1. 290) through school and college, protected by the kindly cloud of Dulness, only to lose whatever sense or morals he has in the palaces and stews of Europe. One young sprig is presented to the Goddess, having, with relief, 'Drop the lumber of the Latin store' (1. 319) in Rome, and 'gather'd ev'ry Vice on Christian ground' (1. 312). 'With nothing but a Solo in his head' (1. 324), he is a fit prey for all the smooth gentlemen who want to deprive him of his money, such as the fraudulent dealer in antiquities, embodied in Annius, the 'crafty Seer, with ebon wand, / And well disssembled em'rald on his hand' (ll. 347–8). Or if the young man does not want to become a connoisseur, he can devote himself to a hobby, atomising flowers or pursuing butterflies.

These harmless activities are chosen as examples of the tyranny of things which, like the tyranny of words, excludes the holistic vision. This, as Pope saw it, was the danger of empirical science. The Goddess is well pleased if men spend their time in disconnected studies of isolated physical phenomena. She wants them to 'See Nature in some partial narrow shape, / And let the Author of the Whole escape' (ll. 455–6).

At this point the gloomy Clerk, or religious sceptic, steps forward and promises it shall be so. He will guide a new generation down the 'high Priori Road' laid down by Hobbes, Descartes and Spinoza, showing it how to:

> ... reason downward, till we doubt of God:
> Make Nature still incroach upon his plan;
> And shove him off as far as e'er we can:
> Thrust some Mechanic Cause into his place (ll. 472–5).

The gloomy Clerk's promise corresponds to the final, most profound and secret truth imparted to Virgil's hero during the Eleusinian Mysteries – but it is the antithesis of it. In the *Aeniad* the speaker is Anchises who tells his son that, far from being a mechanism, 'The sky and the lands, the watery plain, the moon's gleaming face, the Titanic Sun and the stars are all strengthened by the Spirit working within them, and by Mind, which is blended into all the vast universe and pervades every part of it, enlivening the whole mass.'[21] This passage Warburton interprets, not as an expression of pantheism, but as proof that the ancients knew there was a supreme God, akin to the Biblical one.

In Warburton's commentary of Book VI of the *Aeniad*, the lessons its hero learns in Purgatory and Tartarus have purified him and he is ready to enter Elysium, where he will be instructed in the Greater Mysteries that prepare him for his future destiny. In the *New Dunciad* the young Aeneas, misled, then ruined by his education, is returned a 'finish'd son' to Dulness (l. 500). 'From Priest-craft happily set free' (l. 499), he is ready to take his place in a homocentric universe. He has lost his full humanity under the spells of various enchanters, and is no more than a wraith as he prepares to enter the Elysium of Walpole's England.

This he can do when he drinks from the cup proffered by the 'Wizard old' (l. 517), who is Walpole himself. It is at this point that, as Warburton's notes to the poem tell us, Pope begins the 'celebration of the *greater* Mysteries of the Goddess' (l. 517n). Walpole is the supreme image in Pope's version of the Eleusinian rites because the poet believes that, however likeable he found the Great Man as an individual, the example set by his cynical amorality accounted for much of the corruption in contemporary society. The drink he offers his adherents, like the waters of Lethe, makes them forget. Whoever tastes of the Wizard's cup leaves behind everything that might inhibit him from pursuing a career of squalid self-interest. In Virgil's Elysium the hero found patriots, lawgivers 'who brought mankind from a state of Society, virtuous and pious priests, and Inventors of Arts mechanical and liberal' (*Divine Legation*, 1: 275).

In the English Elysium the lawgiver casts an ambitious eye on the star and plumed hat of a Knight of the Garter, whereupon 'A Feather shooting from another's head, / Extracts his brain, and Principle is fled; / Lost is his God, his Country, ev'ry thing' (ll. 521–3).

The Greek words for death and initiation being similar, when a participant in the Eleusinian Mysteries is initiated, he is reborn. After 'errors and uncertainties; laborious wanderings; a rude and fearful march through night and darkness', the reborn enter on a new scene. 'A miraculous and divine light displays itself; and shining plains and flowery meadows open on all hands before them' (*Divine Legation*, 1: 277–8). In Virgil's *Aeniad* the Eleusinian Mysteries culminate with the initiate looking into the future. As Aeneas walks through the bright fields with Anchises, he is shown the glory of Rome, the city he is to found. In contrast Pope concludes by describing how 'The sick'ning stars fade off th'ethereal plain' (l. 636). No glorious civilization awaits as 'Art after Art goes out' (l. 640) and 'Unawares Morality expires' (l. 650). The 'dread Empire, CHAOS is restor'd ... Universal Darkness buries All' (ll. 653 ff.).

The *Divine Legation* is not the only source of Pope's poem.[22] However, looking specifically at the *New Dunciad* in the light of Warburton's commentary on Book VI of the *Aeniad* helps us in two ways. We can judge more precisely the extent to which Pope made his desired escape from politics into philosophy by taking the theologian as his mentor. We also see the structure of the poem more clearly. The seemingly unwieldy chunk of 200 lines or so on formal education takes its place as one of the many ordeals the aspirant must undergo, before he is initiated into anti-Truth. The poem moves dynamically towards its finale.

Pope was almost too successful in his secondary aim of throwing Nicholas Paxton off the scent. He threw many other readers off the scent as well. On 3 April 1742 *Universal Spectator* complained that the *New Dunciad* was 'too allegorical' and therefore obscure. While it was all a bit too much for Lord Hervey who said, there 'is a Darkness to be felt in ev'ry Line.'[23]

Notes

1. Spence, 508.
2. Spence, 951.
3. A.W. Evans, *Warburton and the Warburtonians* (Oxford University Press, 1932), p. 273. The speaker is Richard Hurd.
4. Ibid., p. 276.
5. *Corr.* 4: 236.
6. *Corr.* 4: 238n.
7. George Harris, *Life of Lord Chancellor Hardwicke*, 3 vols (London, 1847), 1: 475–6.
8. *Corr.* 4: 369.
9. Horace Walpole to Sir Horace Mann in 1741, quoted W.E.H. Lecky, *A History of England in the Eighteenth Century*, 7 vols (London, 1878), 1: 394.
10. *Dunciad in Four Books*, ed Valerie Rumbold (London: Longman, 1999), ll. 22, 35–6, 43–4. This edition is quoted throughout the chapter.
11. Spence, 49.
12. Frances A. Yates, *The Rosicrucian Enlightenment* (London: Routledge & Kegan Paul, 1972) chapter 4 and *passim*.
13. Maynard Mack, *Collected in Himself* (Newark: University of Delaware Press, 1982), p. 412. Later on Pope acquired Gay's copy of Fénelon's work in French.
14. G.D. Henderson, *Chevalier Ramsay* (London: Nelson, 1952), p. 109.
15. *The Travels of Cyrus*, 4th edn (London, 1730), viii.
16. *Corr.* 4: 373.
17. See D.P. Walker, *The Ancient Theology: Studies in Christian Platonism from the Fifteenth to the Eighteenth Century* (London: Duckworth 1972).
18. *The Divine Legation of Moses*, 4th edn, 5 vols (London, 1764–65), 3: 476. This edition is quoted throughout the chapter.
19. *Corr.* 4: 251 and 341n.
20. *Corr.* 4: 251.
21. *The Aeniad*, trans. W.F. Jackson (Harmondsworth: Penguin Classics, 1956), Book VI, sections, 724–8. This translation is quoted throughout the text.
22. See Rumbold, *op. cit.*
23. *A Letter to Mr. Cibber* (1742), quoted J.V. Guerinot, *Pamphlet Attacks on Alexander Pope 1711–1744* (London: Methuen, 1969), p. 296.

CHAPTER TWENTY-SEVEN

Putting Things in Order

As soon as Warburton started thinking of himself as the poet's mentor, he became Bolingbroke's rival, though their mutual friend was reluctant to face the fact. When Bolingbroke inherited the family home in Battersea and returned to England, Pope looked forward for a couple of years to Warburton's meeting with 'the only Great Man in Europe' who knew 'as much as he.'[1] However, the two men, who were temperamental and intellectual opposites, avoided one another.

Bolingbroke returned from France in April 1742 when his father, whom he called Old Frumps or Le Père Éternal, died at the age of ninety, to the financial relief of his heir.[2] In the first place Bolingbroke stayed in England for about five weeks to settle the details of his inheritance and, as ever, Pope spent as much time as possible with him during the visit. When his friend went back temporarily to France in May, to arrange his affairs there, the poet gave him all Warburton's works in preparation for a meeting later on.

For some time Pope had intended to revise the whole of the *Dunciad*, with a view to republishing it as soon as he got the copyright back. This took some time. In 1743 he brought a suit in Chancery against Henry Lintot, to prevent him issuing the poem in three books, on the grounds that the copyright, granted a publisher in 1728 for fourteen years only, should now revert to himself. Increasingly, in his last years, Pope went to law to settle disputes. Gone were the days when he roasted Curll in pamphlets, still less laced his drink. In 1741 Pope had taken his old foe to Chancery over the 'pirated' letters. This case had resulted in a landmark judgement by Lord Hardwicke stating that letters were the personal property of the writer of them, which meant that no one else had a right to publish them without permission.[3] Pope also succeeded in his suit against Lintot two years later, so clearing the way for the publication of the *Dunciad* in four books.

It is possible that word was going around London as early as 1742 that the revised *Dunciad* was to have a new hero – Colley Cibber. Cibber was a much better choice for the role than Theobald, who was relatively obscure and had not even been mentioned in the recent Book IV.

Since the days when the laureate had been a target in the *Craftsman*, the Opposition had not let up in its campaign against him. Nor was the *Craftsman* without support. As early as 1731 the *Universal Spectator* devised a convention for contemporary poets, presided over by the Goddess of Dulness, at which the crown was awarded to Cibber.[4] This was because Dulness was predominantly a matter of moral obtuseness and Cibber's opponents thought he was an unprincipled opportunist. Cibber was a popular actor and a prolific author who gave the public what it wanted. He produced insipid odes for his royal master whenever the occasion demanded it, but then so had other laureates. The Opposition did not object so much to any of these things as to the fact that he was the artist of whom the state approved who, as Fielding said, preached and practised 'an absolute submission to our superiors.'[5] Accordingly he reaped the rewards he so obviously prized, invitations to Court functions and membership of White's. His contemporaries could either be amused or irritated by his cheerful self-satisfaction. When he published his autobiography in 1740 it was said of it, that chastity was 'almost the only Virtue which the great Apologist hath not given himself.'[6]

No one knows why Cibber, who for years had ignored the jibes about him in the Horatian satires and elsewhere, suddenly decided to go on the offensive against Pope in 1742. A plausible explanation is that he heard about the new honour the poet was about to bestow on him. It would have been in character for Pope to make sure he did hear he was to become the *Dunciad*'s hero. If Cibber reacted it would not only provide useful advance publicity for the revised poem, but would make the work appear motivated by personal rather than political hostility. It was the same technique Pope had employed with the earliest version of the *Dunciad*, when he encouraged Government hacks to think he was merely responding to their pamphlets about him. However, if such was the poet's plan, it was yet another of his stratagems that went wrong.

The attack came in late July in the form of *A Letter from Mr. Cibber, to Mr. Pope*. The poet had just obtained a copy of it when he visited Richardson's studio. There, he sat down to read it, remarking lightly, 'These things are my diversion.'[7]

In the *Letter* Cibber had summoned up the ghost of Pope past, reminding him of the days when they used to go to Button's, soon after the poet had begun to translate the *Iliad*. He was thinking particularly of one night when the young Lord Warwick suggested it would be a good joke to take the 'little Homer' to a bawdy house near the Haymarket and 'slip' him at a 'Girl of the Game.' The laureate described how the three of them arrived at the 'House of Carnal Recreation', whereupon the 'smirking Damsel', who served them with tea, 'happen'd to have Charms sufficient' to 'tempt the little-tiny Manhood of Mr. Pope into the next Room with her', much to the delight of Warwick. After a while Cibber decided the poet had been there quite long enough if he was not going to hazard his health. So – he went on, in his bluff, familiar fashion, 'I ... threw open the Door upon him, where I found this little hasty Hero, like a terrible *Tom Tit*, pertly perching upon the Mount of Love! But such was my Surprize that I fairly laid hold of his Heels, and actually drew him safe and sound from the danger.'

Richardson, who was watching Pope read all this, could see his face

27.1   Colley Cibber. George Beare

contorted with anguish. Cibber rounded off the tale by relating how Warwick, who was tittering in the doorway, cursed him for spoiling the sport, and how he defended himself 'with great Gravity' by asserting he had saved the English Homer from the pox for the 'Honour of our Nation.'[8]

Pope insisted the story told by Cibber was 'an absolute lie' as to 'the main point.' Though he recalled accompanying the laureate and Warwick to the place in the Haymarket, he denied going off with the 'smirking Damsel' or any other woman there.[9] However, few wanted to believe the poet just sat in a brothel drinking tea. For a few weeks the *Letter* was the talk of the London coffee houses and, if that was not enough, at least four separate engravings were made of the 'Tom Tit' episode and displayed in all the bookshop windows. Cibber has the dubious honour of penning the most devastating of the hundreds of attacks on Pope. The *Letter* is a minor masterpiece.

Although Warburton encouraged the public to think so, the laureate's anecdote was not the reason he became the hero of the *Dunciad*. Within two weeks of the *Letter*'s appearance, Pope mentioned Cibber to a friend saying, 'I have ready, actually written ... all I shall ever say about him', thereby implying the revision of his poem was complete.[10] Like so many of Pope's targets, Cibber was in the *Dunciad* because he was on the other side of the political fence.

During the summer of 1742 much of Pope's time was taken up by a stalwart opponent of the Administration, the octagenarian Duchess of Marlborough, who was now crippled with gout, her once fiery hair faded and thin. She summoned him continually to Windsor Lodge – apparently to discuss Plato. He got on very well with 'Mount Etna'.[11] He played the part of her courtier, while maintaining his independence by refusing her offers of lavish gifts. She had wanted to buy him a coach and the house at Twickenham but, wary as ever of being on anyone's payroll, he fought her down to an armchair and a mention in her will. Their meetings were always agreeable because he genuinely admired her. He was also happy to flirt with her, inviting her to a moonlight supper in his grotto, suggesting that had she been younger and he 'stronger by twenty Years' they 'might have made a match of it.'[12] When they were not philosophising, they talked politics, their conversations on that subject focusing on the disappointing aftermath of Walpole's resignation, which had come at last in February. Sarah Churchill's shrewd assessments of men, who had or wanted power, were always worth listening to. To the poet and his Opposition friends she was the 'Oracle in the Woods.'[13]

As a result of his attendance on the Duchess, Pope was not free to accompany Warburton when he travelled with Allen to Bath in August and was unable to join them at Prior Park until about the second week in October. Then the poet and his editor had a few weeks together so that, by the end of the year, work on the final edition of Pope's works was well under way with *An Essay on Man*, *An Essay on Criticism* and the *Pastorals* newly annotated.

Once back in Twickenham Pope was deluged with enough dismal news from his political friends to make him wish he had stayed in Bath. The resignation of Walpole had not brought about the regeneration of England. As predicted, Pulteney accepted a peerage and as Earl of Bath joined Walpole, the new Earl of Orford in the Upper House, only to be greeted by his realistic rival with, 'Here we are, my lord, the two most insignificant men in the kingdom.'[14] The Government was now led by Wilmington whom, as Spencer Compton, Walpole had once supplanted. Under this nonentity a committee of enquiry was set up to investigate corruption under the former regime, but all it produced was a cover-up. Richard Edgcumbe was moved up into the Lords so that he would not have to give evidence about corruption in the Cornish boroughs. Officials who distributed Secret Service money (an eighteenth-century slush fund) refused to testify. The Commons and Lords alike combined to shield Walpole and themselves. Pope was not surprised but was depressed nonetheless, writing to Allen at the end of the year, 'My Heart is sick of this bad World (as Cato said) and as I see it daily growing worse.'[15]

Pope spent most of the winter of 1743 quietly at home, usually indoors. During the day he worked on the final edition, using the new notes for his poems as fast as Warburton sent them from Newark. His career was drawing to a close and from now on he would be mainly concerned with perfecting his complete works, so that future generations would have the best possible basis for assessing his reputation as a poet.

Pope, at the age of fifty-four, had already outlived many of the men who had been around when he had first arrived in London, bent on dominating the literary world. His Scriblerian allies, except for Swift, were dead and so were most of his foes at Button's. He thought of himself as an old man and he was, for although he still had plenty of mental energy and 'a most excellent memory',[16] he was becoming ever more physically decrepit. Candlelight now strained his eyes, so in the evenings he picked up 'a poor Scholar or two' who could 'get no employment' to come and read to him.'[17] Poet and reader sat in the study, Pope, a slovenly beau, in snuff-stained black, presiding from the Duchess's red armchair, which he called his 'Throne of flame-coloured Damask.'[18] Over the next few hours, he plied his guest with wine and ended up drinking more of it himself than was good for him. He sometimes gave up wine for a while, but always went back to it as it made him feel cheerful. He also got Swift to send him Irish whiskey, even though spirits made him feel gloomy.[19] As we have already seen, Pope was fond of good food. What was more surprising in an eighteenth-century gentleman, was that he liked to cook, once regaling William Kent, another gourmand, with accounts of 'the many good things' he 'could make.'[20]

However, austerity was all too often forced upon him in 1743, as his health deteriorated, albeit by fits and starts. He was in the habit of writing frankly about his ailments to Hugh Bethel, thinking that, because this old friend was also a chronic invalid, he would be more interested than most correspondents and might, perhaps, make helpful suggestions. In a letter he wrote on 20 March, Pope said that his asthma had been getting worse since the beginning of year, so that he could no longer walk upstairs or even turn over in bed without losing his breath. He also said he now got one cold after another, despite staying by the fireside as much as possible.

At the end of March Mrs Blount died, which renewed the poet's anxiety to see Patty financially secure and settled, preferably away from Teresa. Early in this year he made enquiries for an annuity for her, which would give her an additional £100 a year. If need be he was willing to put up the money for this himself.

Lord Hervey also died in 1743 on 5 August at the age of forty-seven. For some months before that it had been obvious that he was a very sick man, as he dragged himself with his coffin face to operas and assemblies. In 1740 Walpole had brought him into the Cabinet by seeing that he was made Lord Privy Seal, but he did not keep that position for very long after the fall of his patron. As well as accelerating his illness, his abrupt dismissal, after a lifetime of loyal service made him so angry that he changed sides, attacking the Ministry vigorously in pamphlets and in the House of Lords. He did not change his opinion of Pope however. He rejoiced in Cibber's *Letter* and wrote his own *Letter to Mr. C-b—r, On his Letter to Mr. P.*, congratulating the laureate but telling him he had not gone far enough. The poet was no longer concerned. When he heard of his enemy's death, he merely said '*Requiescat in pace*' (May he rest in peace).[21]

By the time Hervey was buried, Pope was at Prior Park, having decided to go there in the summer rather than risk a journey in the cold weather later. On this visit things went badly wrong, so that the poet and Allen were not on speaking terms for months afterwards.

As well as Warburton, the guests at Prior Park in 1743 included Patty Blount, for whom the poet had cadged an invitation and Mrs Allen took against Patty. Elizabeth Allen was a conscientious wife, concerned with seeing no one took advantage of her good natured husband. As the manager of the household, she must always have found the invalid poet's lengthy visits a trial. He was a demanding guest. His wish on this occasion to bring his female companion would not have eased matters. Patty's careless bonhomie, which so delighted Pope, was unlikely to appeal to her correct hostess. Nor would the rumours about Patty being the poet's mistress have helped the relationship between the two women along. Even so, as long as nothing happened to confirm the rumours, the visit might have passed off without incident.

Unfortunately, Allen's favourite niece, a girl of sixteen named Gertrude Tucker, noticed Patty going into the poet's bedroom round about six o'clock each morning. One day curiosity overcame her and she stood listening at the door, after which she went off to tell the Allens. She also told Warburton, who was to make an advantageous match when he married her a couple of years later.

Although no one said anything, the atmosphere at Prior Park was highly charged after Gertrude told her story. Pope decided it would be diplomatic to leave right away with another of the guests who was going to Bristol. He set off, under the impression that Patty was not to stay 'a Day longer' in the house after he left.[22] However, she had difficulty finding transport, so the next thing that happened was that the poet got a distressing letter from her. She told him that, as she packed up all her things, 'Mr. and Mrs. Allen never said a word' and, she added 'Mr. Warburton takes no notice of me.' She was excluded from the conversation at dinner and what was 'most wonderful' no one drank the poet's health after he went.[23]

Pope was horrified when he got Patty's letter. He wrote back by return, interspersing a flurry of practical suggestions, as to how his friend might get away from Prior Park, with denunciations of the 'impertinent' Mrs Allen who was 'a Minx', and calling Warburton 'a sneaking Parson.'[24] Always somewhat prone to paranoia, he did 'not wonder if Listeners at doors should open Letters.'[25] Now we are left to wonder what Gertrude heard as she stood eavesdropping outside the bedroom? Perhaps Pope and Patty were speaking their minds about Mrs Allen and others in the house. On the other hand, it would be foolish to rule out the possibility that some kind of sex game was being played out on the other side of that door.

At no stage did Pope blame Ralph Allen for what had happened, supposing he had been overruled by his wife. The opportunity for a tentative reconciliation came before the end of the year, when Allen fell ill, and Pope wrote expressing his sympathy and concern. From then on both men were looking for an opportunity to get their relationship back on its former footing.

On 29 October the revised *Dunciad* in four books was on sale. By this time Robert Dodsley was Pope's preferred bookseller. Dodsley was a well read and talented ex-footman who became a successful dramatist. Pope had encouraged his literary ambitions and, in 1735, had given him £100 to set himself up in business, publishing and selling books in Pall Mall. This gave Dodsley a steady income and he was grateful. Always the poet's devoted admirer, he had willingly co-operated in stratagems to prevent Curll cashing in with editions of Pope's letters.[26] When Pope enabled Dodsley to buy his bookshop, he was continuing a practice he had initiated several years earlier. After 1728 Pope no longer dealt with the major figures in the publishing world. Instead he set up his own men, financing Henry Woodfall and possibly John Wright as printers, as well as Lawton Gilliver as a publisher.[27] This made sound business sense because he got better terms from his protégés than from Tonson or Lintot. It also meant he was given every facility in overseeing the actual production process of his books as meticulously as he wished. [28]

The *Dunciad* in four books was the last new work Pope published. By the time it came out, his health, which had been a little better during the summer, was worse than ever. Over the next few months he moved restlessly from one friend's town house to another, and then home again, to see if a change brought any improvement. By the middle of October Bolingbroke was back in England for good, so the poet often hugged the fire at Battersea, listening to the friend who, having lost none of his power as a spell-binder, engaged him 'in the most agreeable Conversation' he knew 'and the most instructive.'[29]

By the New Year Pope was emaciated, his once melodious voice thin and dry, so that he compared himself to Homer's old men who chirruped like grasshoppers, and said he lived 'like an Insect in the hope of reviving with the Spring.'[30] Even though by February he realized he was 'going, and that not slowly, down the hill',[31] he had survived so many illnesses since boyhood, he thought there was a chance he might pull through this one. He took simultaneous advice from six doctors before the end, two of them in Bath and the rest in London. One very bad day, Bolingbroke, in sheer desperation, added to them by calling in the quack Joshua Ward, whose 'magic' pills had earned him a couple of references in the Horatian satires. Not that Ward's pills, which consisted mainly of antimony, sound any more bizarre to modern ears than the orthodox medications the poet took, containing mercury, crabs eyes and soap.

During 1743 the war had gone better for England. Pope, along with other patriots, rejoiced when George II led his troops to victory at Dettingen in June. However, by the end of the year there was a new crisis, as the Ministry learned the Jacobites were planning another invasion. On 21 February 1744 the French fleet was sighted off Dungeness, whereupon the Ten Mile rule was re-imposed on Papists. Pope, ever careful to obey the Penal Laws, returned home to Twickenham, though he made a couple of quick visits to the Royal Hospital in Chelsea to see Cheselden who, he believed had recently saved his life, during a particularly severe asthma attack he had had at Bolingbroke's house.

At the beginning of March Pope had still not brought Bolingbroke and Warburton together. But the two men did meet finally over dinner in Murray's house in Lincoln's Inn Fields, where they promptly quarrelled about religion. Afterwards Pope overheard Warburton and Hooke 'talking of Lord Bolingbroke's not believing in the moral attributes of God.'[32] Pope was taken aback and asked Bolingbroke about it, who said Warburton had been mistaken, much to the poet's relief.

Pope was also relieved when Allen came to see him at Easter. Because the early morning was still the best time for him, he invited his guest to come to his bedroom before breakfast on Good Friday. He was hoping to find out the exact cause of the trouble at Prior Park. Allen was embarrassed and therefore vague, but said enough to confirm that the difficulty had been over some scandal involving Patty. Referring to her and to his wife, he spoke of 'mutual dissatisfaction' between the two women, and added that Mrs Allen 'must have had some very unjust and bad thing suggested to her' about Miss Blount. With that Pope had to be content, especially as Allen said, 'he never in his whole life was so sorry at any disappointment.'[33]

Pope was realistic about his future, though he was determined not to give up until he had to. So he had made his will and more significantly, perhaps, had given away his beloved dog Bounce to Lord Orrery.[34] At the same time, before the renewed restrictions on Catholics drove him from London, he thought of buying a house in an airy part of town, so as not to be a burden on his friends. Once back in Twickenham again, he continued working. In addition to putting poems together for Warburton, he found the energy to read Mark Akenside's labyrinthine *Pleasures of the Imagination* which Dodsley had brought him one day, to ask whether it was worth the £120 the author wanted for it. The poem, a minor literary landmark, anticipated Wordsworth in the role it gave to the imagination in the poetic process. Pope, with his usual critical acumen, told the publisher, 'not to make a niggardly offer; for this was no everyday writer.'[35]

However, the bell tolled for Pope at the end of March 1744, when Bethel recommended that he try yet another new doctor. This was Thomas Thompson, who already included the Prince of Wales and Henry Fielding among his patients. He began treating the poet towards the end of April, having decided he was suffering from dropsy, not asthma.[36] His method of curing this was to institute a ferocious regime of vomits and purges. At first Pope supposed these were making him better. Although he felt lethargic, he was able to go out in his chariot on fine days. The relief was temporary and, although it is doubtful whether Pope could have recovered anyway, with Thompson in charge he soon became utterly debilitated. By the second week in May he was on his deathbed and knew that he was.

Notes

1. *Corr.* 4: 505.
2. Bolingbroke's father, who had dedicated himself to wine and women, viewed his restless and ambitious son with laconic humour. 'Ah, Harry', he remarked, on learning his offspring was made a lord. 'I ever said you would be hanged, but now I find you will be beheaded.' Spence, 888.
3. Pat Rogers, 'The Case of Pope v Curll', *Essays on Pope* (Cambridge University Press, 1993), ch. 11.
4. *Universal Spectator*, 6 February 1731. The Opposition kept up the campaign. So throughout 1740 Fielding's *The Champion* launched attacks on Cibber.
5. *Joseph Andrews* (1742), ch. L.
6. Ibid.
7. Samuel Johnson, *Lives of the English Poets*, ed G.B. Hill, 3 vols (Oxford, 1905), 3: 187.
8. J.V. Guerinot, *Pamphlet Attacks on Alexander Pope 1711–1744* (London: Methuen, 1969), pp. 293–4.
9. Spence, 251. Nevertheless, Cibber's tale was suspiciously like an old slander about Boileau being humiliated in a house of ill fame behind the Hotel de Conde. Boileau, *Oeuvres* (1716), 1: 241.
10. *Corr.* 4: 415.

11. 'Mount Etna' was Hervey's nickname for Sarah Churchill. *Lord Hervey and his Friends 1726–1738*, ed Earl of Ilchester (London: John Murray, 1950), pp. 87, 90, 92, 99, 100, 181.
12. *Corr.* 4: 412.
13. *Corr.* 4: 444.
14. W.E.H. Lecky, *A History of England in the Eighteenth Century*, 7 vols (London, 1878), 1: 398.
15. *Corr.* 4: 429.
16. Spence, 532.
17. *Corr.* 4: 437.
18. *Corr.* 4: 398.
19. *Corr.* 3: 93, 97, 192.
20. *Corr.* 4: 150.
21. Robert Halsband, *Lord Hervey* (Oxford: Clarendon, 1973), p. 305.
22. *Corr.* 4: 463.
23. *Corr.* 4: 462.
24. *Corr.* 4: 464.
25. Ibid.
26. Harry M. Solomon, *The Rise of Robert Dodsley: Creating the New Age of Print* (Carbondale and Edwardsville: Southern Illinois University Press, 1996), pp. 46–8. Dodsley became the bookseller associated with the Opposition. He published Glover's *Leonidas* which turned out to be a 'literary gold mine', p. 58.
27. John Nichols, *Literary Anecdotes of the Eighteenth Century* (1812), 1: 30.
28. David Foxon, *Pope and the Early Eighteenth-Century Book Trade*, revised and edited by James McLaverty (Oxford: Clarendon, 1990), pp. 131–5.
29. *Corr.* 4: 463.
30. *Corr.* 4: 499.
31. *Corr.* 4: 501.
32. Spence, 290.
33. *Corr.* 4: 510.
34. At Orrery's house Bounce was bitten by a mad dog and had to be shot. Pope wrote her epitaph, the couplet being the last lines of verse he composed. *Corr.* 4: 517. For Pope's succession of dogs, all called Bounce, see Spence, pp. 629–30.
35. Johnson, *op. cit.*, 2: 463. Johnson was himself a writer whose talent was spotted by Pope. After reading *London* (1738) he tried, without the author's knowledge, to get Johnson a job. *Corr.* 4: 194.
36. *Corr.* 4: 521 and note.

CHAPTER TWENTY-EIGHT

The Death of a Public Figure

A steady stream of visitors began arriving at Twickenham as soon as word spread that Pope was dying. Some of them the poet invited. Others came anyway. A few such as Bolingbroke, Marchmont, Hooke and Spence were at the villa almost constantly during the last days. Spence was there, not only as a friend, but to record a public event for posterity. He saw himself as Phaedo, the faithful disciple who attended his master in the Athens prison, though when he said so, Pope replied, 'That might be, but you must not expect me to say anything like Socrates at present.'[1]

Indeed for days on end Pope was unable to say anything that made sense to his hearers. On 6 May he lost his mind for the whole of a Sunday. After that he was confused, complaining that the thing he suffered from most was not being able to think. His vision was blurred. He saw things as if looking at them through gauze and found himself seeing 'false colours on objects.'[2] Soon he began to have hallucinations, some of them bizarre, others beatific. Once he asked Dodsley, 'What great arm is that I see coming out of the wall?' Another time he 'pointed in the air with a very steady regard', asking 'What's that?' Then looking at Spence said, 'with a smile of pleasure and with the greatest sweetness and complacency, 'Twas a vision.'[3]

The hallucinations could have been due to an insufficient supply of oxygen reaching the brain – a condition associated with congestive heart failure. Pope was dying because he had heart disease. The first sign of imminent danger had been those asthma attacks at the beginning of 1743, which he said he was having more often than before. After over forty years of suffering from kypho-scoliosis (compound curvature of the spine) due to tuberculosis, his chest was so deformed that his lungs were compressed. Naturally he had difficulty in breathing. His circulation was also impaired. Both these handicaps put a strain on his heart. Cardiovascular disturbances were also a likely cause of ascites (excess fluid in the abdomen) which Thompson thought was dropsy.[4] Perhaps an eighteenth-century doctor cannot be blamed for not recognizing ascites, but it was unfortunate that the one to whom Pope entrusted himself not only made a wrong diagnosis but, mistaking a symptom for a cause, based the regime he prescribed on an assumption that dropsy was the main thing wrong with his patient. Thompson's prescriptions were not helpful. In fact they did harm, because the repeated vomits and purges he inflicted on Pope were dehydrating, and severe dehydration is enough in itself to cause mental confusion.[5]

Pope's friends and his other physicians were dubious about the treatment he

Nicholson, C., *Writing and the Rise of Finance: Capital Satires of the Early Eighteenth Century*. Cambridge University Press, 1994.

Porter, D. and R. Porter, *Patients Progress: Doctors and Doctoring in Eighteenth-Century England*. Cambridge: Polity Press, 1989.

Porter, R., *English Society in the Eighteenth Century*. Harmondsworth: Penguin, 1982.

———— *Enlightenment: Britain and the Creation of the Modern World*. London: Allen Lane, 2000.

Rogers, P., *Eighteenth-Century Encounters: studies in literature and society in the age of Walpole*. Brighton: Harvester, 1985.

Siebert, F.S., *Freedom of the Press in England 1476–1776: The Rise and Decline of Government Controls*. Urbana: University of Illinois Press, 1952.

Siskin, C., *The Work of Writing: Literature and Social Change in Britain 1700–1830*. Baltimore: Johns Hopkins University Press, 1998.

Speck, W.A., *Society and Literature in England 1700–1760*. Dublin: Gill & Macmillan Humanities Press, 1983.

Stone, L., *The Family, Sex and Marriage*. London: Weidenfeld and Nicolson, 1977.

Szechi, D., *Jacobitism and Tory Politics*. Edinburgh: John Donald, 1985.

Thomas, K., 'The Meaning of Literacy in Early Modern England', in *The Written Word: Literacy in Transition*. Oxford University Press, 1986.

Thompson, E.P., *Whigs and Hunters: The Origin of the Black Act*. Harmondsworth: Penguin, 1973.

Varey, S., '*The Craftsman*: A Historical and Critical Account', unpub. diss., Cambridge University, 1976.

———— '*The Craftsman*', in *Telling People What to Think: Early Eighteenth-Century Periodicals*, eds, J.A. Downie and T. Corns. London: Frank Cass, 1993.

Walker, D.P., *The Ancient Theology: Studies in Christian Platonism from the Fifteenth to the Eighteenth Century*. London: Duckworth, 1972.

Yates, F.A., *The Rosicrucian Enlightenment*. London: Routledge & Kegan Paul, 1972.

Creativity

Albert, R.S., ed., *Genius and Eminence*, 2nd edn. Oxford: Pergamon Press, 1992.

Bloom, B. and L. Sosniak, *Developing Talent in Young Children*. New York: Ballantine Books, 1985.

Boden, M.A., *The Creative Mind: Myths and Mechanisms*. London: Weidenfeld and Nicolson, 1990.

Csikszentmihalyi, M., *Creativity: Flow and the Psychology of Discovery and Invention*. New York: HarperCollins, 1996.

Eissler, K.R., 'Notes on the Environment of a Genius', *Psychoanalytic Study of the Child*, 15 (1959), 267–313.

Eysenck, H.J., *The Natural History of Creativity*. Cambridge University Press, 1995.

Feldman, D., *Beyond Universals in Cognitive Development*. Norwood, NJ: Ablex, 1980.

Findlay, C.S., and C.J. Lumsden, 'The Creative Mind: Towards an Evolutionary Theory of Discovery and Innovation', *Journal of Social and Biological Structures*, 11 (1988), 3–55. [The whole of this issue of the *JSBS* is devoted to creativity.]

Gardner, H., *Creating Minds: An Anatomy of Creativity Seen Through the Lives of Freud, Einstein, Picasso, Stravinsky, Eliot, Graham and Gandhi*. New York: Basic Books, 1995.

———— *Extraordinary Minds*. London: Weidenfeld and Nicolson, 1997.

———— *Frames of Mind: The Theory of Multiple Intelligences*. London, Heinemann, 1984.

Goertzel, V. and M.G. Goertzel, *Cradles of Eminence*. Boston: Little, Brown & Company, 1962.

Greenacre, P., 'The Childhood of the Artist', *Psychoanalytic Study of the Child*, 12 (1957), 47–72.

Gruber, H. *Darwin on Man*. University of Chicago Press, 1981.

Gruber, H. and D.B. Wallace, *Creative People at Work*. Oxford University Press, 1989.

Jacobson, E., 'The Exceptions', *Psychoanalytic Study of the Child*, 14 (1959), 135–54.

Lykken, D.T., 'The genetics of genius' in *Genius and the Mind*, ed A. Steptoe, Oxford University Press, 1998.

Ochse, R., *Before the Gates of Excellence: the determinants of creative genius*. Cambridge University Press, 1990.

Pinker, S., *How the Mind Works*. London: Allen Lane, 1998.

Steptoe, A., ed., *Genius and the Mind: Studies in Creativity and Temperament*. Oxford University Press, 1998.

Sternberg, R.J., ed., *Handbook of Creativity*. Cambridge University Press, 1999.

Storr, A., *The Dynamics of Creation*. New York: Atheneum, 1972.

Winner, E., *Gifted Children*. New York: Basic Books, 1996.

Index